# FLAMES
## IN THE SAHEL

### THE 2012 TUAREG WAR IN MALI

## YUSUF GAMAWA

ISBN 978-1-957943-61-9 (paperback)
ISBN 978-1-957943-62-6 (digital)

Rushmore Press LLC
1 800 460 9188
www.rushmorepress.com

Printed in the United States of America

'To Douglas Stephen Cunliffe, the departed
Prince, for his friendship'.

# Contents

# List of Abbreviations and Acronyms

ADEMA: Alliance Démocratique du Mali

ADIDE: Association des Démandeurs et Initiateurs d'Emploi

AEF: Afrique Equatoriale Française

AFISMA: African-Led International Support Mission to Mali

ALM: Armée de Libération Nationale du Maroc

AOF: Afrique Occidentale Française

AQIM: al-Qaeda in the Islamic Maghreb

ARLA: Armée Révolutionnaire de Libération de l'Azawad

ATNMC: Alliance Touaregue Niger Mali pour le Changement

BAUA: Base Autonome de Timétrine **Base**

CAR/Nord: Consolidation des Acquis de la Réinsertion au Nord

CNID: Comité National d'Initiative Démocratique

CRN: Conseil pour la Réconciliation Nationale

FAO: Food and Agriculture Organization

FIAA: Front Islamique Arabe de l'Azawad

FLN: Front de Libération Nationale

FNLA: Front National de Libération de l'Azawad

FPLA: Front Populaire pour la Libération de l'Azawad

FPLSAC: Front Populaire pour la Libération du Sahara Arabe Central

FULA: Front Unifié pour la Libération de l'Azawad

GARDL: Indenous or Middle East based organizations active in emigration issues in Mali.

GBV: Gender Based Violence

GIA: Groupe Islamique Armé

GSPC: Groupe Salafiste pour la Prédication et le Combat

JMAC: Joint Mission Analysis Center.

ICRC: International Committee for the Red Cross

ILO: International Labour Organisation

MDG: Millennium Development Goals

MDJT: Mouvement pour la Démocratie et la Justice au Tchad

MFUA: Mouvements et Fronts Unifiés de l'Azawad

MINUSMA: Multidimensional United Nations Mission to Mali

MNJ: Mouvement des Nigériens pour la Justice

MNLA: National Movement for the Liberation of Azawad

MPA: Mouvement Populaire de l'Azawad

MPGK: Mouvement Patriotique Ganda Koy

MUJWA: Movement for Unity and Jihad in West Africa

MUSTABAL: It is a Middle east based organization that is active i emigration issues in Mali.

OCHA: Office for the Coordination of Humanitarian Affairs

OCRS: Organisation Commune des Régions Sahariennes

PAREM: Programme d'Appui à la Réinsertion des ex-Combattants au Mali

PDS: Parti Démocratique Soudanaise

PFLP: Popular Front for the Liberation of Palestine

POLISARIO: Frente Popular para la Liberación de Saguia el Hamra y Rio de Oro

PSI: Pan Sahel Initiative

PSP: Parti Socialiste Progressif also Parti Progressiste du Soudan

TSCTI: Trans-Saharan Counterterrorism Initiative

UDPM: L'Union Démocratique du Peuple Malien

UMADD: Union Malienne pour la Démocratie et le Développement

UNESCO: United Nations Educational, Scientific and Cultural Organization

UNMAS: United Nations Mines Action Service

UNICEF: United Nations Children's Fund

UNIDO: United Nations Industrial Development Organization

UNFPA: United Nations Population Fund

UNHAS: UN Humanitarian Air Service

UNHCR: United Nations High Commissioner for Refugees

UNIDIR: United Nations Institute for Disarmament Research

UNOPS: United Nations Office for Project Services

USAID: United States Agency for International Development

US-RDA: Union Soudanaise–Rassemblement Démocratique Africain

UXO: Unexploded Ordinance Detection

WFP: World Food Programme

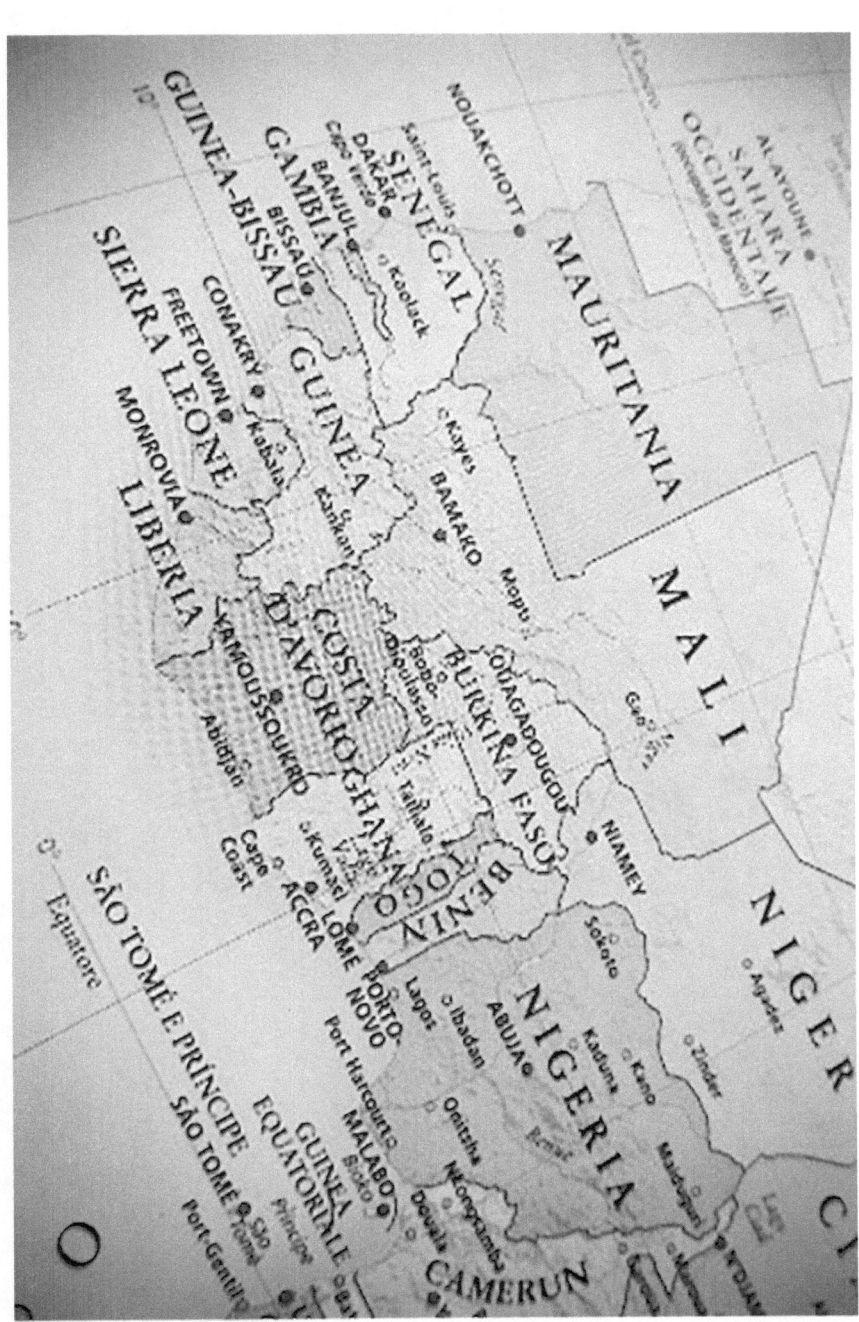

istock-521291713

*"The flames [fire] have remained and burnt for quite long In our unconsciousness For the burnt livestock and older dead [people] At the entrance of Kidal, we must gather And fight As powerful or strong as you maybe you will burn in your flame [fire]"*. Chatma song.

– Ibrahim Ag Alhabib
Tinariwen Tuareg Musical Band
[Rebel Songs, The New Yorker].

# Prologue

*They were the men and the women of the sand, of the wind, of the light, of the night. They appeared as in a dream, at the crest of a dune, as if they were born of the cloudless sky.*

– J.M.G. Le Clezio [Goodreads].

The Sahel Region is now a shadow of itself. The countries in the Region appear to have lost their significance and the region and its once valued trade routes have turned into hubs and routes of violence and crime, unlike in the great days of the Empires, when they were known as centers of learning and great industry, including Mali. Ibn Battuta, the Arab traveler described the Mali Empire saying *'the Sultan has a lofty pavilion...where he sits most of the time... there came from the gate of the palace about 300 slaves, some carrying in their hands bows and others having in their hands short laces and shields...'* [Orias, U.C. Berkeley]. Thus, describing the magnificence of the ruler and the greatness of the Empire. Prior to the period of colonial conquest in the African continent, the Mali Empire [1230-1600 CE], as it was known in those days, was one of the most powerful African states, equal in status only to the likes of the Kanem-Bornu Empire [1380-1893] in terms of wealth and control of trade in the continent.[1]Leo Africanus [Al-Hassan ibn-Muhammad al-Wazzan al-Fasi - c1460 - 1554] was quoted describing the Kanem Borno Empire in a book titled 'History and Description of Africa', written by Alfred James and Andrea Overfield, in the following words: '*They have a most powerful prince. ... He has in readiness as many as three thousand horsemen and a huge number of foot soldiers; for all his subjects are so serviceable and obedient to him, that whenever he commands them, they will arm themselves and will follow him wherever he leads them. They pay him no tribute except tithes on their grain; neither does the king have any revenues to support his state except the spoils he gets from his enemies by frequent invasions and assaults*', Africanus went ahead to describe the ruler of the Empire in these words: '*And yet the king seems marvelously rich, because his spurs, bridles, platters, dishes, pots and other vessels are made of gold. The king is extremely covetous and would rather pay his debts in slaves rather than gold*'. Like the empire of Kanem-Bornu, the Mali Empire has remained a reference point for sophisticated African societies that flourished before the advent of European traders on the African continent. The descriptions by Battuta and Africanus provide insights into not only the strength and power that the old African Empires possessed, but also tells a lot about their status alongside others. It shows how vast they were and how firm the rulers' control over their subjects, as well as the army is. It also provides for further discourse on pre-colonial African societies and issues that relate to development, human rights, and welfare among several others. In the fourteenth century, Mansa or Emperor Kankan Musa made the pilgrimage to Mecca, and news reached Europe of his generosity with gold in Cairo. It was Musa that brought to the empire architects and scholars that made Gao and Timbuktu important centres of Islamic learning. These cities were subsequently lost to the rising Songhai Empire, and in 1591, Morocco invaded the Mali Empire in search of gold. In 1747, a Tuareg prince from the north, whose ancestors had founded Timbuktu in the eleventh century, regained control of the city. In the south, the Bambara people rose to power and by 1712 a Bambara kingdom had been established at Segou. It is claimed that the influence of Bambara is still felt in Bamako and other cities. And in the nineteenth century, the Fulani or Fulbe[2], Macina and Tukulor empires of the Fulani peoples became powerful under ambitious leaders. After series of wars that took place between the years 1818 and 1844, a Fulani Islamic theocracy was established which extended to Djenne and Timbuktu. From 1854 to 1864, its leaders fought both the Bambara and the early French colonisers to expand the Fulani Empire from Segou to Timbuktu while other tribal leaders continued to battle one another, and in the end all finally surrendered to the French.

The French rule in Mali and West Africa, in general, is regarded as a form of direct rule as opposed to the British colonial policy of indirect rule. The French pursued a policy of assimilation, which is said to have had its origins in the French Revolution and its ideas of freedom, equality, and fraternity, which were to be applied to anyone who was French irrespective of race or colour. The French initially considered all its colonies as extensions of France as a country. The assimilation policy was clearly an idea that stemmed from the assumed superiority of French culture and civilisation. However, the French, having realised the impossibility of the former, reverted to a new system of colonial relations called 'association'. The policy of association implied respecting the cultural and political values of Africans and the general belief that Africans should not be forced to become black French people. However, in practice, the association policy proved difficult to administer and instead Africans and their traditional authorities became subordinates in the colonial administrative setup and carried out policies dictated by French officials without any real consultation. African societies were made into districts, and traditional authorities considered not subservient were deposed and replaced without due regard. French colonies in general, and, of course, Mali remained under the control of conservative local elements and colonial military force.

Mali gained independence from the French in 1960. It is considered a relatively poor country, with a population of about 15.8 million, of which 64% are said to be living below poverty line. Between 1960 and 1991, the country remained under the control of either one political party or military dictatorship. This was seen to have led to the informalisation of state institutions by corrupt elites, which affected and politicised not only the military in Mali but also other state security agencies in the country, leading to further weakening of the Malian state. It was only in 1992 that democratic rule returned to Mali, and at that time the country did not have any credible foundation for democratic governance or any democratic institutions in place. However, between 1992 and 2012, the country became a reference point in democratic governance in the international community, especially within the West African sub-region.

A careful study of the economic structure of Mali as a country reveals its weakness and fragility economically and structurally. Mali has been described as one of the poorest countries in the world, with its population of 15 million people, a GDP of 10.31 billion in 2012, a GDP growth of -1.2%, and an inflation rate of 5.4%. According to reports of the world development indicators released by the World Bank in 2014, Mali achieved a GDP of 10.31 billion USD in 2012, which was the result of a growth of -1.2%, and an inflation rate of 5.4% in 2012. And that between year 2000 and 2012 Mali's GDP witnessed a total growth of 5.2% and a growth of 4.0% between 2012 and 2013, and 5.2% between 2013 and 2014. The -1.2% growth rate was prior to year 2012, perhaps between 2011 and 2012, which was not a positive growth, meaning in fact a negative growth rate or deficit kind.

The Malian economy had gone through several reforms in the 1970s, which saw the economy transform from a state economy to an open private economy. However, economic growth was only seen to have improved around 1994 after a period of contraction in the

1980s, which was marked by an average GDP growth rate of -1.2% between 1980 and 1986. Between 1987 and 1993, the growth of the Malian economy was recorded at 3%. The GDP per capita was seen to have risen from $240 in 1994 to $380 in 2004, with an average increase of 4%. Following the devaluation in 1994, the economy appeared to have recorded more growth and was recorded at 5.4% in 2006. Between 2005 and 2007, Mali's GDP growth witnessed a decline; in 2007 the GDP was 3.2% as against 5.3% in 2006 and 6.1% in 2005. In 2008 and 2009, GDP growth was 5% and 4.5%, while in 2010 and 2011 growth was recorded at 5.8% and 2.7% according to the *Global Finance Magazine* country data on Mali. Mali was ranked number 134 in the human development index in 2002, and in 2011 Mali was ranked number 175 out 187 countries on the human development index, which provides an overview of indicators such as life expectancy, education, and income levels. Infrastructural development that supports production related to energy and agricultural development remained a challenge just as the economy remained stagnant due to decline in agricultural production as a result of poor climatic conditions. The entire Sahel region has been constantly facing drought, which has led to food insecurity and migration among its population. The above analysis shows clearly how weak Mali is economically as a country.

The Malian economy is largely dependent on activities related to agriculture, which represent about 40% of GDP and three quarters of export revenues. Agricultural production is mainly centred on local food commodities such as sorghum, rice, millet and cotton, which is considered a cash crop and usually grown in the south of the country. Malian agriculture relies mainly on human labour and is not mechanised. This usually results in low yields. Small farmers are engaged in farming and usually sell about 15% to 20% of their produce. Cotton production and profitability is usually determined by the world market fluctuations. In the northern part, livestock breeding is the main preoccupation, and most economic activities are concentrated in the areas irrigated by the Niger River. Most industrial activities in the country are also centred on agricultural activities.

The growth rate of agriculture has declined to an estimated 2.6%. The decline and weakness of the agricultural sector in Mali has been a major source of concern, especially considering the fact that the low-income households, who constitute the majority, depend on agriculture for their livelihood. The growth of the agricultural sector annually represents about 20% of GDP growth and usually comes from rice and cotton farming. Rice and cotton are seen to represent about 20% of agricultural value added and usually have an annual average growth rate of between 7% and 4.5%. Other crops, which include cereals and livestock, represent 35% and 28% of agricultural value added and have witnessed an increase rate of 1.6% in cereals and 2.9% in livestock. The weakness in the agricultural sector also further exposes the weakness of Mali as a country since most activities in the country are centred on agriculture. Food security remains an important feature of strong-standing nations or states and it is critical to the survival of any state.

Apart from agriculture, gold also accounts for a large part of Mali's income as a country. Mali is the world's sixteenth largest producer of gold. Mali produced an estimated 48.8 tonnes of gold or 1.63% of the world's total production in 2011, valued at $2.3 billion. Gold is said to constitute a larger percentage of Mali's GDP than any nation, an estimated 18.98%, and accounts for 75% of the country's foreign earnings. In the year 2010, a projected increase in gold production of up to 52.2 was anticipated according to a Reuters report in December 2009. Gold is said to account for about 15% of Mali's GDP.

In terms of infrastructural development, Mali's infrastructure networks appear to be a reflection of the population distribution. The distribution of Mali's economy and demography differs greatly between the north and south. The south has a higher population density, and is where most of the nation's natural resources are to be found, as well as economic activities. The north, on the other hand, has important tracts of land that are important for agricultural production, but such land has not as yet been fully exploited. As a result of these marked differences, the density of transport, power, and ICT infrastructure is concentrated in the south. Mali is said to have one of the most spatially or unequally developed infrastructure networks on the whole of the African continent. Apart from a few roads that link to certain scattered mining sites and irrigation areas, northern Mali is said to be an inaccessible desert. The entire country appears to depend heavily on regional corridors and regional infrastructure for transport and water development. About three regional international trade corridors link Mali to the sea, and the country depends on the ports of neighbouring states for its imports, the administrative capacity of which remains weak. Regional railway networks remain disconnected in the region, making railway interconnection difficult, while road corridors are accorded higher importance. Mali plans road regional connectivity, which is presently absent. Double carriage way paved quality regional roads and a national connectivity of one-lane paved quality roads is planned. Mali aims to construct rural roads that will give access to about 14% of agricultural production, which at present is lacking and has stagnated agricultural growth in the country. In the area of power, Mali is a member of the West African Power Pool [WAPP] but is yet to be interconnected with other countries apart from Senegal and may require to generate 284 megawatts of electricity to achieve about 39% of internal electricity coverage, which currently stands at 13% coverage, another index of Mali's weakness, considering the importance of power to the industrialisation of the country and its economic growth. Mali has also developed infrastructure related to ICT and has developed a fibre optic network that is connected to the SAT submarine cables at two different locations in Senegal and Cote d'Ivoire. The country aims to achieve universal access to GSM signal and public broadband facilities.

However, for Mali as a country to meet its infrastructural needs and link up with other developing countries, it must be able to meet the targets it has outlined for itself, some of which have been highlighted above. In meeting these set targets in the areas of roads, power, ICT, and water resources, it is estimated that the country would require about $1 billion per year. The water and power sectors are estimated to about gulp $300 million each, while transportation and ICT may gulp about $236 million and $178 million, respectively. The costs related to the water sector are in line with the millennium development goals target for water and sanitation globally, while those of the power sector aim at 284 mws of new electricity generation to meet the planned 39% coverage of the country. Clearly, Mali's infrastructural spending needs are too high for the country's GDP and would cost about 19% of the country's annual GDP for a decade.

In terms of Mali's political development since Independence, Mali's leader at independence was Moddibbo Keita who was elected under the US-RDA party. Keita was overthrown by Traore in 1968. Musa Traore ruled for about 20 years and was also overthrown by Col Ahmadu Touré. It was Ahmadu Touré, who came to power in 1991 through a military coup that handed over power to a democratically elected government in 1992 when Alpha Oumar Konare emerged as the civilian president in the 1992 elections. Ahmadu Touré again joined politics in 2002 and succeeded in winning the elections in the same year as well as for another term in the 2007 elections. It was while the country was about to hold another round of elections In 2012 that a war was declared in the northern part of the country by the Tuareg group by the name of the National Movement for the Liberation of the Azawad [MNLA]. The cities of Kidal, Gao, and

Timbuktu, often considered as the areas of the Azawad, were taken over by the rebels.

Armed conflicts and the search for peace and security have for a very long time become issues of serious concern not only among African states in the post-independence period but globally. Many international and regional organisations within Africa, as well as at other global levels, have for many years become engaged in solving one conflict or another among African states; yet insecurity still bedevils the continent. The African continent is believed by many scholars to be composed of artificially created nation states, imposed by the colonial masters. Many have also tried to explain the manner in which state structures developed in Africa, which they view as having developed mainly through coercive mechanisms, as well as centralised political and economic control through the use of army, policy, and bureaucracy. The consequences of this are seen to have resulted in the emergence of a political culture that is largely based on ethnicity and authoritarian patterns of governance. As such, the control of a state and its economic resources becomes the basis of political competition in many African states.

Most scholars appear to have heaped the blame for many of the problems facing the African continent on the creation of nation states within Africa without any regard to the ethnic diversity of the various peoples across the continent lumped together by the colonial powers. The scramble for and partition of the African continent in many cases subjugated several ethnic groups within certain particular political regions. This overtime came to constitute a problem and resulted in many wars and conflicts across the continent in the post-independence period. According to several sources, beginning from the 1960s, a total of about twenty-four African states engaged in one military conflict or another and that about twenty-two had had to make serious efforts to avert the breakout of war and conflict within their respective states.

A study conducted by the Institute Catalá Internacional per la Pau [ICIP], Barcelona, and published in its working papers in June 2010, showed that an estimated fourteen armed conflicts had taken place across the African continent by the end of the cold war[3]. These armed conflicts were reported to have taken place in Angola, Guinea Bissau, Liberia, Rwanda, Sierra Leone, Somalia, Sudan, Uganda, Democratic Republic of Congo, and Eritrea-Ethiopia. Mali was excluded from the list despite the fact that Mali was among those states which started to witness armed conflict and violence at an early stage after gaining independence from the French in 1960. Most of the conflicts affecting the African continent were seen to have possessed certain similar characteristics. For instance; most or all were internal conflicts which were also regional in nature and sometimes even internationalised or transnationalised. Many organisations and actors were involved in these conflicts, either in the management of the conflict or in the resolution process, and this led to the creation of complex scenarios. Local armed groups became involved and the conflicts were usually accompanied by grievous humanitarian consequences. It is estimated that over five million people may have died as a result of the armed conflict in the Democratic Republic of Congo. In Sierra Leone, it was reported that about two million people were displaced. In Rwanda about 1 million people were killed in what came to be known as the Rwandan genocide while in Darfur about three hundred thousand people were reported to have perished[4].

The situation in many African states stirred up a debate revolving round a new concept, namely what came to be known as 'weak states', 'fragile states', or 'failed states'. There is still heated debate among scholars about such terms or concepts.[5] While many agree, others oppose the entire idea. Similarly, while some are selective with regard to the different terminologies and appear to favour the use of *fragile*, others prefer to use the term *weak* instead of *failed states*. Such states are also sometimes referred to as 'quasi states', a term often used by Robert Jackson.[6] These states, according to Jackson, have '*de jure*' but not '*de facto*' sovereignty. He argued that they have *de jure* sovereignty as a result of their acceptance in the international community but are not recognised by their citizens as a legitimate authority. However, it has been observed generally that the majority of development agencies appear to have agreed with the term *fragile states* when referring to certain states within the African continent and parts of Asia and South America. These agencies generally define the term *fragile states* to mean 'a fundamental failure of states to meet the citizen's basic needs and expectations'. These states are described by the development agencies as incapable of ensuring basic security, maintaining the rule of law and justice and providing basic services and economic opportunities for their citizens[7].

Those who contest the concept generally argue that *fragility* is not a condition and that it varies along a continuation of performance across areas of state function and performance. As a result, nowadays many development agencies prefer to use the term *fragility* or *fragile situations*. F. Stewart and G. Brown define *fragility* while describing nations that are failing or at high risk of failing in three different dimensions that include authority failure, service failure, and legitimacy failure.

The other term frequently used is *weak state*. *Weak states* here are described as poor states, suffering from significant gaps in security performance and legitimacy. These states, according to the Brookings Institution[8], lack control over certain areas of their territory as well as the capacity to combat internal threats of terrorism or insurgency. Yet another term is that of *failing states*, which is used to describe states that are failing the citizens in achieving economic growth. *Failed states* are states whose central government has collapsed and have no authority to impose order, resulting in loss of physical control of territory. A *collapsed state* is a term used to describe states that have failed and have virtually ceased to exist.

In recent times a critical analysis of these terms has emerged according to which such terms imply that all states move along set trajectories and imply a concept of an '*end state*', when in reality states recover from failure or collapse. The terms are also criticised for not offering a solution or a way of theorising with regard to competing systems of governance. It has also been observed that characterising *failed, collapsed states* or *anarchic* situations completely absent of order and system of governance can be misleading. Current researches have revealed how alternative forms of order, security, and governance emerge and sustain themselves in the absence of a formal state. According to W. Zartman, societies continue to function and to offer sources of legitimate authority and that contemporary collapse does not mean societal or civilisation collapse[9]. T. Hagmannand Hoetine argues that the *state-failure* debate is based on fundamental conceptual flaws that render its insight and recommendations unconvincing in the light of empirical evidence. They contend that scholars are quick to equate the lack of central government with *failed states* or *anarchical states* and that contrary to this state-centred approaches, life goes on with non-state actors performing many functions usually associated with states. However, despite all the criticisms associated with these various terms, it is clear that *weakness, fragility*, or similar situations definitely exist. The argument that non-state actors perform the functions of a state cannot stand since non-state actors cannot be recognised to represent such states in international organisations such as the UN and similar bodies. Since our discussion is centred on sovereign states, then to consider any role played by non-state actors is to digress or evade the central argument or topic of discussion. As such, one may conclude that though there may have been disagreement among scholars on the use of the terms discussed above, it is misleading to say that *weak, fragile*, or *failing states* do not exist. Even if it is true that they may recover, the fact cannot be disputed that they had at a particular point in time *failed* or appeared to be *failing* or *weak*.

The present conflict in Mali would appear to bear all the marks of the various armed conflicts highlighted above with only slight differences. It should be stated at the outset that though the focus of this work is the 2012 Tuareg war in Mali and France's intervention, it must, however, be understood that the Mali conflict did not start in 2012 and can therefore not be discussed in isolation from previous revolts that have taken place in the country, which date back to as early as 1963, only three years after Mali gained independence. The conflict in Mali can to a certain extent also be categorised as an ethnic or regional conflict, like most of the other conflicts affecting the African continent – as noted above. Essentially the conflict is one between the Tuareg group inhabiting the northern part of Mali on the one hand and the Malian state on the other, which is perceived to be dominated by southerners, mainly the Bambara-Malinke.

It is argued that the Tuareg are not an ethnic group but a race. Nevertheless, the conflict is generally seen to be an ethnic and regional one though a thorough study of the nature and complexity of the problems between the Tuaregs and the Malian state will reveal that physical and not only linguistic characteristics constitute a major difference between the southern Bambara-Malinke people and the Tuaregs along with other Arab peoples inhabiting the northern part of the country. While the Tuaregs are light skinned and have physical characteristics similar to those of the Arabs or the Berbers, the southerners are dark-skinned typical of the populations of sub-Saharan Africa. Issues relating to superiority in racial terms have generally complicated the relationship of the two groups though it is also true that the Tuaregs had regarded the French in the colonial period in a similar manner. When the French occupied Mali, the Tuaregs made it clear that they were not interested in being part of any such arrangement and as a result they constantly rebelled against the French. For instance, Alla ag Albachir openly opposed and led a revolt against the French just as his son, Elledi ag Alla Albachir, was to do in post-independence Mali. The revolts against the French explain why the Tuaregs came to be exempted from forced labour and enlistment in the army during the colonial period. It was exempted from these programmes by the colonial government in order to preserve the peace as revolts by the Tuareg had caused the French a lot of damage. As a result the Tuareg were permitted a relative degree of independence.

It is therefore possible that the Tuareg never opposed the Bambara-Malinke people per se but were rather bent on preserving their independence and identity and for this reason desired total political independence and refused to accept any form of control or domination by any people, be they French or Bambara-Malinke. Studies have shown that the Tuareg had once occupied a far larger area in the past and dominated other groups wherever they settled.[10]. Rodd, for instance, alleges that the group earned a reputation for treachery and was never loved by other peoples. The Tuareg's sense of their superiority may perhaps have derived from glories of their history as a warrior nation. According to Rodd, having been converted to Islam by the El Merabat, the Sanhaja Tuareg formed a desert confederation on a distinctly religious basis.[11] It was this league of desert tribes that captured Fez and established what came to be known as the Almoravid dynasty [Rodd, 2013], a dynasty which at one time prevailed over the whole of the Maghreb and Spain, where it was responsible for the glories of architecture, science and the arts which characterised Moorish rule.

In Mali the group found it difficult to accept the idea of servitude to the French and later to the Malian state and it was largely for this reason that the Tuaregs resisted the French incursion and revolted several times in the post-independence period against the Malian state. The rebellion in 2012 was something of an exception, especially if those involved and their objectives are considered. Whereas previous wars saw the participation of mainly civilian Tuaregs and associations and were aimed at independence, the 2012 war saw the participation of jihadist groups whose aim was the Islamisation of northern Mali. The participation of groups such as Alqaeda in the Maghreb [AQIM], Ansardine, and Movement for Jihad in West Africa [MUJWA] gave a new dimension to the 2012 revolt that was unknown in earlier Tuareg uprisings in Mali. The general situation in the Sahel region, in particular, the fall of Gaddafi, which saw Tuareg returnees fleeing from Libya, and the emergence of organised crime appeared to have led to or assisted in the emergence of these groups. However, the demands and grievances of previous revolts remained significant issues, especially as voiced through the Movement for the Liberation of the Azawad [MNLA], largely seen as a Tuareg movement distinct from the jihadists.

Since it gained independence from the French in 1960 and prior to these developments, Mali had remained one of the relatively stable countries in West Africa. Though considered poor, it nevertheless proved to be a very important player in the West African sub-region as a result of the steady growth of its democratic institutions. Despite being a small country, Mali was accorded tremendous respect in Africa, particularly among the nations of West Africa and since 1975 it continues to play a prominent role in the regional integration process of the West African sub-region under the ECOWAS initiative. Mali has held the chairmanship of the regional body as a result of its commitment, progress, and maturity in democratic governance. Mali's foreign policy has largely been restricted to the West African sub-region, where it has been seen to be involved in the promotion of regional cohesion and cooperation among West African states. The country became deeply involved in mediating in conflict resolution as well, especially after its President, Alpha Oumar Konaré, assumed the chairmanship of ECOWAS in 1999.

Furthermore, Mali's concerns in the sub-region extended to border security relations with its immediate neighbours, which include Mauritania, Niger, Tunisia, and Algeria. This resulted from the lingering problems it faced with the Tuareg in the North. Though Mali's influence in the region is sometimes explained in terms of its progress in democratic practice, the country remained a weak state, with a relatively weak government and economy and inadequate resources. Mali lacked the capacity to influence any country in the region and, in fact, instead continues to depend on Nigeria for economic and security assistance[12].

Generally speaking, conflicts, peace, and security issues in Africa have remained subjects of international debate to the extent that they have overshadowed other important issues taking place in the African continent. Conflicts and crises in the continent have tended to be given negative considerations, and most often the blame has been laid on the misbehaviour of African leaders or the general uncivilised conduct of the African people. The armed conflicts, the failure of the economies of African states, as well as the decline in democratic culture have generally been blamed on factors confined to Africa, highlighting the failure of the continent to adjust to the changes brought about by globalisation.

Such views, however, have not gone undisputed; and as such, other factors responsible for the situation in the continent have been identified and discussed by several scholars, and the general conclusion, therefore, is that the evolution of postcolonial Africa must be contextualised by two major factors. The first remains within a historical and international context. It is generally argued that African political, economic and cultural heritage must be looked at in the light of the colonial legacy[13]. It has been argued that any analysis of the situation that fails to take into consideration the European legacy in Africa will not be sufficient for a valid analysis of the African situation or condition. The second factor has mainly been to do with the negative image of Africa, in which the international media has played a leading role in propagating. It is believed that for any evaluation of the security and stability of the African continent to be meaningful, a broader and all-inclusive approach must be developed in order to grasp the reality of the African predicament[14].

The recent war in Mali—a rebellion in the North by the Tuaregs - is thus a phenomenon that has remained consistent since the 1890s, with outbreaks in 1910, 1963, 1990, and 2002. The process did not begin in 2012, and many reasons had been advanced by many writers and scholars for the continuation of the Tuareg rebellion in Mali.[15]. One explanation advanced was the killing of herdsmen and the poisoning of wells during the 1963 war, as well as the poor implementation and sometimes breaching of peace accords and decentralisation initiatives in the 1990's and the 2000's.

Generally, scholars have tried to view such problems, including the one in Mali and other former colonies in Africa, as stemming from a divided political heritage that was inimical to territorial cohesion. Mali, like most countries in Africa, faced the problem of achieving unity as a modern state as a result of artificial borders created by the colonial masters prior to the independence of many African states. These colonial borders did not take into consideration the diverse socioeconomic realities that existed in different parts of Africa, including Mali; and, as such, citizenship has in many cases remained an abstract concept in many parts of Africa even today[16].

In the past, several efforts had been made towards creating a single state for the semi-nomadic Tuareg group, which is scattered across the Sahel region to places like Libya, Algeria, Burkina Faso, Mauritania, and Niger. Mali's government since independence appears to have been under the control of the settled Africans, and successive governments had tried to deal with the cultural differences that existed between the group and the Tuaregs. The Tuaregs generally felt isolated from political power and at the same time felt deprived of certain basic rights by the Malian government. As a result of these grievances, two successive revolts were launched by the group in 1963 and 1990, respectively, which brought about a division and clear confrontation between the group and the Malian authorities. The two revolts were violently suppressed by the Malian authorities but led to the migration of many Tuaregs of Mali origin into various countries within the Sahel region.

The rebellion on 17 January 2012 by the Tuaregs and the MNLA saw the driving out of the Malian forces from the North and its occupation by the various rebel groups that collaborated and fought the Malian authorities. The three other groups, which are radical Islamists in nature, include al-Qaeda in the Maghreb [AQIM], MUJWA and the Ansardine, whose ambition is the Islamisation of Northern Mali. Obviously the objectives of the two Islamist groups differ from those of the MNLA, which is fighting for certain basic rights and for greater involvement of the Tuaregs in the affairs of the Malian government. As such, soon after the takeover of the northern part of Mali, the two radical Islamist groups pushed out the MNLA and took control of the northern cities, immediately imposing and declaring the region to be under Sharia or Islamic law.

Meanwhile, the success with which the rebels took over the northern part of the country led to serious criticism of the Malian government's failure to counter the insurgency, particularly within the military. This triggered a military coup. Part of the Malian army tended to blame the civilian government's response to the rebellion, which was seen to have exposed the weakness of the Malian state. The 22 March, 2012 coup ousted the government of Ahmadu Touré and replaced it with a military regime under Captain Amadou Sanogo. The coup in Mali was condemned by ECOWAS and the international community in general and led to a resolve to intervene in the Mali conflict, particularly by ECOWAS, the regional body in West

Africa that, since the establishment of the ECOMOG peacekeeping force during the Liberian, Sierra Leone, and Niger crises, has had an established mechanism for peace and conflict resolution. The body was initially involved in mediation efforts between the rebel groups and the civilian administration in Mali prior to the coup and made efforts to broker a peace deal through its council of ministers. ECOWAS responded to the coup with a set of sanctions against the new government in Mali. Under these sanctions, Mali was suspended from the regional body as a member, and this included a travel ban within the West African region, and all ambassadors of ECOWAS states were withdrawn from Mali. At the same time all the borders of ECOWAS states with Mali were closed. Thereafter, the military junta stepped down and an interim administration took over. It was the interim administration that requested for the intervention of France, in the face of the continuing rebel advance on the capital, Bamako.

The book is divided into four parts. The prologue is followed by Part One, which is entitled 'From Empire to Independence' Part One deals mainly with the history of Mali, from its pre-colonial past through the period of colonial rule, as well as its postcolonial history. It deals with the physical geography of Mali, the terrain, climate, rainfall, and general weather conditions, providing or making an environmental assessment possible.

Part One goes on to deal with the French incursion into Mali and the subsequent imposition of colonial rule. This part tries mainly to look at French colonial interests in Mali, where, initially, the French seemed to have regarded Mali as a link to its possessions in the Senegal basin. The last part of the chapter takes a look at post-independence developments in Mali. This part tried to analyse relatively briefly the various governments and administration and their policies in the country. It examines the various problems, initiatives and responses of the different administrations in Mali, from those of Modibo Keita, which took over as the first indigenous administration in 1960 at Independence, to the elected government of Boubacar in 2013.

Part Two, entitled 'Past Tuareg Wars in Mali', goes back to the early history and origin of the Tuareg as a people. It tries to deal with the controversies attached to their origins as well as the difficulties experienced by scholars in differentiating between the Tuareg group and other Arabic peoples inhabiting the Maghreb areas of North Africa. Certain physical characteristics and their desert life style have led many to assume that the Tuaregs belong to these Arabic-speaking people, though they have their own distinctive dialect. The second part of the chapter tried to look at the relationship between the Tuaregs in Mali and the Malian state, one that has clearly never been a good one. The Tuaregs, as mentioned previously, had maintained a measure of independence even during French colonial rule in Mali and they consequently showed little interest at all in being part of any arrangement or any country but their own.

The 1963 rebellion is discussed in detail. It examines their social organisation along clan or *tewsit* lines and the progress of the rebellion. This brings us to the next major rebellion which is 1990 – al-Jebha - for which the Tuaregs were a lot better equipped and more organised than in 1963.

Part Three, entitled 'The 2012 Tuareg War and French Intervention in Mali', is the main focus of this book. However without a proper grasp of the past Tuareg wars, it would be very difficult to understand the rebellion- the background, causes, and outbreak of the 2012 war. Here, the 2009 rebellion that was said to have been initially started and ended with a negotiation is briefly discussed and then how the French responded to the request of the Malian president and began armed intervention, resulting in the the retreat of the rebels towards the massif of Adrar des Ifoghas and Algeria. It looks at African and foreign responses to the crisis and examines French policy and motives for intervening, as well as the impact on Mali of that intervention.

Part Four goes on to examine the post-conflict period. It examines the consequences of the migration caused by the crisis and the increasing insecurity and food scarcity. Issues related to human right violations and abuses are discussed in the second part of this chapter and post-conflict stabilisation efforts by the EU and United Nations and its partners and their activities in the cities of Kidal, Timbuktu, and Gao. The activities of UNMAS, which organised sensitisation training regarding land mines and was also responsible for clearing the remnants of contaminated weapons across the north, are described. Some of the weapons found or seized from the rebel groups in the post-conflict period became important documents and this documentation brings the chapter to an end.

An epilogue is provided at the end of the book followed by the notes and bibliographical section and the index section.

# PART ONE

## From Empire to Independence

## Mama Africa

*"She gave birth to the world Ask the Degan tribe in Mali or ask I ancestors Her origin is divine".*

– Richard Nnoli

*"All they say is you are uncivilized Using policies to publicly undress you From Lesotho to Libya, Mali to Malawi, Zambia to Zimbabwe Raping justice and reaping where and what they sowed not".*

– Lydia Jerotich

## CHAPTER ONE

# Land and People of Mali

*We need self-confidence in our ability to build Africa. I
trust in Mali, and I trust in music.*

– Rokia Traore

M ali is a landlocked country located in the West African
sub-region of Africa, covering an area of about 1,240,000
square kilometres and making it the eighth largest
country in Africa. Mali shares a long border with seven countries. It
shares a border with Algeria that stretches about 1,376 kilometres;
Niger, 821 kilometres; Burkina Faso, 1,000 kilometres; Cote d'Ivoire,
532 kilometres; Guinea, 858 kilometres; Senegal, 419 kilometres; and
Mauritania, 2,237 kilometres[17]. Covering half the country from the
north is the Sahara, consisting of the shifting sand dunes of Erg Chech,
the salt deposits of Taodenmi, and the rocky plains of the Tanezrouft
region[18]. To the east and north is the Ifoghas massif, a 600-metre
eroded sand stone plateau that extends from the Ahaggar Mountains of
the central Sahara. At the centre of the country is the Hombori Tondo,
which at about 1,155metres or 3,800 feet and is Mali's highest point.
The Bandiagara plateau and escarpment are also located in the same
region[19]. From the south-west border with Guinea, the Fouta Djallon

3

Massif extends into the Madinque plateau, which has highland areas of up to 640 metres [2,100feet] and deep river valleys.

In terms of climatic condition, Mali is characterised by three seasons as a result of the combination of annual rainfall with temperature changes. The weather is usually dry and hot from February to June, wet and mild from June to November, while it becomes cooler and drier from November to February. The weather pattern is responsible for the emergence of three climatic zones in the country. The northern part, which is located in the Sahara, has virtually no rainfall at all. It's mean daily temperature is [119 degrees Fahrenheit] and lower temperatures of 5 degrees Celsius [41 degrees Fahrenheit]. The Sahel region between the Sahara and Equatorial Africa records an annual rainfall of between 100 and 200 millimetres [4–8 inches], with a daily mean temperature of 29 degrees Celsius [84 degrees Fahrenheit]. The Sudan region or zone records about an annual rainfall of 700–1,300 millimetres [28–51inches] with a daily mean temperature of 27 degrees Celsius[20].

There are two major rivers in Mali and they have consistently been the main source of water for both human use and for agriculture. These are the Niger and Senegal River. The former, together with its inland delta system, is considered the most significant source of water in Mali. Its source is in the north-eastern tip of Sierra Leone. It then flows inland through Guinea and enters Mali through its south-western border. It is dammed in three different locations in southern Mali: at Selingue, Sotuba, and Markala. The navigable course of the river runs for about 1,600 kilometres from Bamako's port, north-east, past Timbuktu, and then east and south towards Gao. Its course is straight in the Macina region, from Mopti to Kabara, and then spreads out into a system of lakes and wetlands. At Lake Faguibine, about 400 kilometres west of Timbuktu and narrows dangerously, preventing navigation during the dry season. It widens in the south upstream of Gao and is navigable south of Asongo.

The Senegal River is another important source of water in Mali, located in the south-western part of the country. Starting from the confluence of the Bakoye and Bafing rivers near Bafoulabe, it flows northwest past Kayes to form a border between the neighbouring countries of Mauritania and Senegal[21].

With a total of about 15.3 million, the population of Mali consists of several ethnic groups, who speak over fifty different languages. In the year 2010 about 47.2% of the population consisted of people between the ages of zero and 14, about 50.6% between 15 and 64 and 2.2% above. Between 2005 and 2010, Mali recorded 680,000 births per year with a death rate of 221,000 per year[22] and between 2012 and 2013 a total fertility rate of 6.1% with a crude birth rate of 38.8% in both urban and rural areas[23] - a relatively high population growth in Mali.

Mali is a multi-lingual country with a diverse ethnic identity. The vast majority, who are dark in complexion, live in the south and west, including the descendants of Mali's ancient empire. These areas are the historical centres of power and support a variety of occupations[24]. In the northern desert live those whose ancestors are reported to have originated in the Maghreb.[25] It is they who brought Islam into the country. They are estimated to number about 1.2 million at present. An estimated 90% of the population of Mali is Muslim, mostly Sunni, and belong to the Maliki School of jurisprudence[26]. About 5% of the population is Christian and includes both Roman Catholics and Protestant denominations while the rest of the population adheres to traditional indigenous religion[27].

In the south-west are the Mande people, who, according to many sources, constitute the majority or about half of Mali's population. The Bambara are the largest subgroup of the Mande people and make up the majority of the population in Bamako, which is the Malian capital. The descendants of the Bambara and the Kaarta kingdoms of the early centuries were traditionally farmers and craftsmen. The Bambara language is the first or second largest language of about 80% of the people of Mali[28]. Other Mande people include the Solinke and the Malinke. The Bozo people are considered as the descendants of the Solinke, who migrated from the old Ghana Empire and are well-known fishermen. The Fulani people constitute about 15% of the total population of Mali, and historically they are considered the descendants of the Peul, Macina, and the Tokulor kingdoms. Their language is referred to as Fulfulde, with cattle rearing as their main occupation and as a result they are settled all over the grazing ranges on the north and south of the River Niger.

Then there are the Senufo people, who constitute about 12% of the total population of Mali. They include the Mamara Senufo, speaking Minyanka, and the Bomu. They are mostly found along the border with Burkina Faso and Cote d'Ivoire where it is claimed their ancestors ruled the ancient kingdom of Kenedugu [1650-1898]. The main preoccupation of the Senufo is farming. It also retains strong traditional religious beliefs.

The Dogon peoples constitute less than 1% of the total population of Mali. Their architecture in the Bandiagara cliffs near the centre of the country is well known and has been recognised as a World Heritage Site by UNESCO. Many Dogon artefacts have been collected by international collectors. The Dogon speak over forty different dialects, some of which are considered separate languages.

The Songhai people make up about 6% of the total population of Mali and are located mostly in the eastern part of Mali along the Niger River, where in recent history they are known to be fishermen and farmers. The Songhai are descendants of the last ancient West African empire, the Songhai Empire, which prevailed in Mali and parts of Niger republic between the 15th and 16th centuries. After the demise of the empire, the Tuaregs assumed.

The Tuaregs and Maure peoples are located in the deserts of the northern part of Mali, and together the two peoples constitute an estimated 5–10 % of the total population of Mali. For several centuries, the Tuareg group has been known to be nomadic and is mostly found in northern Niger, Algeria, and Libya. They are known as the 'blue men of the desert', who refer to themselves as Kel Tamasheq, which means speakers of Tamasheq. The Tamasheq is generally recognised as the language of the Berbers and is completely different from other languages spoken in Mali. The Maure people, historically known as the Moors are to be found in the West, overlapping into Mauritania. They are generally considered to have descended from the Berbers and call themselves Amazigh[29], speakers of the Semitic Hasanya language, which is the official language of Mauritania.

Mali is well known to outsiders on account a number of its cities, which served as either important centres of trade in the ancient period during the trans-Saharan trade or as important learning centres that attracted people from far and wide. A brief on some of these important cities will shed light on the importance the cities occupied not only in Malian history but in ancient African history as a whole since the cities were mostly founded before the founding of the Malian state and in the days of the great African empires of Kanem-Bornu [1380-1893], Old Oyo [1300-1888], Mali [1230-1610], Songhai, as well as the Asante and Fante empires of Ghana [c 400 to c 1200]. A brief discussion of some of these cities will provide a glimpse of the complexity of the composition of some of those groups of people mentioned above and the general political divide within Mali.

Bamako is Mali's capital and is located along the Niger River in the southern part of the country. The name of the city is derived from the Bambara word 'Bamako', which means Crocodile River, and is mainly Bambara-dominated. History has it that Bamako was where Sundiata Keita defeated the Ghana Empire and founded the Mali Empire in the thirteenth century.[30] Declared the capital of French

Sudan West Africa by the French in 1908, Bamako is the most densely populated city in Mali. In 2009 there were about 1.8 million people living in Bamako and it was rated as the fastest-growing city in Africa and the sixth fastest-growing city in the world.

Djenne is reputed to be the oldest city in sub-Saharan Africa. The Jenne-Jeno trading centre dates back to 250 BCE. The present city is currently located on an island where the Niger and Bani rivers meet where it has been since the eleventh century. It is regarded as the hub for the trans-Sahara gold and salt trades and was conquered by the Songhai, the Fulani, as well as the Tukulor peoples before it was finally occupied by the French. The great mosque of Djenne is recognised as a World Heritage Site by UNESCO and considered the world's largest adobe edifice.

Timbuktu, famous throughout the world, is also among Mali's most popular cities. It is located at a point where the River Niger meets the Sahara. Arab geographers wrote about the wealth of Timbuktu in the fourteenth century and so also did the nineteenth-century Europeans, among whom many died attempting to explore its environs. The city became an important centre of learning and trade in the fourteenth century. According to Tuareg tradition, the name Timbuktu means 'a mother with a large navel'. Timbuktu was designated as a World Heritage Centre by UNESCO in 1988. At different times, it served as the capital of the ancient Mali Empire as well as the Songhai Empire. The Tuareg are the dominant population group in Timbuktu.

Kidal is a small Saharan city located in the north-east of Mali. The city has for long been occupied by the nomadic Semitic peoples of Mali. Many paintings dating back to the twelfth century are to be found in the city. In recent times it has become a centre where armed rebels seeking self-governance are to be found.

Gao was founded in the seventh century and it is located on the southern course of the River Niger in the eastern part of Mali. Early Arab histories showed that the city was initially known as Kawkaw and was the capital of the Songhai Empire. It was reported that in the fourteenth century the ruler of the empire, Askia Muhammad embarked on a pilgrimage to Hajj and upon return converted its inhabitants to Islam. The tomb of Askia Muhammad at the great mosque of Gao is recognised as a World Heritage Site by UNESCO.

Mopti, another important city in Mali, is inhabited by a diverse population including the Fulani, Bambara, Dogon, Songhai, Bwa, Tukulor, and Bozo. The city lies at the confluence of the Niger and Bani rivers in the Macina region of Mali. It is built on an island, has a very busy port and is considered an important centre of fishing and livestock-rearing. The city of Segou is located along the Niger River, between Bamako and Mopti. It was an important city in the time of the Bambara kingdom in the 18th century. It is the third largest city in Mali and is well known for its Sudanese colonial architecture, pottery, and cloth markets.

Sikasso is in the southern Sudan zone and has rainfall all the year round. It was the capital of the Senofu kingdom of Kenedugu in the nineteenth century and was also the last to hold out against conquest by the French. Koulikoro, mainly occupied by the Soninke, Bambara, and Malinke, who are the majority, links the nomads in the north with the farmers in the south of the country. Commercial activities such as oil and soap production flourish in the city. In 1892 Kayes was the first headquarters of the colonial French Sudan. Prior to this period, a Tukulor leader, Umar Tal, was said to have laid a siege against the French at a nearby city, Medine Tukulor. Koulikoro is linked to Dakar in Senegal by rail.[31]

## CHAPTER TWO

# The Ancient Mali Empire

*I salute you all, sons of Mali, and I salute you, Kamandjan. I have come back, and as long as I breath, Mali will never be in thrall-rather death than slavery. We will live free because our ancestors lived free.*

– Sundiata, The Epic, p 56.

The origins of present-day Mali are traceable to the ancient kingdom or empire of Mali, which existed between 1230 and 1600 CE. Initially, in 1217, the Mali Empire started out as a local Madinka under their ruler, Sundiata Keita.[32]However, under Sundiata's 25-year rule it soon transformed and grew into an empire.[33] The empire succeeded in extending its influence over a large territory within West Africa, reaching as far as the Atlantic Ocean, an area far larger than the present Malian state. Most of the literature available about the ancient empire appeared in the writings and works of Arab geographers and renowned scholars such as Ibn Khaldun [1332–1406], as well as Ibn Battuta or Shams ad-Din[1304-1369] and Leo Africanus [Al-Hassan ibn-Muhammad al-Wazzan al-Fasi - c1460 - 1554] who was quoted in his decription of Mali in the book 'History and Description of Africa' as saying: *'In this kingdom there*

*is a large and ample village containing more than six thousand families,*
*and named Mali, which is also the name of the whole kingdom. Here the*
*king has his residence. The region itself yields great abundance of wheat,*
*meat and cotton. Here are many craftsmen and merchants in all places:*
*and yet the king honorably entertains all strangers. The inhabitants are*
*rich and have plenty of merchandise. Here is a great number of temples,*
*clergymen, and teachers, who read their lectures in the mosques because*
*they have no colleges at all. The people of the region excel all other Negroes*
*in wit, civility, and industry, and were the first that embraced the law of*
*Muhammad'.*[34] It is certainly very unusual in those days for a village
to shelter up to six thousand families. What he describes is a city
state, especially when it is stated that 'the name of the village is the
name of the entire kingdom'. The quote made clear the occupation
of the inhabitants to be either farmers, craftsmen, or merchants. He
describes the people as knowledgeable while at the same recognizing
the ruler to be universal in his outlook as he entertains all strangers.
Mali at the time, based on such description by Al-Hassan Ibn
Muhammad could have been the most advanced African kingdom
and the first to embrace Islam. In his famous travels from Morocco
in the Sahara, Ibn Battuta travelled south by caravan, stopping at
the oases and the salt mines on the way until after two months he
reached the junction of the trans-Saharan trade route. From there
Ibn Batuta was able to reach Timbuktu, which was then a provincial
city and proceeded to Gao, which was an important centre for trade
at that time[35].

Ibn Batuta's accounts of Mali have been recorded in many books
and reveal a lot about the importance that the Mali Empire occupied
at that time as well as the activities taking place in the empire. Ibn
Battuta[36] was quoted describing some of the activities in the empire
in these words: *'The black men come up from their country and take*
*away salt from Taghaza. In the towns of Mali it sells for twenty to thirty*
*Mithqals*[37] *and sometimes as much as forty. The Negroes use salt as a*
*medium of exchange just as gold and silver is used in other places; they*

*cut it into pieces and buy and sell with it.'* The production and trade in salt influenced the precolonial economy of west African societies throughout the 2nd millennium C.E. Sources and control of salt trade continued to shift within the sub-region as kingdoms and empires rise and fall. Taghaza as described in the quote remained the only source of salt in the Sudan up to the 15th century C.E, it was a very rare commodity in the Savannah region. Many of Ibn Khaldun's[38] works also record the genealogy of the Malian Empire and its history, which is preserved and passed down. According to this genealogy, the empire was formed in the thirteenth century at the battle of Krina in 1235. Mansa Musa[39] made the pilgrimage to Mecca in 1324 in the fourteenth century. Timbuktu was sacked by the Mossi in 1391, and in 1430 a North African Tuareg, Sunni Ali Ber, seized Timbuktu. By 1493, the Songhai had seized Teghaza, and in 1610 the entire empire fragmented. According to many sources, gold has been the major source of Mali's wealth. It was agreed that the availability of large deposits of gold as well as Mali's position and control over the trans-Saharan trade gave Mali its significance worldwide in the ancient period. In the days of the empire, Gao and Timbuktu, both located at the edge of the Sahara, served as important centres and trade routes through the desert to the Levant and to Europe. The two major commodities, gold and salt, were usually exchanged for different goods far and wide. The gold was usually exported north of the empire while the salt travelled to the south. Leo Africanus [Al-Hassan ibn-Muhammad al-Wazzan al-Fasi - c1460 - 1554] was explicit in his description of Timbuktu and Gao that is contained in the book written by Alfred Andrea and James Overfield. His accounts of Timbuktu is as follows;

> *'All its houses are ... cottages, built of mud and covered with thatch. However, there is a most stately mosque to be seen, whose walls are made of stone and lime, and a princely palace also constructed by the highly skilled craftsmen of Granada. Here there are many shops of artisans and merchants,*

*especially of those who weave linen and cotton, and here Barbary merchants bring European cloth. The inhabitants, and especially resident aliens, are exceedingly rich, since the present king married both of his daughters to rich merchants. Here are many wells, containing sweet water. Whenever the Niger River overflows, they carry the water into town by means of sluices. This region yields great quantities of grain, cattle, milk, and butter, but salt is very scarce here, for it is brought here by land from Tegaza, which is five hundred miles away. When I was there, I saw one camel-load of salt sold for eighty ducats. The rich king of Timbuktu has many plates and scepters of gold, some of which weigh 1,300 pounds, and he keeps a magnificent and well-furnished court. When he travels anywhere, he rides upon a camel, which is led by some of his noblemen. He does so likewise when going to war, and all his soldiers ride upon horses. Whoever wishes to speak to this king must first of all fall down before his feet and then taking up earth must sprinkle it on his own head and shoulders. ... [The king] always has under arms 3,000 horsemen and a great number of foot soldiers who shoot poisoned arrows. They often skirmish with those who refuse to pay tribute and whomever they capture they sell to the merchants of Timbuktu. Here very few horses are bred. ... Their best horses are brought out of North Africa. As soon as the king learns that any merchants have come to the town with horses, he commands that a certain number be brought before him. Choosing the best horse for himself, he pays a most liberal price for it.... Here are great numbers of religious teachers, judges, scholars and other learned persons, who are bountifully maintained at the kings expense. Here too are brought various manuscripts or written books from Barbary, which are sold for more money than any other merchandise. The coin of Timbuktu is gold, without any stamp or inscription, but in matters of small value they use certain shells from the kingdom of Persia. Four hundred of these are worth a ducat, and six pieces of Timbuktu's golden coin weigh two-thirds of an ounce. The inhabitants are gentle and cheerful and spend a great part of the night in singing and dancing throughout the city streets. They keep large numbers of male and female slaves, and their town is greatly vulnerable to fire. At the time of my second visit, almost half the town burned down in the space of five hours'.*

Al-Hassan Ibn Muhammad's lavish description of Timbuktu is indeed remarkable. He most certainly was astonished by what he saw during his visit. He not only described the architectural perfections of the city and its details but went further to explain how such expertise was imported from Granada at the time, further confirming the level of sophistication that obtained. He described the industriousness of the people as they engage in agriculture and trade. His generous account of the ruler and his enormous taste for gold and other ornaments is vivid and shows the ostentation attached to his rule as the king. The military strength and striking ability of the city was not ignored, and so is the intellectual aspect of the city's life when it was explained that manuscripts were brought into the city from other Maghreb states. Leo Africanus went ahead to describe Gao city in the following words as captured in the same book by Alfred Andrea and James Overfield titled 'History and Description of Africa';

*'Here are very rich merchants and to here journey continually large numbers of Negroes who purchase here cloth from Barbary and Europe. The town abounds in grain and meat but lacks wine, trees and fruits. However, there are plenty of melons, lemons and rice. Here there are many wells, which also contain very sweet and wholesome water. Here also is a certain place where slaves are sold, especially upon those days when merchants assemble. A young slave of fifteen years of age is sold for six ducats, and children are also sold. The king of this region has a certain private palace in which he keeps a large number of concubines and slaves, who are watched by eunuchs. To guard his person he maintains a sufficient troop of horsemen and foot soldiers. Between the*

*first gate of the palace and the inner part, there is a walled enclosure wherein the king personally decides all of his subjects controversies. Although the king is most diligent in this regard and conducts all business in these matters, he has in his company counsellors and such other officers as his secretaries, treasurers, stewards and auditors. It is a wonder to see the quality of merchandise that is daily brought here and how costly and sumptuous everything is. Horses purchased in Europe for ten ducats are sold here for forty and sometimes fifty ducats a piece. There is not European cloth so coarse as to sell for less than four ducats an ell. If it is anywhere near fine quality, they will give fifteen ducats for an ell, and an ell of the scarlet of Venice or of Turkish cloth is here worth thirty ducats. A sword is here valued at three or four crowns, and likewise are spears, bridles and similar commodities, and spices are all sold at a high rate. However, of all other items, salt is the most expensive. The rest of this kingdom contains nothing but villages and hamlets inhabited by herdsmen and shepherds, who in winter cover their bodies with the skins of animals, but in summer they go naked, save for their private parts. … They are an ignorant and rude people, and you will scarcely find one learned person in the square of a hundred miles. They are continually burdened by heavy taxes; to the point that they scarcely have anything left on which to live'.*

It is obvious that the city of Gao must have been a very huge market for slaves at the time. Slave trade was a very important commercial activity at the time, and it perhaps explains why the ruler keeps many concubines as mentioned in the quote. It is however worthy to note the sophistication of the bureaucracy described and the kind and number of officials in the service of the king. Elaborate indeed! Also worthy of attention is the types of trade activities that existed between the city and the rest of the world even in that age. Cloths and horses among others were brought from Europe and Turkey to the city, and other items out of the city to other parts of the world.

The Mali Empire reached its zenith under one of its famous rulers, known as Mansa Kankan Musa, whose reign made Mali known all over the world, especially after his famous pilgrimage to Mecca in 1324. The accounts of his travel revealed not only a lot about Mali's wealth to the outside world but also its power and strength. Mansa Musa was accompanied to the pilgrimage by 60,000 men. It was reported that eighty camels carried hundreds of pounds of gold dust, and about 12,000 slaves each carried four pounds of gold bars during the trip. Mansa Musa was reported to have spent so much gold in Cairo to the extent that it caused inflation that lasted about a decade after his trip. Mansa Musa's display of wealth during the trip caught the attention of Western scholars and mapmakers and as a consequence attracted the attention of Europeans, making Timbuktu and the cities of Mali famous[40]. One account of his travels was described in these words: '*This man flooded Cairo with his gifts. He left no court Emir no holder of a royal office without a gift of a load of gold. The people of Cairo made incalculable profits out of him and his men in buying and selling and giving and taking. They exchanged gold until they depressed its value in Egypt and caused its price to fall*[41].

Mansa Musa brought to the empire architects and scholars that made Timbuktu and Gao important centres of Islamic learning. Ibn Battuta describes religious practice in Mali in these words during his travels: '*Another of their good qualities is their habit of wearing clean white garments on Fridays. Even if a man has nothing but an old worn out shirt, he washes it and wears it to the Friday service. Yet another is their zeal for learning the Quran by heart. They put their children in chains if they show any backwardness in memorizing it, and they are not set free until they have learnt it by heart*[42].' The city of Timbuktu continued to grow into a centre of Islamic scholarship and learning up to the fifteenth century apart from being a centre for trade. The city's population continued to increase, and in the sixteenth century, Timbuktu alone was recorded to have housed between 150 and 180 Quranic schools, where basic reading and recitation of the Quran were taught. The schools had an estimated peak of between 4,000 and 5,000 students while the city's population was recorded at about 100,000.

After the reign of Mansa Musa, the ancient Mali Empire began to witness a period of gradual weakness and eventual collapse. In 1391, the city of Timbuktu was sacked by the Mossi who originated from neighbouring Burkina Faso where they remain the dominant ethnic group. The Mossi are said to be the direct descendants of the Dagomba in Ghana[43]. The group lived in villages of extended families and grew so powerful that they began conquering the surrounding villages and states including Timbuktu. By 1493, the Tuaregs also seized Timbuktu, and the Songhai defeated Mali in the same year[44].

The Songhai are a group who settled on both banks of the middle Niger River and ruled by a dynasty of royal family of Sonni since the thirteenth century and became independent of Mali, establishing their own state known as the Songhai Empire with Gao as their capital.[45]

The conquest by Songhai was followed by an invasion from Morocco in the fifteenth century in search of gold. With an army of between 3,000 and 4,000, as well as 8,000 dromedaries, they attacked and crushed the Songhai army, thereby taking over all the important cities of Mali from the Songhai[46]. However, by the sixteenth century the empire had split up and this led to the rise of many different groups. In 1747, a Tuareg prince regained control of Timbuktu, a city claimed to have been founded by the Tuaregs in the fourteenth century. In the southern part, the Bambara had risen to power and established their presence and rule at Segou. Between 1818 and 1844, a Fulani theocratic [Islamic] system of government was established and extended from Djenne to Timbuktu; and eventually a conflict ensued between the Fulani and the Bambara, which lasted from 1854 to 1864, with the arrival of the French colonisers in Mali, all the peoples in Mali ultimately were forced to submit to the colonizers.

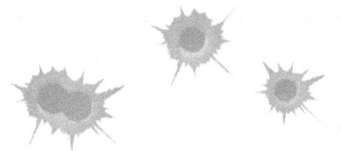

## CHAPTER THREE

# Colonialism and Post-Colonialism [1899-2013]

*At sunset when you pray to God, say over and over that
each man is a brother and that all men are equal.*

– Sekou Toure [Grandson of Samori Toure]

The interest of France in the West African sub-region can be traced back to 1637when the French built a fort at the mouth of the Senegal River with the aim of exploring the interior. France, Netherlands, and Portugal came into fierce competition for trade in the Senegal area. In addition to the North, France had taken Algiers in 1830 going on to conquer Algeria. Throughout the 19th Century French colonists settled in Algeria.

Changes in technological development in the eighteenth century led to a renewed interest in African exploration among Europeans generally. The invention of instruments such as the compass, and marine astrolabe made movement across oceans less difficult leading to the emergence of what came to be known as the Age of Exploration. In this way, first the Portuguese and the Dutch, British and the French were able to access the entire coastline of Africa and the first result of this was the notorious Atlantic Slave Trade.

Scientists and explorers followed. During the Napoleonic Wars, in the region of 2.000 scientists participated in a scientific expedition, to catalogue the artefacts of modern Egypt and its natural history after Napoleon succeeded in capturing the country. The exploits of other Europeans like Richard Burton [1821-1890] in West and East Africa, John Hanning Speke [1827-1864], who discovered Lake Victoria, one of the sources of the Nile and journeyed down it, David Livingstone [1813-1873] and Henry Morton Stanley [1841-1904] in South and Central Africa but above all Mungo Park [1771-1806], who was the first European to trace the complete length of the River Niger.

Such explorations attracted Europe's interest in Africa and alerted them to its natural resources. Soon the European powers were at loggerheads as they 'scrambled' to take possession of Africa's riches. The Berlin Conference, convened between 1884 and 1885, by the European powers was supposed to provide criteria and a set of rules for colonisation and trade activities on the African continent. Participants at the conference agreed that 'effective occupation' should determine how nations would lay claim to any territory on the African continent[47]. This agreement naturally accelerated the pace of European invasions.

Many reasons have been advanced regarding the primary interest of France in Mali. The legendary wealth and the gold deposits of the old Mali Empire might have played a part but in actual fact France's primary interest in the area was the need to link up its holdings in Senegal and Algeria, which had been occupied earlier, as well as to provide access to the Congo and its resources through Lake Chad[48]. The French Sudan was a set of colonies that between 1865 and 1960 was administered as the Federation of French West Africa, namely Senegal, Guinea, Cote d'Ivoire, Upper Volta [Burkina Faso], Niger, Mauritania, and Dahomey [Benin]. Algeria had remained an important part of the overseas empire of the French since its annexation in 1830 and in 1848 it subsequently became a department in metropolitan France.

As has been seen, Mungo Park was the first European to travel through Mali to the River Niger but was drowned at the Bussa rapids in present-day Nigeria. A companion of Mungo Park, Alexander Gordon, was killed by the Tuaregs after a successful journey to Timbuktu in 1826. In 1828, the Frenchman, René-Auguste Caillié became the first European to visit Timbuktu and live to tell the tale. Between 1880 and 1881, a French colonel, Paul Flatters, led an expedition to survey a railroad that would cross the Sahara. His expedition was composed of 300 camels, 10 French soldiers, and 78 native guides and porters. When Flatters attempted to cross the territory controlled by the Tuaregs in the Sahel, the Tuareg leaders rejected the idea and as a result laid ambush for the French team[49]. Many of them were killed and others died as a result of injuries sustained and the harsh climate and topography. As a result there wasn't a single survivor.

The French then dispatched heavily armed military missions from Algeria, Senegal, and Congo in 1899, led by Captain Paul Voulet and Adjutant Lieutenant Julian Chanoine. They were accompanied by 2,000 soldiers, 100 guides and interpreters and over 1,000 porters. The mission was reported to have burnt villages, enslaved the population, and killed those that were considered superfluous to their needs[50]. As a result of the atrocities committed by the Voulet-Chanoine-led mission to Mali, the French had to make a reassessment of its military-led pacification strategy of the Sudan region and replaced Voulet with Lieutenant Colonel Klobb, who was killed by Voulet, thus complicating the entire issue. Nevertheless it was the expedition by Voulet and Chanoine which marked the beginning of French attempts to impose colonial rule in Mali.

This was only achieved after some years of bitter struggles and determined resistance, in particular the heroic and epic campaigns of Samori Touré, whose well-organised empire straddled much of West Africa. His army too was well-organised and repeatedly defeated French forces sent to subdue him. The French were forced to admit defeat and sign treaties with him, which they regularly broke, until eventually he was forced to abandon his original state and establish another centred on Cote D'Ivoire. Ultimately, French fire-power proved too much for him. He was captured and exiled to Gabon.

The introduction of colonial rule saw a transformation in the structure of the Malian society politically, economically, and socially. It saw the emergence of a totally new administrative system, implemented by new officials. In pre -colonial Mali, people did not draw any distinction among the regimes or reigns of particular individuals or of any general political order. The paramount factor justifying rule and the acceptance of rule was the notion of '*fanga*' – in other words the power to rule. This was the essence of rule and provided the *raison d'être* for any institution of rule or leadership. Rule derived its hegemony from the capacity to suppress any manoeuvring between competing political factions – what is called '*fadenkele*'. Leadership in pre-colonial Mali was evaluated on the basis of its performance: the capacity to maintain social harmony as well as to ensure the well-being of the community. However, the latter was sometimes and it was sometimes assumed that *fanga* alone was sufficient.[51] Perhaps this may have aided the imposition and acceptance of colonial rule in Mali, which, even though it was strongly resisted, relied largely on force, whether it was accompanied by other political and economic tools or not. As a result it would appear that adaptability to the colonial system in Mali may not have been as difficult as expected.

Colonial rule in Mali saw the rise to power of new families and individuals from the lower hierarchy of colonial native administration. French colonial rule altered the previous socio-political order, especially in southern Mali. There was a shift in political legitimacy. Two new types of political elites emerged in Mali during the period of colonial rule. The French replaced the previous ruling families with others who were traditionally considered to be inferior in status. Literacy, geographic and occupational mobility provided advantages to individuals from all social backgrounds to occupy positions in the colonial administration and benefit from new and growing trade opportunities. New moral and legal codes introduced by the French subverted historic values and social culture as they proclaimed the equality of man and thus made it possible for people of lower social origin to rise in status. As such, previous influential families were forced to acknowledge and accept gradually that there had been a power shift through the introduction by the French of new systems and policies.[52]

As touched on in the prologue, in general, French colonial policy was a form of direct rule in sharp contrast to Lugard[53] and others' Indirect Rule as implemented by the British in their East and West African colonies. The French had tried various policies overtime in its different colonies, the earliest of which was known as 'assimilation' which tried or aimed to transform Africans into Frenchmen. The policy derived its ideological roots in the egalitarian ideals of the French Revolution - freedom, equality, and fraternity. Not all social forces in France however approved of such an approach. Conservatives, monarchists and the Catholic Church were opposed to it.

Despite its apparent democratic and egalitarian gloss, the assimilation policy was in essence based on an assumption of the superiority of French culture and civilisation. It was a policy that was seen to have little or no belief in the value or validity of African cultures, histories or civilisations.[54]

With the expansion of the French colonial empire in Africa in the late nineteenth century, many different African peoples came under

French rule and there was a growing dissatisfaction with the policy of assimilation. This prompted a debate on existing colonial policy. While some argued that Africans were racially inferior and incapable of full assimilation, others argued that the strenuous efforts required in education in order to make assimilation a reality were not realistic. However, above all these, was the growing realisation and recognition that the Africans had their own very distinctive cultures. This debate was said to have triggered a change in colonial policy to a new policy of 'association'. Association meant the recognition of African cultural and political values and that economic activities were, ostensibly, to be of mutual benefit to the Africans and the French. The policy also meant the retention of traditional customs, laws and religion but in reality it became very difficult to implement, as the French divided African societies into cantons or districts and chiefs considered not subservient were deposed without any regard for their status.

The application of the policy of 'association', just like that of 'assimilation' produced many contradictions. For instance, in Mali, the country was divided into multiple chiefdoms and village confederations that varied in size and degree of political centralisation. A lot of chiefdoms came under the control of more powerful chiefdoms. This relationship only came to be known during certain occasions such as annual tribute collection or during settlement of conflicts among political factions. All chiefdoms in Mali had maintained influence over various regions through the use of military force and, in less-centralised chiefdoms, it was the capacity of a clan to mobilise the labour for production and for military expeditions that determine the clan's political position.[55] The policy of association was also seen to have brought about a high degree of authoritarianism and saw the usurping of the rights of African peoples as the colonies remained under the control of military and conservative elements.

In terms of development, great efforts were made to increase exports and to build railways into the interior in order to assist these efforts. This placed a heavy burden of taxation on the population. Economically speaking, French businessmen and traders benefited most from the system, followed by the Lebanese and the Syrians in collaboration with the French, to the detriment of the African people, who could not compete with the Lebanese and the Syrians who had access to credit facilities that were not available to the indigenous African people[56].

A mark of the oppressed and inferior status accorded to the populations of the French colonies was the 1887 *Code de l'indigénat* legal system whereby all natives in France's colonial possessions occupied an inferior status and were excluded from the rights of the citizens of France. The Code provided for taxes, forced labour, separate courts, corporal and –though outlawed in practice - capital punishment.

Though in most African states anti-colonial agitation was ongoing during the colonial period in the form of migration, revolts, strikes and movements for greater participation in government or self-rule, the process of decolonisation in Africa became accelerated after World War II, and many African countries began to witness a rise in nationalism and the desire for self-determination. It was a time when most European economies were experiencing a decline as a result of the devastating effects of the war and, as a consequence, found it extremely difficult and expensive to maintain their respective colonies. Combined with the economic problems were the emerging militant nationalist movements across Africa demanding self-rule from the colonial powers. The Mau Mau rebellion against the British in Kenya broke out in 1952; meanwhile, the French also tasted a similar fate with the outbreak of what came to be known as the Algerian war of independence against the French colonial administration in Algeria, which lasted from 1954 to 1962. Accounts of the Algerian war is detailed in book entitled 'Wretched of the Earth', written by Frantz Omar Fanon also known as Ibrahim Frantz Fanon [1925-1961], a French West Indian Psychiatrist and political philosopher. The publication was an attempt by Fanon to provide a psychological and psychiatric analysis of the effects of colonialism on the people and different nations that were under colonial domination and was published in 1961 shortly before his death. Fanon describes the process of decolonization in his book as a process that is violent in nature and espoused what came to be known as the 'revolutionary theory of violence'. The consequences of the war for both sides were huge both in terms of resources and casualties, with a death toll of between 960,000 and 1.5 million people, according to Algerian sources, and about 350,000, according to French sources. During the war, France was said to have devoted about 400,000 soldiers to the war, a development that led to the fall of the French fourth republic, which saw the return to power of General Charles de Gaulle. Upon coming to power, General de Gaulle made a declaration in 1959 that self-determination was the preferable solution to the Algerian War. And his words were followed by referendums in both France and Algeria, after which, albeit after many negotiations, the independence of Algeria was granted[57].

Generally, the politics of decolonisation in French Africa differed from that in other parts of Africa. Most of French West Africa tended to side with Vichy France[58] while French Equatorial Africa remained loyal the Free French under General de Gaulle. The participation of many African soldiers contributed to the liberation of metropolitan France from the Nazis during World War II and was to have been made possible as a result of those who fought on the side of Paris. Their participation in the war was obtained on the basis of what came to be known as the 'blood-for-rights principle'.[59] In 1944 by the Brazzaville Declaration de Gaulle promised Africans more rights, as well as the abolition of the *Code de l'indigénat* and its replacement with citizenship within a new order to be known as the French Union. It was a promise kept by de Gaulle but which only became a reality over time as the gradual process of decolonisation unfolded across French colonial Africa. Elections were organised for the first time in

French Africa in 1945, where African candidates presented themselves to electorates of African origin to the Constituent Assembly, which became responsible for the drafting of the constitution of the fourth republic.

The French Sudan, which Mali was part of, elected Fily Dabo Sissoko as its representative. The French Union came into being by 1946 and the *indigenat* system[60] was abolished and replaced with citizenship of the French Union. Under the new system, Africans were given the right to establish their own assemblies, which were referred to as Conseils Généraux. This process was followed by the creation for political parties within the French Union, as well as the proposal of certain reforms by General de Gaulle of the French Union and the French republic. Under the new reform, the various territories within the French Union would become independent states or republics with authority over all areas with the exception of foreign policy, defence, and finance. A referendum was held where all French colonies voted in favour of the new union in September 1958; and by November 1958, the colony known as the French Sudan[61], which comprised of Mali, came to be known as the republic of Sudan and a member of Communauté Française, or community of French countries or French Union, with its own assembly and a ministerial cabinet presided by a governor [French] but with full participation of politicians of Sudan origin[62].

The emergence of the new order was seen as a setback by many Africans who saw the transfer of authority from a federation of French West Africa to the various semi-independent states as a form of divide and rule; it was seen as setback for those territories that hoped to remain united with one another. The consequence was the search for some form of regional integration, and in this regard the Union Soudanaise [US-RDA], a political party led by Modibo Keita, took a leading role. Two visions emerged within the West African Rassemblement Démocratique Africain [RDA]. The first one was espoused by Modibo Keita and known as the US-RDA while the Senegalese PDS remained under Leopold Sedar Senghor, who generally advocated for a West African federation of states. The second vision was espoused by the Ivorian PDCI-RDA, which under Houphouët-Boigny favoured a West African federation that would be in close collaboration with metropolitan France.

In 1958 delegates from the French Sudan—which included Senegal, Benin, and Burkina Faso—voted in favour of the independent federalist alternative led by Modibo Keita, Leopold Senghor, and their respective political parties. Following this development, French Sudan received independence from France in 1960. The Sudanese republic [Mali] and Senegal were joined in a federation. This was not to last long and a few months later Senegal withdrew, and the Sudanese republic was renamed the republic of Mali[63].

After the attainment of independence, bureaucrats that had occupied lower positions under the colonial administration became no longer accountable to their French masters. Political party leaders that had taken leading role in the nation's independence struggled and took over various positions in the new setup with the consent of the colonial administration, which had given recognition to the political leaders as representatives of what was in the best interest of the new emerging nation state. However, in many parts of rural Mali, especially the south, the population was unwilling to acknowledge the leadership of this new emerging class, who was seen to have come from inferior social origin. Usually, political parties, especially the leading US-RDA under Modibo Keita who emerged as the president from independence, tried to justify their claims to power by referring to their leading role in the anti-colonial struggles as well as to their socialist orientations, which they claimed was the surest way of reclaiming the authentic Malian culture, which colonialism had destroyed. The regime tried to do this by using historians and artists to show some kind of continuity in their works between the new modern state and the old traditions and history, as seen in the adoption of the name Mali for the new republic instead of Sudan.[64]

It was not only in the rural south of Mali that the US-RDA-led administration faced the problem of convincing the population and consolidating its rule but in the northern part of Mali as well. Keita and his party came under attack for its high modernist socioeconomic policies, which were considered unrealistic, unnecessary, and untenable in certain parts of the country. The patronising attitude of the regime was criticised and was characterised by stereotypical ideas, which caused a build-up of tension among the northern populations consisting mainly of the Tuaregs. The Keita regime appeared to lack an understanding of local work ethics, gender relations, social dynamics, as well as political power structures. This led to the imposition of policies by the regime that was very much resented among a section of the population that favoured the preservation of the colonial socio-political legacy, particularly in northern Mali.

The presence of a French air force base in Mali raised the fears that the Malian government was pursuing a neo-colonial line.[65] The Northerners felt that the French were becoming too involved in the internal affairs of the country. When later Algerian fighters of the FLN were invited to Mali by Keita, their presence became an exacerbating factor as they developed comradely relations with the Tuareg group, with who they shared similar political objectives. The situation was further complicated as rumours of attack by the Tuaregs in collaboration with FLN and certain French elements started going round. Though unfounded, it was an indication of the distrust and mutual suspicion that existed between the Tuareg group in the north and the Keita regime.

The Tuaregs[66] on their part accused the Keita regime of isolating them from the political equation of the country. They had participated in the US-RDA anti-colonial struggles, and quite a number of them had indeed acquired Western education. However, it was not clear if they wanted to play a greater part in the government of Mali or not be a part of the new Mali at all. However, what became clear was that even if they wanted to remain, they would only do so so under certain conditions. This became clearer as the Malian state became more and more concerned to establish its identity. This lack of trust, uncertainty and build-up of tension between the Keita-led Malian regime and the Tuaregs finally led to what is known in the Tuareg language as Affelaga or rebellion in 1963 against the Malian state.

Modibo Keita remained the president of Mali from independence in 1960 until 1968 when an army general known as Moussa Traoré overthrew the Keita regime in a coup d'état. Under Traoré, Mali was transformed into a police state where political activities were completely forbidden. The military regime of Traoré lasted for two decades and was characterised by brutality and the repression of the Malian people. By 1970, it was clear that the welfare of the community could not be taken care of by the various leaders of Mali from independence, and by this time the state resources had diminished due to mismanagement and the economic adjustment measures imposed by international economic organisations or agencies such as the World Bank and the IMF.[67] In March 1991, Colonel Ahmadu Toumani Touré, who was a minister in the Traoré regime, joined a group of pro-democracy forces after Traoré ordered the shooting of several students who had protested against his regime in Bamako, the capital, and several hundreds of students were killed in cold blood[68]. The Traoré regime was also faced with another Tuareg rebellion in the same year. The result was the regime collapsed and Colonel Ahmadu Toumani Touré came to power, becoming the president of Mali in the same year.[69] Upon coming to power, Touré promised to relinquish authority to a democratically elected government after one year and true to his promise Touré launched a new political process in 1992 that saw elections taking place in the country. It was the first time the country had witnessed a democratic election since the election of Keita at independence. The outcome of the 1992 elections was generally lauded both within and outside Mali and Mali became a model of democracy particularly within the West African sub-region. Touré handed over the reins of power to Alpha Oumar Konare, who emerged winner of the 1992 elections.

In 1997, Konare indicated interest in contesting for the next election and was successfully voted in for another five-year term. His administration was noted for the restoration of democratic values in Mali, as well as the management of the Tuareg problem [see p. below]. Konare was also opposed to death sentence and commuted the death sentence passed on the erstwhile military dictator, Moussa Traoré, and his wife to life sentences. His government was, however, noted for corruption, particularly among official officeholders.

Under Konare Mali continued to play a significant role in the regional integration process under the ECOWAS[70]. At the end of Konare's second term in 2002, Mali again went through another round of elections where twenty-four candidates presented themselves to the electorate to contest the office of the president. At this time the former Malian military president Ahmadu Touré had joined politics and was among the twenty-four contenders and in the end emerged victorious and was announced the winner of the election. Mali's democracy under Touré was described as a success story among African states and finished the first five-year term in 2007 and was again re-elected in 2007[71]. In 2012, the government of Touré came to be criticised for its inability to handle an uprising in the northern part of the country by the Tuareg group and their al-Qaeda affiliate groups. Touré's second tenure in office was to end in 2012, and it was while his government was making preparation for another round of elections that the rebellion in the north broke out and all attempts by the Touré government to find a solution to the crisis did not yield any result. It was while Touré was making efforts to contain the insurgency in the north by involving the ECOWAS that a certain Captain Amadou Sanogo staged a military coup in March 2012, ousting the regime of Touré, which had ruled Mali from 2002 to 2012. After the coup, Touré was forced to flee the country while the United Nations, ECOWAS, France, United States, and other organisations condemned the coup and called for the restoration of constitutional order in Mali. Following this development, ECOWAS became involved in the affairs of Mali and negotiated the establishment of an interim administration with the Sanogo military junta and under an arrangement where the parliamentary leader, Dioncounda Traoré, emerged as the interim president of Mali[72]. The interim president took over power and prepared the country for elections in July 2013 after a French-led force had restored order in the country. The election was won by Ibrahim Boubacar Keita after a run-off in August in which he defeated Soumaïla Cissé to become the new democratically elected president of Mali.

# PART TWO

## Past Tuareg Wars in Mali

### *Imidiwan Afrik Temdem [Friends from all over Africa]*

*I have an inquiry, One that disturbs my soul Brethren Is the revolution like those trees whose branches will grow if they are watered? I have lived with such passion for a decade I have come among brethren My friends what are your thoughts? These people have lived degradation since birth They cannot make these trees grow with their water.*

– Tinariwen Tuareg Musical Band
[Rebel Songs, The New Yorker]

## CHAPTER FOUR

# The Tuaregs

*A desert Hosts us, a language Unites us, a culture Binds us.*

– Terakaft [Caravan] Tuareg Musical Band

A ccounts and traditions about the origins of the Tuaregs vary. They are sometimes conflicting and complicated, sometimes confusing and inaccurate. This relates not only to the locating but also to providing a general description of the group. However, most agree that very little is known about them – and for this reason, their identity is often confused with that of other peoples who share a location, a related language or have a similar appearance. In particular they are often confused with another indigenous North African people, Berbers.

The Tuaregs differ distinctly from the Berbers in many significant ways. Herodotus, the acclaimed father of history, referred in his writings to the indigenous people of North Africa as Libyans. He noted that among the Libyans there exists a group of nomads whom European travellers call the Tuareg - or Tawarek, after the name given to the group by the Arabs. The livestyle of this nomadic group differed greatly from that of the sedentary populations of the Mediterranean region. As knowledge and exploration of the Sahara increased, the presence of the Tuaregs was reported in many distant places, including Fezzan along the Niger[73].

Information relating to the group's complex social organisation and individual characteristics, the vast areas it inhabited and how numerous it was became available only gradually. Berth and Richardson were among the first European writers to reach the conclusion that the Tuareg was not a tribe but a race[74] of people of many different clans, which occupies a large area in North Africa and ranges as clans or confederations of tribes all over the central Sahara, southern Algeria, Tunisia, Tripoli, and north of Sudan[75]. They are also to be found in the East from Murzak-Kawar Oasis along the Tripolitanian coast in Libya as far as Chad, further to the west and south to Timbuktu. The Tuaregs dominate the regions they inhabit though they exercise little influence on the activities of the sedentary populations. They are known to control the three central caravan routes from the Mediterranean to Central Africa, which run from Fezzan to Lake Chad, Nigeria, and other tracks to Niger at Timbuktu and Gao. The Tuaregs have also penetrated sub-Saharan areas around the Niger River. Wherever they come in contact with other groups, they become the masters. Nowhere have the Tuaregs been considered or treated as slaves or underdogs. They ruled in Bornu, south-west of Lake Chad; they held sway from Algeria to Timbuktu; and they took control of all lands as far as the Atlantic Ocean until the arrival of the Moors and the French in the sixteenth and eighteenth centuries, respectively.

Generally, the Tuaregs are described as nomads whose means of livelihood revolves around raiding neighbouring communities. They were described by Rodd as a 'mendacious[76] people', whose tactics in warfare were characterised by surprise. The Tuareg have no-one's good opinion. They have never been beloved of other men. Instead they earned a reputation among their rivals for 'lies' [Rodd] and 'treachery'. Their knowledge of desert warfare is legendary and they fight with swords, lances as well as rifles when they can lay their hands on them.

The Tuareg is easily recognized because of certain physical characteristics they possess. These characteristics were described in a categorisation of the Libyan people by the renowned Italian anthropologist, Giuseppe Sergi [1831-1946], author of *L'Antropologia della Stirpe Camitica* and *The Mediterranean Race*. He categorised the Libyan people as belonging to three distinct groups based on their physical characteristics. The first category which he termed *dolichocephalic*[77] accurately describes the general structure and appearance of the Tuareg people[78]. This has not varied over the centuries. In the sixteenth century, Al-Hassan ibn-Muhammad [Leo Africanus], compiled a similar classification of groups in inner Libya between the Atlantic area and the Nile. He divided them into six different categories, namely Sanhaja, Guenziga, Zanziga, Jedala, Ketama, Targa, and Lenta. Interestingly all these groups identified by Al-Hassan ibn-Muhammad belong to the *muleththemim* or veiled category of people.

According to Al-Hassan ibn-Muhammad, the Sanhaja Tuaregs formed a desert confederation after the advent of Islam in the region and became responsible for the conversion to Islam of all Tuaregs of the west. They referred to themselves as El Merabat. El Merabat was later adopted as the name of the desert tribes which captured Fez and established what later came to be known as the Almoravid dynasty. This was the dynasty which conquered and occupuied the entire Maghreb and most of the Iberian Peninsula in Europe after successfully defeating a coalition of Castilian and Aragonese armies led by the Castilian king, Alfonso VI, at the battle of Sagrajas [or Zalaca/Zalaqa] in 1086. The victor was the Almoravid king, Yusuf ibn Tashfin. The Almoravids were responsible for the spectacular stimulation of science, architecture and the arts as well as the preservation of much of classical literature of antiquity, thus contributing to the glory of Western civilisation. The impetus and drive of the Almoravids was according to Rodd provided by the Tuaregs themselves who had inspired the Almoravid movement itself and all that it was able to achieve[79].

In Mali, despite their description as a nomadic war-like race the Tuaregs do have and are indeed familiar with social and political organisation as war itself requires some organisation and preparation. Although the degree as well as form of socio-political organisation certainly differs between various groups that exist in Africa and other places, the western Tuaregs, to which the Mali Tuaregs belong, have a hierarchy and a concept of clan or what is referred to as the *tewsit*[80] in the Tamasheq or Tuareg[81] language as the two main bases of their socio-political organisation. The *tewsit* or clan is seen to be common among all Tuaregs in general wherever they may be and is described as a semi-kinship group that is based on family lineage and ideology but which differs from one family or clan to another. Understanding the *tewsit* is of great importance in understanding the history and structure of the Tuareg society and politics.

Although the meaning and interpretations of the word, *tewsit,* has often been confused and misrepresented. The Tuaregs themselves have sometimes used the word to describe certain internal administrative organisations within their own society. But so far, in anthropological terms, the word has been translated to mean *clan*. And here, the clan and genealogy are seen to form a kinship structure as the two are also considered to be interrelated.

In the Tuareg society several genealogies exist, and these include groups such as the Imghad, or former slaves, as well as other groups considered poor or weak in the society, known as the Tilaqiwin[82]. And so a *tewsit* in this regard is considered as a socio-political group formed around a certain lineage or clan considered to belong to a particular category such as either the Imghad or Tilaqiwin in kinship terms. The male 'spine' of the *tewsit*- known in the Tamasheq language as the 'Aran Meddan'– are the paternal male cousins. The 'Tegeze' is the relationship between sister's children and mother's brother. These two, the 'Aran Meddan'and the 'Tegeze', are considered the most significant relations regarding kinships in western Tamasheq society and in Mali. These two relations mean unrestricted material support and protection to nephews and nieces by mother's brothers and, on the other hand, loyalty and protection to the uncle by the sisters' children and vice versa for the 'Aran Meddan', which is on the paternal side. These relations are extended from generation to generation.

All the various *tewsiten* [plural of *tewsit*] are incorporated and organised under what is known as an *ettebel*. The *ettebel* is explained as a grouping of clans and other age groups into a political unit in hierarchical order under a single leader known as the *amenokal* or owner of the land. The literal meaning of *ettebel* is 'federation'; and in the Tamasheq or Tuareg society, federations are seen to rise and fall, depending, of course, on the strength and the organising ability of the dominant groups politically[83]. They are spread across to Libya, Algeria, Niger, Tunis, Morocco, and Burkina Faso. The Tuareg in Mali consist of the Kel Adrar, Kel Tademekkat and the Kel Atazam. The Kel Ahaggar and Kel Ajjer are found in Algeria while the Kel Gress, Kel Air, and Kel Dinno are located in Niger. Although no groups are indicated as being in the other countries, the Tuaregs nevertheless exist in these states.

## CHAPTER FIVE

# The Tuareg in Mali

*Oh, you that are organized Moving together Hand in hand You're living a path that is empty of meaning In truth You're all Alone.* Amassakoul 'n' Tenere *[Traveller in the desert]* Song.

– Tinarewen Tuareg Musical Band
[Rebel Songs, The New Yorker].

Since the advent of French colonial rule in the French Sudan and later in Mali in the nineteenth century, the Tuaregs strongly resisted the French and recorded many successes against them. [84] As a result, the French were forced to formulate a separate policy towards the group in order to maintain their control over the colony.

The first phase of colonial rule was a period of confrontation between the French and the Tuaregs. In the second phase, the Tuareg tended to treat the French colonial administration with a haughty indifference. The Tuareg refused to participate in all colonial programmes and policies and also showed no interest in the colonial politics of the time. Failing to understand it, the French termed the reserved Tuareg attitude 'reserved' and 'deceitful'. However, despite this, the

French showed great interest in the culture of the Tuaregs in their territories. Certain aspects of their culture such as the matrilineal transfer of power as well as their hierarchical nature and structure of their society reinforced their reputation as the mythical lords of the desert, whose political system came to be compared with that of the European feudal system[85].

The myth surrounding the Tuaregs or Tamasheq as the lords of the desert had tremendous influence on French colonial policy towards the group. While the French were seen to pursue a policy of transformation and modernisation across the rest of the Sudan, they maintained a policy described as 'protective' towards the Tuaregs and their culture. The Tuaregs were exempted from forced military sercvice, forced labour and French education, considered to be diametrically opposed to the Tuaregs' way of life. The French attitude was one of sympathy and attraction. Nevertheless the Tuareg were kept under strict surveillance by the French authorities. It was a policy full of contradictions – sympathy and attraction on the one hand and suspicion and surveillance on the other.[86]

A serious consequence of French attitudes to the Tuareg was the French tendency to identify with and adopt certain beliefs and prejudices held by the Tuaregs regarding the rest of the peoples of the French Sudan. The Tuareg considered themselves the natural lords and masters of the black inhabitants of the French Sudan. Their views relating to social and racial relations tended to be credited and accepted by the French colonial administration, leading to an official colonial belief in the superiority of the Tuaregs over other groups. Naturally such a policy encouraged the division between the Tuaregs and other groups within the French Sudan and later the Malian nation.

Another issue that became a source of concern regarding the Tuaregs during the colonial period, was slavery. While the suppression of slavery was a general policy of the colonial masters, the French appeared reluctant to take action to end it in the French Sudan where it was prevalent among the Tuareg. The slave problem came to be known as the '*bellah* question' in Malian history. The Tuaregs were identified as slaveholders and raiders and as such responsible for the continued perpetuation of slavery in the Sudan. The French colonial adminstration did not aid the emancipation of slaves in the North as the critical infrastructure needed for such emancipation was not created in areas dominated by the Tuareg. For instance, it failed to create liberty villages as they did in the other parts of the Sudan, and no army recruitment or labour was created to offer the slaves an alternative occupation to the servitude they rendered to the Tuaregs. Thus French policy regarding slavery was described as one based on political interest. Certain clans among the Tuaregs, including the Kel Hoggar and Kel Adagh, had been allowed to retain their slaves and could also acquire more if they so wished[87]. Thus, the actions, policies, and decisions of the French colonial administration over time came to be interpreted by other groups inhabiting the Sudan as prejudicial and favouring the Tuaregs.

At the onset of political activities, which, as we have seen, came to be dominated by in effect three major political parties, namely the Keita-led Union Soudanaise [US-RDA], which became the dominant party in the French Sudan, the Senegalese Parti Democratique Soudanais [PDS], which remained under Leopold Senghor, and the PDCI-RDA, which came under Houphet-Boigny. These political parties attitude to the Tamasheq or Tuareg societies was that they did not conform to the norms that existed across the Sudan, including those of the French colonial administration. Among the various issues raised by the emerging political parties which became the main instruments of anti-colonial struggle in the French Sudan, some related to Tuareg society, such as the slave question. The nationalist parties demanded the emancipation of all slaves[88]. These parties were supported to a large degree by the masses – including the peasants and the slaves.

Thus pre-independence political parties were seen to be opposing Tuareg interests, who had always been seen to be the favourites of the French colonial administration[89]. It was such developments that laid the foundation of post-colonial relations between the Tuareg and the rest after the attainment of independence in 1960.

With the separation of Senegal from the Sudan republic after independence and the emergence of Mali as a republic, the Keita-led US-RDA came to dominate all political offices and activities in Mali as the founding ruling party in the new republic. Although at this time many Africans did not show much interest in political affairs in Mali, it was noted that as in the pre-colonial period, the Tuaregs once again stood aloof from post-independence national[90] politics. Though it is true that a limited number of Tuareg did participate, they confined their activities to their own domain. Even then they did not present themselves for election to national or local government offices.

A comparative analysis of nomad voters and sedentary population voters to the 1946 constitutional assembly showed that in the Kidal area, which is a Tuareg region, 243 people, or 1.7% of the total population, participated in the election; and among these people, only 73 were Tuaregs[91]. It was generally based on statistics of this kind that some argued that the Tuareg might indeed participate in elections. It was, however, observed that the participation of the group remained minimal despite the fact that at that time the chief of the Tuaregs[92] had also established a party, Parti Socialiste Progressif [PSP]. However, several reasons were advanced for the lack of real participation of the Tuaregs in the political affairs of Mali, both during the pre-independence period as well the post-independence era. The first explanation for the group's low participation in political affairs had to do with geographical location. The Tuaregs generally remained in villages as nomads and as a result became isolated from the political centre as all major political activities were concentrated in the urban areas[93]. The second pointed to the general lack of interest in representative politics by the group. Their leaders were tribal chiefs who relied on the French authorities for their influence and did not appear to have either interest or confidence in the emerging post colonial order, which they perceived as a threat to their way of life and their interests[94]. The third reason derived from Tuareg antipathy to western education, which they had resisted since it was first introduced by the colonial administration. This was seen to have impacted negatively on the collective achievements of the group as it denied the group many opportunities and positions in both the colonial administrative set up, as well as in the post-independence politics of the newly emerging Malian state[95].

In newly independent Mali, the governing US-RDA, led by Modibo Keita, who was Mali's president at independence, introduced many changes into the nation's socio-economic and political sectors. These were to have a profound effect not only on the Tuaregs but also on the country at large. The Malian economy at this time was redesigned in line with the new political system or ideology, which the US-RDA Keita-led government envisioned for the Malian people. At independence the president was quoted as saying that socialism was the best option for Mali as a political system or ideology, a system he called African socialism. Under such a system, a planned economy would be put in place, supervised by Keita through his cabinet; and in accordance with such a policy two basic sectors of the Malian economy, which received little or no attention from the past colonial administration, would be strengthened, namely the agricultural and industrial sectors.

The new economy was designed by foreign experts, a team headed by the Egyptian economist, Samir Amin. Others included Jean Bernard and Jean Leroy, who were all well-known Marxists, as well as Eli Lobel, an Israeli planner[96]. According to these experts, the plan was designed to fit the realities of the new emerging nation, and in part aimed mainly at agricultural and rural modernisation. In accordance with the new plan, farmers across the nation were to be organised into cooperative groups and a credit scheme was introduced as well as the introduction of modern farming equipment and education to all Malian farmers.[97]

The regime envisioned the reshaping of Malian peasant society based on modern scientific socialist principles combined with tradition and the Mande 'spirit of industriousness'. Modibo Keita, who is also of Mande origin, appeared to have formed an opinion that the Mande people were serious, hardworking, stubborn, patient, and loyal, which are qualities that he hoped would form the character of the new Malian nation. The regime saw the Malian nation as originally communally based and that such communality was destroyed as a result of the introduction of the monetary economy during colonial rule.

Fundamental adjustments were made by the regime as a result of which many modern, young, and disadvantaged groups came to be promoted, among them women and other members of the lower castes and former slaves. Rural development schools were established all over the country with the sole aim of providing education in modern agricultural techniques while elementary schools were established to teach courses based on the structure of the new Malian government's ideology of Marxism/Leninism as well as the aims of the US-RDA as a party. The new changes were expected to propel the transformation of the Malian society into a modern, prosperous nation as envisioned by the Keita-led US-RDA government.

In order to achieve such economic objectives, the Keita-led government had to take certain measures they deemed necessary. The regime also realised that certain groups within the country were opposed to the newly introduced policies[98], and this largely led to the formulation of more policies that would ensure the implementation and actualisation of the core economic policies. It was, however, observed that in spite of all the efforts to have good and workable economic policies, they were resented by the Malian people, the Tuaregs in particular. The Malian state at independence lacked the resources necessary for the development of the country, especially under its new economic policy. And as a consequence, the regime created what came to be known as human investments.[99] This meant that the Malian population was expected to work on a voluntary basis to ensure the development of the country. The regime further introduced a policy that entailed the conscription of young people into labour brigades, which came to be organised under agricultural schemes throughout the country.

For some time the Keita administration remained optimistic about its new economic policies in the country. However gradually it became apparent that they were a failure. There were a number of reasons for this. It was observed that the regime had sought to effect the envisioned modernisation of the Malian economy by sheer willpower. It wrongly assumed that the mentality of the Malian people could be transformed from a traditional to a modern outlook overnight and that this was the only possible way of achieving the government's objectives. Here, it is argued that the regime appeared to have confused political change and economic transformation. Political change does not necessarily mean a change in the economy.

The two programmes referred to above, namely the human investment and the youth labour brigades, revived the painful memories of the Malian population of the policies of the past colonial administration. While the new human investment policy came to be closely associated with the forced labour under the colonial governments, the *service civique*, which forced young people to work in various agricultural schemes across the country, it came to be seen as a replica of the 'little farming soldiers' of the French colonial administration in Mali.

The immediate consequence of the two new policies by the Keita-led administration was that it led to the emergence of what was previously known during the colonial administration as labour migration[100]. The people resisted being forced to work, and to avoid any confrontation with the authorities, they resorted to migration to other cities both within and outside Mali. During the French colonial rule in Mali, the French Sudan served as a labour reserve for other colonies in the Congo and sometimes the Middle East. People had reacted to the colonial policies and migrated in their thousands across the West African region to avoid being taken to any of these colonies to work. And so when the Keita regime insisted on these policies, the system of labour migration returned to Mali[101], and the government was now looking for a way to put a stop to such migration as it was naturally affecting the new economic policy negatively. Several attempts were made to put a stop to such migrations but failed, and as such, the government introduced what came to be considered as travel permits[102], which enabled people to travel within the country. People were migrating from the countryside to towns such as Bamako in order to enable them to further migrate from these urban centres to neighbouring states. The government hoped that the introduction of the permits would stop such movements both within and outside the Malian state.

Migration then came to represent a kind of resistance by the Malian people against the policies of the Keita government. Although the reasons for migration were explained in different ways, many agreed that it was to avoid taxes, forced labour, as well as payment of dues to the Keita-led US-RDA political party that was made mandatory to citizens.

Of all the groups present in Mali, it appeared that the new policies affected the Tuaregs the most. It was reported that between November and December 1962, hundreds of Tuaregs living along the western part of the Niger bend, around Hombori and Douentza, migrated to Upper Volta [Burkina Faso][103]. Many reasons have been advanced to try and explain why the Tuareg felt most disturbed by the new policies. During the period of the French colonial rule the Tuaregs were the only group exempted from forced labour and military recruitment in Mali. As such, the policies appeared completely strange to the group; in fact, what made it worse and in fact totally unacceptable was the Keita government's practice of forced labour for the women. In the Tuareg tradition, women were free from work and only performed their domestic responsibilities of cooking and fixing tents. Those women who did other work in the Tuareg societies were considered to be of lower social status, but even then, they only performed the rôle of goat herders. In the Tuareg society, the domestic slaves usually undertake all sorts of manual labour such as fetching water and firewood. Thus the general world view of the Tuareg inhabiting the North and their concept of labour was totally at variance with that of the other peoples inhabiting southern Mali, in particular the Bambara and Mande.

Many argued that right from the inception of the new country, the historical foundations of the country were based on the history of the Mande and the Bambara nation[104]; and Keita himself, who emerged as president at independence, was of Mande descent. It was maintained that the elements that made up national discourse and identity-building were derived from the Mande culture and history.[105] It was also observed that even the adoption of the name Mali was a reflection of the ancient Mali Empire, which was founded by the Mande and Bambara peoples. At independence many African states changed their names and took neutral names to avoid ethnic problems as colonial borders came to place diverse peoples in one country irrespective of their history and culture. Nations such as Benin, which was formerly known as the kingdom of Dahomey, changed to Benin Republic for such reasons just as the Gold Coast avoided adopting the famous Asante empire name and took a new name known as Ghana. These countries avoided their famous ancient names mainly to avoid ethnic tension in their various emerging states. On the contrary, the adoption of Mali underlined the dominance of a part of its population, namely the Mande or Bambara people, in the affairs of the new state.[106]

The above perception is sometimes used to explain why the Tuaregs of the North, since the founding of the new nation, continued to consider themselves separate from the Malian nation and government. Scholars tend to explain the independence and the indifference of the Tuareg group to the Malian state as that of competing nationalisms. The Tuareg had maintained such attitude even during the colonial period. However, it became more pronounced after independence. The Tuaregs, from their actions, did not wish to be part of the Malian state and generally envisioned a Tuareg nation that was politically independent. The Malian state, on the other hand, favoured a single state embodying the various groups within it, including the Tuaregs. The Malian state envisioned a truly united country with all the groups promoting the interest of the state. The Tuareg wanted no part of it.

It has been suggested that the Keita regime itself was aware of the sour relations that existed between the Malian state and the Tuaregs and from the beginning formulated policies that were seen to be favourable to the group to create a positive image of the new regime and the Malian state in the eyes of the group. Keita did this by maintaining the tribal chiefs as well as recruiting local administrators from among the Tuaregs for a period of time. [107]

However, the formulation of these new economic policies by the Keita regime, not only succeeded in creating bitter relations between the regime and the Tuaregs but also among other groups that opposed the policies and considered them oppressive within the country. With the Tuaregs, in particular, the economic policies were not the only grievance it had with the regime, but rather the policies formed a part of their motivation for reacting openly and opposing the regime. The Tuaregs blamed the administration for failing to include some of its educated elements in the governance of the new nation even within the northern area, which was considered the base of the group[108]. The Keita administration refused to give any consideration in terms of appointments to the group after it abolished the tribal chiefs system that prevailed in the colonial period. The regime's refusal to appoint the educated Tuaregs was explained by many as a form of distrust[109], which it harboured against the group. But the regime's denial of such appointment further became a source of concern and discontentment among the Tuaregs with the Keita-led government, which in its early days had tried to win its group[110].

Furthermore, prior to the adoption of migration as a form of resistance by the Tuaregs and other groups within Mali that were opposed to the regime's new policies, the Keita government had announced as part of its new policies the introduction of the Malian franc as a new currency[111]. The introduction of the new currency gave the government control over imports and exports from, as well as to, neighbouring countries. This policy did not go down well with the Dioula community, a group of the Mandinka people and descendants of the old Mali Empire who were actively involved in trading activities. Their resentment resulted in a protest by the group in Bamako on 20th July, 1962. The Dioula community protested against the Keita regime with slogans such as 'Long live, France! Down with the Malian franc and down with Mali and its government of infidels!'[112] Following the protest, many people were arrested by the Keita government and tried. The regime accused those arrested of conspiracy against the state and in October of the same year a tribunal appointed to investigate the disturbance made its verdict known. In accordance with the verdict, seventy-seven merchants received various punishments or sentences ranging from one-year imprisonment to twenty years of forced labour in the Kidal prison. Those accused of organising the protest, on the other hand, were given death sentences. These included Fily Dabo Sissoko, Hamadoun Dicko, and Kassoum Touré. The death sentences were subsequently commuted by the government to life sentences with hard labour in Kidal.[113]

After the protests, it became clear that a confrontation was brewing between the Malian government, on the one hand, and other groups within the Malian country, including the Tuaregs. The confrontation came to manifest itself after the migration of some of the Tuaregs that lived in the western part of Niger to Upper Volta. The Keita regime at first did not react to the migration, but Keita was said to have later visited the area and appealed to the people of the area to desist from such migration[114]. At about the same time, some government agents were killed in the area, obviously by the people in the area, which included the Tuaregs. The government responded to these killings by sending two commando units to put a stop to the migration taking place in the area. In a particular clash between the fleeing population and the stationed commando units, about fifty civilians were said to have lost their lives[115].

These two events, the protest by Dioula group and the clash with the Malian soldiers as a result of the migration of the Malian population to foreign countries made it clear that the Keita-led US-RDA regime did not have or was losing control of the country. Though the government did not collapse, it was clear that it was having great difficulty in grappling with the problems that faced it.'[116]

Prior to the occurrence of these two events, resistance to the regime by the Tuareg group had often expressed itself in the form of non-payment of taxes to the US-RDA party[117] and general disobedience to government instructions. The two confrontations described above however led to a rebellion by the Tuaregs in the following year, which came to be known in history as the Afellaga or the Tuareg war of 1963.

## CHAPTER SIX

# The 1963 Tuareg War

*Tuareg men and women Open your eyes Open your eyes Awake we're in a world that is moving fast Who doesn't pay attention will perish.* Keltamashek song.

– Ibrahim Ag Alhabib
Tinarewen Musical Band
[Rebel Songs, The New Yorker]

The 1963 war has been explained from various perspectives. It has sometimes been seen as primarily arising from the increase in taxes by the Malian administration, which was resisted by certain groups among the Tuaregs and other people that were dissatisfied with the Keita regime and its policies, such as the Adagh and the Ifoghas. Yet the Tuareg paid no tax at all. Hence it has been suggested that it was caused by the punishment inflicted on them by the Malian administration with regard to migration.[118]However a closer observation of the rebellion revealed that it resulted from a combination of factors and events that had taken place overtime. Some of these factors may be considered historical, especially if one looks at the politico-historical development of the Tuareg as a group in Mali since the pre-colonial period, the period of colonial rule as well as the relations that existed between the Malian state and the group in the post-independence era.[119]

Since the protests which followed the introduction of the Malian franc and the clash between the commando units and the fleeing population in Mali, which mainly consisted of the Tuaregs, the Malian government became uncomfortable with the situation in the country. If anything, the authorities began to doubt their capacity to maintain full control over the newly emerging country. As a result they began exhibiting certain temperamental tendencies and overreacting on relatively slight issues. The Malian administration made several attempts to win the confidence of some of the various groups among the Tuaregs such as the Adagh and the Ifoghas, as did the French during colonial rule[120]but such attempts did not yield any positive results. Instead they were construed as signs of weakness. Such behaviour led the Tuaregs to presume that this was an opportune time to break away from the Malian state – an objective that they had historically entertained.

Another factor that was seen to have further complicated the relations between the Malian state and the Tuaregs was the spread of rumours, none of which had any basis in concrete fact, and issues became misrepresented and misinterpreted just as the atmosphere continued to create fear and mutual suspicion between the two sides.

The international setting also influenced and magnified the fears of the Malian government, especially concerning its borders and the Tuaregs' settlements along these borders. Many of the Tuaregs located along the border fled to Niger Republic, that opted to maintain ties with the French even after independence unlike the Malian state that chose the socialist path over neo-colonial dependency and broke its traditional ties with France. In Mauritania, too, the presence of the French remained strong and they continued to maintain their troops in the country even after independence. In Algeria, the war of independence was still being waged, though it had not reached the southern part of the country which was still occupied by the Tuaregs. Attempts had been made to include certain groups among the Tuaregs such as the Kel Hoggar and Kel Agger into the Forces de Liberation National [FLN]. There was a strong military presence of the French in Algeria and many officers that served in Mali got transferred after independence of Mali to Algeria[121]. The presence of these former colonial officers that served in Mali and were now serving in these neighbouring states naturally made the Malian authorities very nervous. The Malian government became concerned and suspected the French might be hatching a sinister plan or agenda to stir up some kind of unrest within Mali, using the Kel Adagh. Somehow the Malian administration convinced itself that the French were still interested in regaining their influence in Mali, though there was as yet no concrete evidence for such a suspicion.[122]

However the authorities suspicions were soon confirmed when the Minister of the Interior wrote a letter to the commandant in the North about the presence of French spies and agitators in Mali as far back as October 1960[123]. Added to this was the presence of the French military at the air force base near Tessalit in northern Mali, which it continued to maintain even after independence as well as the presence of FLN fighters, who had initially come on the invitation of the Malian government as a policy of support for the independence of Algeria. These two issues, namely, the presence of the French officers and the FLN fighters and their training camps in the north, an area largely dominated by the Tuareg, were later to become sources of great concern for the Malian state. The result was that the FLN became deeply involved in Mali as they were offered Malian passports and with time began to recruit the local population into their ranks, and this local population mainly consisted of the Tuaregs. The FLN planned to launch a new front in the Algerian war of independence from Mali with the recruited Tuaregs.

Because of location and certain other relations, the Tuaregs came to exert influence over both the FLN and the French officers at the air force base, which were both located in their neighbourhood. All this added to the general atmosphere of confusion, fear, and distrust that characterised the relations between the Tuaregs and the Malian regime.

Then rumours began going round among the Tuaregs of a new cattle policy by the Malian government, which also coincided with an increment in the tax on cattle. Under the new cattle nationalisation policy[124], cattle could now only be sold within Mali. The Tuaregs usually sold their cattle in neighbouring countries; and particularly since the introduction of the Malian franc, they focused on foreign markets in Algeria, Mauritania, and Niger for their cattle. As a matter of fact, the Tuaregs perceived the introduction of the Malian franc as a deliberate policy introduced to curtail the export of cattle. The Tuareg sought clarification from the Malian authorities regarding the cattle nationalisation policy.

In the past, there had existed some misunderstandings between the Tuaregs and certain tax collection officers known as the *goumiers*. During one incident, a *goumier* was engaged in an argument with a Tuareg named Inadjelim ag Ebanzen, a member of the nobility among the Iforgoumoussen clan. In the course of the argument over tax, the *goumier* was reported to have shot and killed Inadjelim. Following this development, a delegation from the Ifogha clan of the Tuaregs made an official complaint about the killing, insisting that the *goumiers* were employing brutal and inhuman methods in collecting taxes from them. At the same time, family members of the killed Tuareg attacked and took revenge on the *goumier*.

These developments exacerbated the tenseness of the situation – thus bringing the possibility of a revolt yet closer[125]- especially as communication between the Tuaregs and the Malian authorities had become difficult, with both parties relying on rumours for information about each other. Fears that the French were planning an attack[126] grew among the Malian state officials, with certain developments taking place in Dakar and the general presence of French troops in neighbouring Niger, Algeria, and Mauritania. The Malian authorities began to suspect that the French might collaborate with the Tuareg groups, who were now dissatisfied with the new policies in the country, and arm them to make war on the Malian state. To make matters worse, they feared that the Algerian FLN fighters might support the Tuaregs in the event of any revolt against the Malian nation. The alliance between the FLN fighters and the Tuaregs was contemplated from a racial point of view as the Algerians and the Tuareg shared certain physical characteristics in contrast with the Africans of the South.[127] The fact that the FLN training camp was situated in the North among the Tuareg and that the FLN and the Tuareg local community had developed close relations with each other did not make matters any better.

It was therefore hardly a surprise when in 1963 the war broke out. It began on 15 May 1963 when Elledi ag Alla, son Alla ag Albachir[128], and Touteka ag Effand attacked a group of *goumiers* and seized their guns and equipment. The *goumiers*, led by Ahyaya ag Quarezza, were on a mission to Timiaouine when the duo of Elledi ag Alla and Touteka ag Effand stopped them and, after taking their weapons, ordered the rest of the group to go and inform certain slaves at a location known as Bouressa that they were around.[129] The Tuaregs were known to keep slaves even though slavery was banned in Mali. The Tuareg had probably concealed these slave in the Bouressa area in anticipation of the encounter with the *gourmiers*, hoping the slaves would come and join them and together fight the Malian authorities. This singular act is said to have marked the beginning of the 1963 Tuareg war against the Malian state. Interestingly, the Afellaga were often linked to the resistance against the French that was led by Alla ag Albachir, a member of one of the Adagh's leading clans known as the Irayaken. At one time he was said to have headed the Ifogha clan, which led all of the Kel Adagh Tuaregs. It was reported that during the period of the colonial rule, Alla ag Albachir refused to obey any power. He refused to recognise the authority both of the French colonisers and that of the local Tuareg's chief known as Amenokal Attaher ag Illi, despite the fact that he was obeyed by all the Tuareg groups[130]. Alla ag Albachir lived as an outlaw and became a very popular hero among the Kel Adagh, in particular, as a result of his defiance against the French colonisers. Elledi ag Alla who kicked off the 1963 rebellion was Alla ag Albachir's son, who was now following in his father's footsteps.

The griots and praise singers of the time generally referred to Albachir as 'old leather pant' or 'the great chief' when describing his bravery and wit. They generally showered praises on his person that sometimes explains how he was feared within the Tuareg society, among the French and in Mali in general. These mythical praises contributed to creating the larger-than-life image associated with his name. It is only in ancient Greece and the mythology of the Greeks that such praises feature. Some versions describe how when he approaches certain Tuareg settlements even the trees would move aside and that war drums would sound across the entire Tuareg world, indicating trouble and danger each time he is seen or sighted. It will perhaps not be wrong to attribute contemporary Tuareg struggle to Albachirs' boldness and fearlessness. It was his role in the resistance against the French in the colonial period that to a greater extent inspired future revolts by the Tuareg, including the 2012 war in Mali.

The Tuaregs had never considered Alla Albachir to be a common bandit, as the French did. To them he was a resistance fighter, one that resisted foreign domination and control, and saw him and all those who resisted the French as the predecessors of the Afellaga [rebellion]. Alla ag Albachir was said to have been killed when Elledi was only about seven years old, and in Tuareg tradition the concept of *egha* [revenge] was considered a matter of honour. It was seen as a debt contracted when the family honour is stained, its prestige compromised or shame caused to it either individually or collectively[131]. Thus, it was expected that when Elledi grew up and came to know those who had assassinated his father, he would avenge the killing of his father.

The significance of *egha* as a reason in the organisation of resistance against a particular people by the Tuareg cannot be downplayed. Elledi was quoted as saying that he became a rebel specifically to avenge the killing of his father under the French administration after a group of Malian security personnel confessed in a boastful manner to have participated in his father's killing while threatening to end his life the way they had his father's. The *goumiers* Elledi attacked at the beginning of the Afellaga were among those who boasted that they killed his father. Elledi it is said specifically made the attack on them with the aim of revenging his father's death according to the practice of *egha* as in the Tuareg tradition, a duty he was bound to perform. Thus, Alla ag Albachir led the Tuareg resistance against the French during the colonial rule while his son Elledi led or at least initiated[132] the resistance against the Malian state after independence.

After the outbreak of the war, a mission of the US-RDA officials and chiefs was sent to negotiate with the rebels, and at this meeting the officials were said to have spelt out the consequences of revolting against the state. In response, the rebels explained their aims and grievances as follows:

> *We fight for our independence, we don't want any of this Mali, and the leaders have no patience. They throw us into prison for no reason. There are heavy taxes and exaggerated custom duties. We are beaten, chained and enslaved in front of our women and children. And the marriage act does not conform to Islamic custom. We are against Mali because all its institutions are anti-religious and against us. We want*

*our independence, that is all we look for, but we cannot stay in Mali. We are against all the principles of the party and government.*[133]

The declaration cited above did not provide a full description of the reasons, feelings or grievances harboured by the Tuaregs against the Malian government. A captured rebel by the name of Amoukson ag Azandeher revealed when interviewed other concerns regarding the revolt. According to him, the Tuaregs or nomads in the North found it inconceivable to accept orders from the black population of the South, whom they had always looked down on as inferiors, servants or slaves. He reiterated that the position of the Tuaregs was one opposed to racial equality. For the Tuareg there was nothing to be gained by Malian independence apart from taxes. He further accused the Malian state of arrogance and feelings of superiority over the chiefs of the Tuaregs without any consideration to their opinion and status in the affairs of the country. He finally accused the Malian regime of high-handedness and general maltreatment through its gendarmerie [soldiers].[134]

What was surprising was the confidence with which so few people, a small minority of the Malian population, could declare a revolt against a whole country that had thousands of well-armed soldiers equipped with modern equipment like tanks, war planes, and heavy artillery. It is true that the Tuaregs are known to be a warrior nation and to have full knowledge of the terrain in the North, which favoured the tactics of ambush in warfare and surprise attacks which they had practised since the pre-colonial period. In addition, the rebels could count on the total support of all the various Tuareg groups. But surely this was not going to be adequate to fight and defeat the armed forces of a modern state in warfare. As a result, many wondered as to what may have reassured and motivated the Tuareg so confidently to take up arms against the Malian nation[135].

It is therefore possible that the suspicions of the Malian government of a possible collaboration between the Tuareg and the Algerian FLN as well as the French were justified. At least it seemed to be evident that the Tuareg expected some kind of support from both the Algerian government and France in their struggles or war against the Malian state. Only the hopes and expectations of support could explain how a handful of people with no adequate arms and equipment would declare war against a state with soldiers, an air force, and sophisticated military equipment. That the rebels harboured such expectations emerged when among those who were taken prisoner spoke about the intentions and hopes of the group regarding the war. They revealed that they did not have a clear idea or hope for victory and when such victory would be achieved and they admitted the Malian military's superiority. Yet they remained hopeful of achieving victory someday. The captured rebels further revealed and confirmed the fears of the Malian authorities that they were counting on foreign support regarding their mission in diplomatic and military terms and specifically they expected support from the Algerian government and France. It was also revealed that though they did not actually have any hope of achieving military victory over that Malian army they cherished the expectation that, as the fighting intensified, independence from Mali could be achieved with the diplomatic support of France and Algeria.[136]

The deposed Tuareg Amenokal [chief], Zeyd ag Attaher, who enjoyed tremendous support from the Tuareg group, was said to have been very optimistic concerning the possibility of an independent Tuareg country and had shared this optimism with other people from among the Tamasheq. Prominent among such Tuaregs with whom he shared such ideas were Amegha ag Sherif, who was among the few educated Tuaregs in Mali and whose early activism in the Tamasheq struggles led to his arrest and subsequent imprisonment by the Malian authorities. Upon his release in 1962, he moved to Algeria where he came to be employed at the French nuclear base.

While working at the nuclear base, he was able to secure employment for many Tuaregs of Malian origin, who in turn gave part of their income as contribution for the purchase of arms by Amegha in preparation for the expected war.

The deposed Tuareg chief had brought together many other personalities by this time among the Tuaregs who also shared his plans and were continuing to make contacts with others from among the Adagh and non-Adagh people as well. These included people like Ayyouba ag Mohammed Adargajoug, who was the chief of Tamesna, which are not part of the Kel Adagh. It was alleged that with the financial help of the Tamesna chief, about thirty rifles were purchased from certain Frenchmen working at the nuclear site.[137]Another group under the Tuareg chief, Zeyd, included Sidi Alamine ag Cheick, who defected from being a *goumier* to fight for the Tuaregs, as well as his brother Issouf ag Cheick. This group proved important in the preparation for the war. Issouf for one broke into an arms depot in Timbuktu and made away with many guns, arms, ammunitions, and uniforms. He then fled to Algeria with his brother to join other rebels at the nuclear site. Another group consisting of the afore-mentioned Elledi ag Alla[138], and his group met up with other groups. Elledi, Zeyd, and the rest of the groups met at Tidjin and took the decision that the time for the revolt was ripe. Elledi's encounter with *goumiers* seemed to have justified their assumption. From a total of about 10 men, the group continued to grow until it reached about 250 men. These men went into battle dressed in green battle dress, not wearing the usual indigo robes, and mounted on camels and holding rifles, mostly out-dated. The uniforms were meant to indicate or represent that of a liberation army for the independence of the Tuareg nation. At the same time they were meant to send a message to the Malian state. However, the choice of the colour green could have been explained from a different angle, namely that it coincided with the colours of the French forces and as such came to be explained as a strategy to deceive the Malian army into believing that the French were invading Mali or in any case were supporting or behind the Tuaregs in their attempt to break away from the Malian nation.[139]

At the beginning of the war, the Tuareg fighters generally organised themselves into three main zones of operation. Although several units were sometimes formed within these zones, these units sometimes fluctuated in nature and size and leadership as the occasion demanded. A normal or average operations unit usually consisted of between twenty and thirty people. It is interesting to note that the unarmed civilian population among the Tuaregs, though they did not take part directly in the war or military engagements, played the role of spies and generally tried to gather as much information as possible about enemy movements and its advances towards the group or its plans generally through various contacts within and outside the Adagh area.

The three zones of operation created by the Tuaregs include the Timetrine zone, which is a plain west of the Adagh Mountains. This zone came under the leadership of Sidi Alamine and Issouf ag Cheick. The second zone came under the leadership the famous Elledi ag Alla and Ikhlou Saloum and was located from Mount Tigharghar and Mount Doriet to Bouressa and southwards to Kidal. The third and last zone came under the control of Azzezen ag Iksa and Mohammed ag Amane and was located at Mt. Quzzein and southwards. In considering the leadership of the various zones, certain factors were taken into consideration, and these factors appeared quite logical. Familiarity of the terrain and area by the leaders of the various zones was considered highly significant, and as such, the appointments of the leaders reflected that fact that they had intimate knowledge of the terrain in the areas to which they were appointed to lead. However, such knowledge was not restricted to the leaders alone but applied also to the members of the units deployed in the various zones[140], who were people who were well acquainted with the terrain. They were also organised according to the *tewsit* or clan affiliation of the respective areas.[141]

The Tuaregs generally mobilised arms from several sources. Algeria, however, remained the main source of supply for the revolt. An arms smuggling outlet had existed since colonial times and arms such as mausers and bouchetas, German and Italian rifles used in WWII, as well as the French MAS-36 rifles, which were cheap and affordable, were readily available to the rebels. Sometimes more sophisticated weapons were available through other sources apart from those mentioned. Many of these were shipped in from Morocco by Mohamed Ali ag Attaher Insar and mainly consisted of battle dress and Egyptian automatic rifles and ammunitions. Camels were used for transportation by the Tuaregs as means of transportation during the war, and this was explained to have been effective since the Tuareg area or northern Mali is usually covered with boulder formations and sharply broken stones and thus a terrain that could be much easier to cross using camels than with mechanised vehicles. The latter were only effective in open terrain and generally encountered a lot of difficulty in most of the area.[142] All Tuareg operations were planned at the Takormiasse base in Algeria, and most attacks were usually in the form of raids on camel back on fixed army posts. Units were usually composed and mount, arms and ammunition distributed, while routes to take to Mali and back to Algeria for distribution of such materials depended on certain factors and information regarding the Malian authorities and army units, which were to be avoided. Units usually moved at night and remained hidden during the day. As a tactic only small enemy forces were attacked. When a rebel was captured, planned operations were usually cancelled to avoid any leak of information on previously planned operations. Attacks in Mali were usually quick, followed by a rapid retreat into Algeria where they were safe from Malian forces.[143]

The Malian government responded to the rebellion at first by deploying the local *goumier* forces but by August, 1963 it became clear that *goumier* forces were unable to suppress the revolt. The Malian government then further deployed the Eighth CCA forces and again the Tenth CCA. As the fighting continued to escalate, the Malian government continued to increase its men steadily. Between September and October 1963, three units were created. The first CCA unit remained at Segou while two other units were created. These included an artillery unit and a motorised Saharan commando unit under the command of Captain Diby Sillas Diarra, stationed in the Adagh area. The commando unit was said to have consisted of about 400 men. By October, about three more units were further deployed to the Adagh area [north]. An approximate 2,200 men, 35 armoured cars, 2 airplanes, and a high number of sophisticated heavy arms had been deployed and used in fighting the rebels, who numbered only about 200 by October 1963. By March 1964, most of the Malian units had retreated and the commando units were further reinforced with 20 vehicles from the Bamako-based tank squadron. The number of men and equipment maintained by the Malian army in the fight against the rebels by 1964 was put at about 1,500 men, 40 armoured cars, 160 vehicles, for examples, tanks and jeeps, and about 20,000 litres of fuel and food were mobilised to Kidal to maintain men and equipment.[144]

Despite the huge amount of arms, equipment, and men deployed by the Malian government against the Tuareg rebels, the Malian army appeared unable to bring an end to the rebellion. Several reasons were advanced for its failure, most of them associated with the geography and terrain of the Adagh region [northern Mali]. The rough terrain of the region helped in demobilising the vehicles of the Malian army, which required constant repair; and in some cases, spare parts were not readily available. This had the effect of bringing about logistical problems in the transportation of men, materials, food, and even fuel to sustain the operation and as a consequence negatively impacted on the effectiveness of the Malian army and its operations. The mountainous landscape of the Adagh area is extremely favourable terrain for ambush tactics, which the Tuaregs have been famous for since pre-colonial times. It was not suitable for motorised forces, and this gave the Tuareg, who rode camels, the advantage over the Malian army. Additionally, the Tuaregs were very familiar with the terrain, the entire Adagh region, and all its surrounding mountains; and as such, it was easy to lay ambushes and launch surprise attacks on the government troops.

Just as numerous factors worked against the victory of the Malian army, others were responsible for the inability of the Tuaregs to defeat or succeed against the Malian army. Two factors in particular were immediately identifiable. The first was an internal factor and the second an external factor. The death of the Tuareg chief, Amenokal Attaher ag Illi II, caused division among the Ifogha clan and resulted in succession disputes among them. Thus, the group became divided between supporters of Zeyd [rebels]—who was the son of the Ifogha Tuareg's chief Ag Attaher, who died—and those of Intalla, the new chief. Zeyd's group generally viewed the new chief and those loyal to him as loyal to the Malian government. The suspicion was justified when the new chief, clearly under instructions from the Malian authorities, contacted the rebels to persuade them to surrender and abandon the war. Many of those who were loyal to the new chief never actually supported the war, rather tending to regard the rebels as a bunch of thieves, and therefore refused to give their support for the revolt. On the external front, the Tuareg did secure a certain amount of clandestine support from France and Algeria. For instance, the rebels enjoyed the liberty of staying in and out of Algeria at any given time. They were also permitted to use the French nuclear site as the base for all their operations. They also received some support in the form of sales of certain arms and ammunitions and medications from the French officials at the nuclear base[145]. But despite this, the high hopes for support from the governments of Algeria and France, which the Tuaregs had entertained, did not materialise. It is not very clear why.

Another factor militating against a Tuareg victory was their general insularity and ignorance relating to geopolitics. They had little conception of the inner workings of international politics. Zeyd was considered a man of great diplomatic skills, and in the Tuareg tradition, personal contact was considered most significant in diplomacy. As a result, Zeyd, having made some contacts in Algeria through the FLN and some French administrative personnel in Algeria, became highly optimistic of the results of his contacts with people from the two countries through some of their officials. Zeyd had expected that the two countries would render total support to the Tuareg cause based on his discussions with their officials[146]. However, these expectations were dashed and Zeyd's hope proved to be unrealistic, especially given that the existing relations at that time between Mali and the government in Algeria were considered excellent. The French, on the other hand, could not risk supporting the rebels since it was already facing violent opposition from the FLN and could not risk some of its highly important interests in Algeria, including the nuclear base; as such, the Tuareg rebels were left to stand alone.

Despite all the realities on the ground, Zeyd still remained optimistic of support and decided to contact the Algerian government again and to remind it of its earlier promise to support the Tuareg cause. Zeyd was said to have made a request to speak with the Algerian president Ahmed Ben Bella, as well as to be provided with transportation to Algiers. Zeyd's requests were met by the Algerian authorities, but unknown to Zeyd, the Malian chief of staff had visited Algeria on 25 September, 1963 and had discussed the revolt with the Algerian government and succeeded in convincing them of the necessity of arresting Zeyd and other rebels whenever they present themselves. Since it has become difficult to put an end to the rebellion, the Malian government resorted to the tactic of arresting the leaders of the rebellion, which was widely seen to be led by Zeyd ag Attaher. Upon arrival in Algiers, Zeyd and other rebels that accompanied him, including Ilyas ag Ayyoub, were arrested and put on a plane to Kidal City in Mali on 1 November, 1963[147].

The Malian government further laid the ground for the arrest of Mohamed Ali ag Attaher Inser, another important figure in the war who had lived in Morocco. Here, also, it appears international politics had worked in favour of the Malian state. The Malian president, Modibo Keita, had been involved in the mediation of a conflict between Morocco and Algeria over the border area of Tlemcen, and the conflict was successfully resolved with the help of Keita who was considered an international statesman of repute and one with great diplomatic skills. In return for Keita's role in mediating fairly the conflict over Tlemcen, Morocco arrested and expelled Mohamed Ali ag Attaher Inser on March 1964.[148] Yet another serious blow to the war, following these arrests, was the capture on 9th March, 1964, at Intacherain Algeria, of the famous and legendary Elledi ag Alla by the Malian force. Elledi was credited with the instigation of the conflict and was considered one of the most important military leaders among the Tuareg rebels.[149]

Following the arrests and capture of the rebel leaders, two options presented themselves to the rebels – either to abandon the fight and seek asylum in Algeria under the protection of the French at the military base or under the protection of the Algerian government or to return to Mali and make an unconditional surrender to the Malian government. The second option came to enjoy the support of the majority. The decision to choose the second option was largely influenced by the fact that the main leaders of the rebels such as Elledi, Zeyd and Mohamed Ali though captured had not been executed.[150] Between May and June, 1964, Intallah ag Attaher, the chief of the Tuareg known to be loyal to the Malian government, toured the whole of the Adagh area, appealing to the rebels to surrender.

Many rebels numbering about forty-eight surrendered to him and were subsequently disarmed. Yet another group of rebels under Sidi Alamine and Issouf ag Cheick did not surrender immediately. On 27 July 1964, Sidi Alamine ag Cheick was killed on the run after a track down by the Malian army while his brother Issouf ag Cheick fled to Algeria with some other rebels that survived the attack by the Malian soldiers. The disbandment of the last group signalled an end to the war. On 15 August 1964, the Malian administration officially declared the war over in the national newspaper *Essor*. The victory was to be celebrated in Kidal on 22nd September, 1964, Mali's third national day[151].

Throughout the war, it was reported that the Tuareg rebels adhered to honourable conduct in warfare. This meant that non combatants shouldnt be harmed in the fighting, and a minimum of civil behaviour was expected also on the part of the Malian forces[152]. However, it was reported that after the imposition of forbidden zone in the course of fighting, after many of the fighters had fled the country with their families, those Tuaregs that remained in the forbidden zone were shot by the Malian army while others died due to the poisoning of all the wells in the Adagh area by the Malian army since the rebels certainly needed water to survive. As a result, many men, women, and children died of the poisoned water[153]. Such conduct was deemed dishonourable by the Tuareg and continued to be a source of *egh*a [the need for revenge] on the part of the Tuareg in later disagreements with the Malian government.

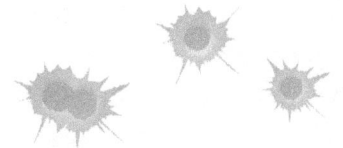

## CHAPTER SEVEN

# The 1990 Tuareg War

*Let the blood boil if it is in your capillary At the break
of dawn grab your weapons and go to the hilltops We
murder our enemies and be like eagles We will free the
dwellers of the desert.* Tamatant Tilay [Death is Here]
song.

– Alhassane Ag Touhani
Tinarewen Musical Band [1983]
[Rebel Songs, The New Yorker]

The second post-colonial Tuareg insurrection took place in
1990 war. It came to be known as Al Jebha. In analysing
this war, we need to take a look at the developments that
took place between the 1963 war and the outbreak of the Al Jebha
in 1990. It would not be possible to fully appreciate or explain what
the 1990 war signified or meant to both the Tuaregs and the outside
world otherwise. Definitely, within the 27-year period, several
changes, both positive and negative, had taken place not only among
the Tuaregs and Mali but all over Africa and in the world at large.
In Africa in particular these changes were profound, as the emerging
nation states across the continent grappled with the problems of
nation building and statehood.

The period succeeding the Tuareg war of 1963 brought about several changes within Tuareg society. These changes were revolutionary as they transformed not only the outlook of the Tuaregs but also certain aspects of their culture. This explained the change in their behaviour and their reaction to certain events both within and outside Mali. However, it must be understood that the changes that took place were the inevitable results of the earlier rebellion and they greatly affected the future and destiny of the Tuaregs as a people. They had a profound effect on all aspects of their lives, including education, economy and politics. The Tuareg were transformed from a desert rural society to an urban one. The economy, which had previously been mainly household-based, was transformed into one based on wage labour and featured the introduction of consumer goods, which were hitherto non-existent. These changes can be attributed to a number of factors. The drought which affected the Sahara in the 1970s and 1980s drastically affected the pastoral life of the Tuareg people. Many of the Tuaregs were forced to abandon their pastoral life and look for new means of livelihood far and wide. In Tamasheq [Tuareg] history this period came to be known as the Teshumara period, a period that witnessed massive movement or migration of the Tuaregs to different parts of Africa, especially within West Africa. In fact, it led to what can only be called a Tuareg diaspora.

Migrations were not new in Tuareg society and history, but the migration that took place during this period remained the most significant as an estimated number of 500 families were said to have taken refuge in Algeria alone.[154] In 1975, following the drought, about 13,000 Malian Tuaregs fled to the Niger republic and about 12,000 moved to cities along the Algerian border where they were met and received by their relatives who had fled to Algeria during or in the aftermath of the 1963 war. Internally, about 47,000 Tuaregs moved to the Gao and Timbuktu regions, where they lived in refugee camps as they did not have the means to migrate abroad.[155]Around

1980, after a repeat of the drought, which by this time had completely crippled pastoral life in Mali, the exodus towards Libya began.

Political developments within Mali after the 1963 war also contributed to the war. The dissatisfaction of the Malian people towards the Keita regime and its economic policies has already been described. In 1968, young military officers ousted the Keita regime in a coup. Keita and his lieutenants were subsequently arrested and sent to prison in Kidal. For the Tuareg the fall of the Keita regime was a relief holding out the hope of freedom and an end to Malian rule.[156] About 400 Tuareg children, orphaned by the previous rebellion and known as the children of the Afellaga, abandoned the government boarding schools in which they had been placed. Caravans were formed, ready to move to Algeria. At this point, the new military regime under the leadership of Moussa Traoré, moved quickly stop them and return the children to their schools.

The new government began to introduce new policies, including opening up the country to foreign investment. However, soon corruption came to dominate the affairs of the new government as all the benefits were enjoyed and controlled by Traoré, his family, and a few people around them. Obviously, this came to have a negative impact on the citizens, especially after the droughts of the 1970s. The drought was so serious that relief aid had to be sought from a number of international agencies such as the FAO and USAID. But even this relief was abused as corrupt officials did not distribute the aid equitably to the people. Instead they stole it and sold it in the market at high prices. A consequence of this was that the Tuareg population in Mali and Niger was forced to migrate further south. A reporter, Phillipe Decraene, described the situation in the refugee camps in Mali as genocide as a result of the failure on the part of the Malian government to address the humanitarian situation due mainly to corruption. Meanwhile, the Tuaregs continued to migrate to other countries, including Nigeria and Libya. Migration to Libya intensified around 1982, when during a speech[157], Libyan leader Gaddafi declared Libya as the country of origin of the Tuareg people[158].

The Tuaregs that did not migrate became seasonal migrants to the cities. Pastoralism no longer existed as the droughts of 1973 and 1984 had left the Tuareg without livestock. They now found employment in cities as salaried herdsmen, guards of villas, construction workers, car mechanics and even fishermen. Their employment was mostly temporary. Others that could not get formal employment engaged in trafficking goods such as sugar, flour, oil, tea, petrol, and dates into Mali and between Algeria, Mali, and Niger. They did this on foot or using camels or donkeys. They then largely used the profits to buy luxury goods and sometimes invest further in the trafficking business. Some set up legitimate businesses within Mali. The changes affected many different aspects of lifestyle – food and clothing included. Many of them no longer wore turbans or veils but jeans with sneakers or sandals. They adopted sedentary habits. As such, the lives of the Tuaregs came to change drastically.

At this time music became an important aspect of the Tuareg social life, especially among the Tuaregs that lived in foreign countries. They sometimes organised parties and invited fellow migrants, including women, to sing songs and dance together. Sometimes at such parties, *griots*[159] also performed, originally from Timbuktu and part of the Tuareg culture. There also developed a new music known as *al-guitara* among the Tuaregs in Libya and Algeria, who learnt to use the electronic guitar and as such formed a band known as the Kel Tinariwen or 'those from the deserts'. The music produced by the newly formed band came to reflect the existence, experiences and sufferings of the Tuaregs, ranging from a quiet blues to militant songs calling for a Tuareg revolution, featuring phrases like: *'The world changes'; 'We sit in ruins'; 'We pull up our trousers and fasten our belts'; and 'We no longer accept the mistreatments we have endured'.*

All these changes were followed by positive developments in education among the Tuaregs both within and outside Mali. In Mali, many enrolled in various institutions and joined different sectors of Malian society - with the exception of the army that had been closed to the group since the 1963 war. Those in Algeria also enrolled in educational institutions. The Ishumar[160], as they came to be known, became more and more radical in their political outlook though, but the better educated among them maintained a more moderate outlook. This sometimes led to disputes between them. The Ishumar[161] continued to call for revolution and independence, sometimes through music, and they used music also to attack the educated Tuaregs for not cooperating on the need for a revolution and independence from Mali.[162]

While all these developments were taking place in and outside Mali, certain events occurred that seemed to favour the Ishumar's call for action and revolution. One such event was the escape of the legendary Elledi ag Alla Albacir from prison in Bamako at the end of 1974. He travelled to Algeria by truck and was received by his former comrades, Amegha ag Sharif, Younnes ag Ayyouba, and Issouf ag Cheick. The four rebels met and deliberated on issues currently affecting the Tuaregs. The discussions centred on whether to continue with the fight for independence from Mali or not and the four agreed to continue with the fight for independence.

Their decision was followed by other activities that set in motion an agenda for Tuareg independence from Mali. Among such developments was the formation of a revolutionary organisation or movement that came to known as the Tanekra[163]. They spelt out the main aims of the Tanekra organization through their songs. In one of their songs, for instance, the *al-guitara* sings: *"Friends, hear and understand me, you know there is one country, one goal, one religion. And united, hand in hand, friends, you know there is only one stance by which you are fettered and only unity can break it."*[164]

As it came into being, the new movement was at first faced with problems of unity among the various clans, which competed for hierarchy among themselves. The intellectuals among the Tuareg discouraged the idea of tribalism and political competition and tried to replace them with political unity and social change and to the uplift of the lives of the Tuareg people in general. The most important force behind the Tanekra movement remained *egha*, or the need for revenge. The concept of *egha* appeared to be common emotion which had a unifying effect on Tuaregs from all the clans. Such emotions found expression in music which mostly dwelt on the 1963 war. In one of the songs the *al-guitara* sings: '*Nineteen sixty three came, and goes on. Its days came leaving memories. It crossed wadis, killing cattle. It killed the elderly and new born children. The brave men died until no one was left. Only grave yards and loneliness came of it*'[165].

The Tanekra movement from the beginning came to be led by the old leaders of the Afellaga, who now found a new means of livelihood in Algeria and were in a position to assist other Tuaregs migrating from Mali and other countries to join them. At this early stage, the movement remained highly secretive in existence and embarked upon enlightening Tuaregs from all works of life on the need to reorganise and reclaim their country and gain independence from Mali. Generally, they used *egha*, reminding the people of those that took part in the 1963 war and who were killed by the Malian authorities. The four rebels earlier mentioned took all the major decisions for the movement. However, the group came to recognise the importance of education to the movement and tried as much as possible to encourage all Tuaregs to seek Western education. They offered the educated from them leading positions, and they played an important part in making contacts with the Libyan and Algerian authorities regarding their struggle for independence. Throughout the 1970s, the movement largely remained invisible and networked silently among its members. It was not until May 1976 that an open name for the group was adopted. The movement then came to be known as the National Movement for the Liberation of Azawad[166], a movement that was destined to play a prominent role in future Tuareg struggles.

As the movement gained momentum, it tended to become more active in Libya. Since the 1963 war, many Tuaregs had fled to Libya when Gaddafi declared Libya as the original country of the Tuaregs. Not only that, the Libyan secret service had supported the struggles of the group and many Tuaregs joined the Libyan army. There are those who allege that Libyan support was largely self-serving as Libya needed soldiers to fight in its own conflicts, namely in Chad and Lebanon. Algeria had in the past made similar efforts to use the Tuareg movement for its own cause when it created the Popular Front for the Liberation of Palestine [PFLP][167] and requested the Tuaregs to join. The Tuaregs declined the offer when they realised that it did not concern or promote their struggle for independence from Mali.

Around 1979, the Azawad movement witnessed a tremendous change. Contact had been made with Libyan officials and army officers[168]. Approximately seventy delegates from various opposition networks in Niger and other places gathered in Libya to discuss various issues, including the possibility of uniting under one umbrella organisation. Such an organisation did emerge - the al-Jebha ash-sh'biyya li Taghrir as Sahara al-kubra al-Arabiyya al wasta [Popular Front for the Liberation of the Greater Arab Central Sahara].[169] The new organisation seemed to have been headed by Nigerien Arabs[170] under the patronage of Libya and was seen to be promoting a Pan-Arab rather than the Tuareg cause. The movement soon came to have a political bureau and a military camp, which was opened to all members. In December 1980, a military training camp was opened for the Tuaregs and was known as Ben Walid due to its location. The camp came to accommodate 2,700 recruits; and by late 1981, about 4,000 recruits had received training. However, owing to diplomatic problems between Libya and Niger, between Libya and Mali and the activities of some of the members of the new al-Jebha organisation, the camp was closed later in the same year.

After the closure of camp Ben Walid, the Tuaregs were left with few options, and they chose to enlist for training and combat in Lebanon with the Palestinian forces instead of either returning to Mali or going to Algeria, especially since they had declined to joining the POLISARIO[171] organisation as requested by the Algerian authorities on the grounds that it did not support their cause. Clearly the Tuareg chose to join the Palestinian army largely in order to gain more military experience in preparation for their anticipated war in Mali.

About 500 Tuaregs volunteered to fight for the Palestinian Liberation army, out of which about 300 chose to return to Algeria while the other 200 stayed behind and underwent military training in different areas such as the use of heavy arms weaponry, tanks, howitzers, Katyusha 40 and 12 calibres, Russian 130 mm howitzers, machine guns, anti-aircraft missiles, US anti-tank weaponry, calibre 106 rockets and anti-vehicle and anti-personnel mines. After such training, the Tuareg volunteers were dispatched to various units where they served in air defence units, together with other volunteers from Libya. By 1982, Israel had occupied Lebanon and started a peace process that would see the end of the conflict, and this meant the end of the presence of all foreign troops in southern Lebanon, including the Tuareg volunteers. In the course of the war in Lebanon, the Tuaregs had lost one man, with five taken prisoners by the Israelis. These were subsequently released and returned to Libya in accordance with the peace process. At the end of the adventure, upon return from Lebanon, the 200 Tuaregs who had gained military skills and knowledge were to later prove useful as they continued to prepare for the impending war against the Malian state, took control of the Tenekra movement.[172].

The Lebanon veterans tried to reorganise the Tanekra movement and gave it a new name - al-Jebha ash-shimalal Mali or the Mali Liberation Front, under the leadership Iyad ag Ghaly. By March 1983, at least two training camps were opened in Libya for Tuareg recruits of Niger Republic origin. The camps came to be known as Ithnam Mars and Camp ar-Rowd and were both located in Tripoli. Though the camps were opened only for Niger Tuaregs, many Malian Tuaregs were able to fake their identities and gain entry. The recruits from these camps were to later serve in the Libyan mission to Chad, further gaining military experience, which would in the future provide the Tuaregs with the experience of creating a well-trained army of their own. The Libyan government paid each of the recruits about 30,000 Libyan dinar, equivalent to about $20,000, and the Tuareg recruits donated one-third of this income to the newly formed al-Jebha organisation. The money was used by the organisation to get more recruits from within and outside Mali as well as to purchase vehicles and equipment.

At this time the al-Jebha members were convinced that the time was ripe to move against the Malian state under Musa Traoré as a result of the deterioration of living conditions in Mali, mainly due to corruption. The group continued to reorganise and strategise but still faced internal problems and divisions that sometimes impacted negatively on the effectiveness of their newly formed organisation, al-Jebha.[173]

On 28 June 1990, an army barracks and an arrondissement office were attacked by armed groups in Menaka, a town in Eastern Mali. A convoy of about four cars, which belonged to a United States NGO, was ambushed by another group of fighters at the same time.[174] These two singular acts came to mark the beginning of what came to be known as the 1990 Tuareg war in Mali or al-Jebha. It was a war that was to last several years, and which differed from the 1963 war in so far as the rebels were better prepared, better organised and more powerful militarily. From June until October 1990, the rebels maintained constant attacks on army camps and administrative posts in all parts of the Adagh and the Azawad area. The rebels attacked many different army formations in different locations at the same time as a strategy, and in this way they hoped to give an impression that they were a large force well organised as such confuse and demoralise the enemy.

In addition, the rebels were able to secure the Algerian border and thus ensure their supply lines. This meant that most attacks were concentrated in the border areas. In this way they were able to seize and supply themselves with much needed arms, materials, weapons, food, ammunitions, and fuel. The rebels succeeded in taking a large number of arms from the Malian army and now had advantage in terms of their training to handle modern weapons, which they had received in the years of Ishumar in Libya, Chad, and Lebanon. The Tuaregs were completely successful in all the attacks they launched during this period as the Malian forces had no combat experience. A crucial advantage was the discrepancy in the motivation to fight. While the Malian soldiers fought as professional soldiers paid by the government, the Tuareg rebels, on the other hand, aimed to achieve the liberation of the Tamasheq country from Malian control. They knew that by starting the war they had only two options: fight and win or abandon the cause and accept whatever consequences that would come with such defeat. As such, the zeal with which the rebels fought could not be compared with that of the Malian forces.[175]

After the first encounter with the Malian forces the rebels set up bases in many different locations. One such was Mount In-Taykaren. From this base they issued repeated challenges to the Malian forces to join battle with them. They did this via radio messages issued from a gendarmerie post in Tarkimt, which they had captured earlier on. Other bases were opened at Essali near Bouressa, and at Tigharghar, which was historically the base of the legendary Alla ag Albachir in the 1940s. The number of bases continued to increase until they reached about fifteen bases in total.

The Malian army on 17 July 1990 responded to the invitation to do the battle with the enemy at Mount In-Taykaren. They mobilised men, weapons, and resources in preparation for an assault. Four hundred infantry men and an artillery unit armed with track-mounted rocket Launchers were deployed to the siege of In-Taykaren. It was reported that after four days of shelling, the infantry assault of the army was easily countered by the rebels who suffered very few casualties. When the rebels counter-attacked, began an offensive, only a day of sniper activity was enough to make the Malian army retreat with the loss of around 40 men. The same operation was repeated in July and August but with more disastrous consequences for the Malian army, which this time lost over 100 men.[176] Every attack aimed by the Malian army at the various rebel bases proved unsuccessful and, realising the invincibility of the rebel bases, where the terrain was virtually impassable by vehicles, the army was forced to retreat. It was impossible to penetrate the interior of the mountains without proper knowledge of the known passages, knowledge the army did not have. By far, the largest victory recorded by the rebel forces was on the night of 4th September, 1990, near the former base of Alla ag Albachir at Mount Tigharghar where about 45 rebels, armed with knives and hand grenades, took on an army unit of 450 soldiers. Making use of knowledge of the terrain, internal organisation of the military camp, and surprise, the rebels succeeded in entering the camp and engaging the government soldiers in close combat, who fled in panic. The rebels claimed killing over 100 soldiers in the raid while losing only fifteen of their own.[177]

After this encounter, the morale of the Malian forces slumped while that of the rebel forces was greatly increased. If anything, the Tigharghar encounter proved that the Malian regular army were no match for the Tuareg guerrilla rebels, and as a result, a quick end to the war appeared almost impossible as the Malian army had hoped initially.

The Malian government was left with no option but to open negotiations with the rebels. It was surprising how a small but extremely skillful group of warriors were able to rout an army ten times its size, killing a large number of soldiers in close combat, man to man.[178] The negotiations between the Malian government and the Tanekra movement or al-Jebha began in October 1990 with a reconnaissance mission and began in earnest by December 1990. It was initiated by the government of Traoré, which was already facing many other problems apart from the revolt from the Tuareg group in the north.

The negotiations were welcomed by the Tuareg rebels, who also for reasons related to lack of resources, weapons, and exhaustion needed time to regain some energy and get more supplies in terms of food and ammunitions for adequate defence, something the Malian forces were not aware of. The first contact was made through some Tuareg tribal chiefs, which the rebels did not recognise as they had not supported the war. As part of the negotiations on 6 January 1991, a ceasefire agreement was signed and a declaration of intent to continue negotiations for final peace was reached in a document that came to be known as the Tamanrasset agreement, which took place under the mediation of the Algerian government, which had shown much interest in the conflict, and not the chiefs. The agreement generally consisted of a ceasefire that stipulated the mutual transfer of prisoners of war, withdrawal of the army from the north, transfer of administration to civil servants, withdrawal of rebel forces from their bases, and the possibility of their integration into the Malian army. Others were the creation of commissions to monitor the application of the agreement made, and a document was also signed that would guarantee a certain amount of autonomy to the north.

However, the Tamanrasset agreement was never fully applied due to many reasons. A split occurred in the ranks of the rebels. One faction saw the ceasefire agreement as a kind of betrayal of the main aim of the revolt, which was independence. As such, they continued to carry out attacks, largely claimed by two new organisations that had emerged out of the Tanekra movement after the signing of the agreement. These included the Front for the Liberation of the Azawad [FPLA] and another Moorish organisation known as Movement Populair de l'Azawad [MPA]. Soon the Tamanrasset agreement came to be violated by both sides. While the Malian government did not fully implement some aspects of the agreement, the Tuaregs on their part continued their attacks contrary to the ceasefire agreement. As such, new negotiations had to be opened by the government, which came to be known as the National Pact on 11th April, 1992, on the eve of the presidential elections in Mali[179]. The terms of the pact contained six points that differed slightly from those of the Tamanrasset agreement. The first is that there should be special social, economic, and administrative status for the Tuaregs. Secondly, there should be tax exemptions for the inhabitants of the north for a period of ten years. Thirdly, there should be a creation of two special funds to reconstruct the north. The fourth called for a decrease in the deployment and withdrawal of army personnel to a limited number of northern towns. The fifth called for the creation of structures to secure the gradual return of refugees after the end of the conflict and the sixth advocated for the integration of former rebels into the Malian armed forces and administration[180].

Like the Tamanrasset, the National Pact was never fully implemented as it became apparent that in reality it was almost impossible to meet or satisfy all the needs or demands of the rebels. While the Malian government made efforts to ensure the implementation of the agreement, autonomy could not be granted to the whole of the north at once as demanded by the rebels. Then on the question of the exemption from tax, it too could not be applied at once and needed to be implemented gradually just like that of autonomy. The reconstruction fund demanded by the rebels also came to be created, but the fund remained empty due to the general lack of resources in the country as a result of the poor performance of the economy. The provision to withdrawal of troops from certain cities was honoured by government. With regard to the return of the refugees, efforts were made to rehabilitate them and the UNHCR made a budget of about $3.5 million available for that. However, fighting was going on as certain groups, such as the FPLA, did not recognise the National Pact. Nevertheless, in the region of 1,468 refugees were repatriated under a pilot project that was later aborted. No further effort was made to repatriate the large number of other refugees who remained outside the country. There were 12,000 in Algeria alone. Again not all rebels could be integrated into the Malian army as there were limited posts or vacancies available, not to mention the money to pay them, while the rebels insisted that all must be integrated. This led to dissatisfaction on the part of the rebels who felt that the Malian government had failed to fully implement the provisions of the pact.

The period following the signing of the pact was characterised by factionalism among the rebel groups, some of which continued the rebellion as they did not agree or fully accept the Pact, which they felt was a betrayal of the independence struggle of the Tamasheq people. Generally, the factionalism was carried out along *tewsit* [clan] lines while on the other hand the Moors formed their own groups such as MPA, ARLA, FIAA, and FPLA, some with an Islamic background and challenged the existence of the pact. These groups tried to challenge the very political structure of the Tuareg landscape.

The same period also witnessed a new development in the form of the emergence of an organisation that came to be known as the Ganda Koy or the Movement Patriotique Ganda Koy [MPGK][181], which was created in April 1994[182]. The emergence of the Ganda Koy was a reaction to the Tuareg war, which had provoked strong anger and resentment towards the Tuareg population on the part of the non-Taureg population residing in the north of Mali. The attacks of the Tuareg rebel forces on several villages in the River Niger area such as Djebock and Bamba created resentment, panic, and grief over the victims and hatred towards the Tuaregs. The rebellion was also considered by these groups to have blocked important trade routes linking certain commercial cities such as Gao and Timbuktu, which had as a result brought commercial activities to a standstill. For this reason, the main backers, founders, and financiers of the Ganda Koy movement came from the wealthier merchants of Gao City. At some point, it became very clear that the sedentary population in the north was not sympathetic to the war and the Ganda Koy militia came to replace the army in protecting the population from the attacks of the rebel Tuaregs. In a pamphlet distributed by the newly formed movement, the Gand Koy stated:

> Fellow citizens of the north, let us sweep away all nomads from our villages and cities, even from our barren land! Tomorrow the nomads will install themselves there as dominators. Black sedentary peoples from Nuro to Menaka, let us take up arms for the great battle that await us; let us send the nomads back to the sands of the Azawad. The existing social balance cannot be modified. The socioeconomic problems of the north need to be solved for all citizens without discrimination. Why are there development projects for the nomads? Why are there army posts for the rebels? Why are there seats in the Parliament for the armed rebel bandits? Because they took up arms and killed? That is inadmissible. The Ganda Koy movement is born. Signed without us, the National pact is against us. The realities in the north show this. We should create insecurity for the nomad as they have created it for the sedentary population.[183]

Generally this expressed the concerns of the non-Tuareg sedentary population inhabiting the major cities in the north. The Ganda Koy followed strategies similar to those of the Tuareg rebels and attacked the civilian Tuareg population. For several months the Tuaregs and the Ganda Koy continued to attack each other. On June 12, the Ganda Koy were reported to have killed between 26 and 60 Tuaregs in Anderamboukane and the following day killed about 25 inhabitants of Lere. On the same day, about 75 Tuaregs were killed in Timbuktu while at the same time a caravan was ambushed on its way back from Taoundeint salt mines, killing 60 caravan drivers. Again, on 19 June 1994, the Ganda Koy attacked a refugee camp near the village of Ber, killing about 160 people. The Ganda Koy tried to interpret the rebellion by the Tuaregs as an attempt to take control of the Niger bend and its inhabitants on the basis of racial superiority. They further saw the various provisions of the National Pact and their accompanying privileges as unfair to the rest of the groups in the north, which had naturally provoked anger, hatred and jealousy towards the Tuareg people.

It was not until October 1994 that it became clear that a military solution could not bring an end to the violence between the Tuareg and the Ganda Koy in the new ensuing conflict[184]. As a result, the Ganda Koy had to be involved in the peace process initiated by the Malian government with the Tuareg group under the National Pact. And from then on, historical discourse was invoked to reconcile the warring parties. According to legends, the Tuaregs and the Songhai were descendants of the same mother; and, due to a curse, the two became enemies. Other sources claimed that the two groups were cousins, and so this history between them was used in bringing about harmony between the two groups. Some international non-governmental organisations also played a significant a role in the disarmament of the respective rebel groups, including, of course, the Ganda Koy, and their integration into the Malian army. Some of these organisations include the UNIDIR and UNDP, which conceived the idea of organising the integration of the rebels. Both the Tuaregs and the Ganda Koy came to be assimilated into the provisions of the National Pact, and from then on, the Ganda Koy never saw the National Pact as against them or favouring the Tuaregs since they were now a beneficiary of the pact.

After this, a second mission known as the round-table conference of Timbuktu was held between 15 and 18 July 1995, which united the Malian government, the MFUA [Tuareg movement], the Ganda Koy, as well as the international donor community. The conference was aimed at allocating funds for the reconstruction of northern Mali and bringing the conflict to a final end. By this time also all the rebel factions had been united under MFUA on the Tuareg side, which further facilitated the peace negotiations. At the end of the conference, an estimated $150 million was promised for the reconstruction of northern Mali, and a fund known as FAR-Nord was created to finance the disarmament and integration of former rebel fighters in the north. The integration was carried out through the creation of special sites in the north, where fighters could present themselves and hand over their weapons, and in return they would be registered in the integration project with the assurance that they would be either integrated into the Malian army or assisted financially in setting up a civilian life. And on 26 March 1996, the conflict was ceremoniously brought to an end in Timbuktu's main market by the public burning of weapons handed in by the fighters at various sites established for the integration of the rebels. It was a ceremony that was attended by elite politicians in Mali, the MFUA Tuareg movement, and the international community. And as the weapons burnt, FPLA leader Zeidan ag Sidi Alamine declared that all the rebel movements including MPLA, ARLA, FIAA, FPLA, and Ganda Koy are now united to be known only as MFUA and that the war, which had lasted for just under six years, was now over[185].

# PART THREE

## The 2012 Tuareg War and the Intervention of France in Mali

*"63 has gone however it will come back Those times left their traces They killed the old and the infants and the newborn They swooped down to the pastures and killed the livestock…63 has passed but it will come back".* Soixanne Trois song.

– Ibrahim Ag Alhabib
Tinarewen Musical Band
[Rebel Songs, The New Yorker]

## CHAPTER EIGHT

# Background and Genesis of the War

*Every time you cross a barrier, the drugs increase in value.*

– Ildefonso Ortiz [The Rolling Stone].

T he 2012 Tuareg war in Mali cannot be discussed in isolation from the general developments that took place not only in Mali but also across the Sahel region after the end of the 1990–1996 Tuareg war. We may recall that that revolt had ended as a result of negotiations and the signing of the National Pact, which was followed by the implementation of provisions of the pact within the Malian nation between the state and the Tuareg rebels, as well as other groups that had risen to challenge the existence of the pact. For some time after the reconciliation and integration programmes that followed the war were implemented; Mali remained relatively peaceful.

Many Tuareg rebels and members of the GandaKoy were integrated into the Malian army, and many others were rehabilitated through various projects. As mentioned earlier the National Pact had never been fully implemented due to many reasons. One of the most challenging aspects of the pact remained the issue of the decentralisation or autonomy promised for the North. As such, it continued to be a source of concern and a potential for future agitation and possible revolt, especially by the Tuareg. All the other reforms related to the National Pact, the integration of the rebels into the army, for instance, were not fully appreciated by the population of the north, including the GandaKoy. Nevertheless, the late 1990s saw Mali emerging as a forerunner of democracy in West Africa as a result of popular participation at the local level as well as the nationwide dialogue that took place throughout the country after the 1990–1996 war[186].

The government had adopted a policy of decentralisation according to which the central government's authority was to be taken over by local and municipal authorities. However, it was alleged that the restructuring of the public service had failed to bring about any significant change. Again, the official recognition of traditional chiefs under the decentralisation policy tended to create confusion and instability among various clans and groups within the Tuareg society and in the North as a whole; as such, groups began to compete for influence and to have one of their own appointed as a chief or otherwise. The decentralisation policy ended up being seriously criticised since it favoured only the elite and the existing power structures rather than create a new setup with new officials from among other social strata. Another problem was that it was very difficult to develop the infrastructure of the northern region because of its sparse and scattered population and the region therefore appeared to have gained very little in terms of aid from both international funding agencies and the Malian state, a situation exacerbated by corruption in central and local government. Politically, the decentralisation policy appeared admirable but for it to be effective needed a great deal of economic investment and good governance and both of these were seriously lacking.

One of the consequences of the implementation of the provisions of the Pact was that it created rivalry in the northern region. This led to internal power struggles which generated general dissatisfaction among the Tuareg, something that was to later lead to the outbreak of a rebellion in 2006. The rebellion was also a protest against the violation of previous agreements such as the Tamanrasset[187] and the National Pact, which it was claimed were not implemented to the latter. And so between 2006 and 2009, Mali was once again engulfed in violence. Though the 2006 and 2009 revolts can hardly be compared to the two previous wars in intensity and impact, it was so serious that the Malian authorities had to open negotiations yet again with the Tuareg rebels, resulting in the signing of a peace accord in Algeria, known as the Algiers Accord.[188] However, in its turn this agreement was soon to become a source of conflict between Tuareg clans such as the Ifoghas, the Berabish Arabs and the Imrad clans.

The rebellion was led by Ibrahim ag Bahanga, who had been among the veterans of the 1990 war. Iyad ag Ghaly, also a former veteran of both the 1963 and the 1990 wars, was also part of the leadership of the new rebellion. Bahanga formed a rebel force which continued to target the Malian army until Bahanga was expelled from Mali in 2009. Libya granted Bahanga asylum after his expulsion from Mali. However, in August, 2011, while continuing to make plans for another revolt in Libya, he was killed in a car crash before his plans came to fruition. It has been claimed that the 2012 war was conceived and planned by Bahanga during his stay in Libya and that after his death the plan suffered some setbacks but was not completely abandoned by his followers.

Meanwhile, a new rebellion was brewing. The Malian authorities, taking advantage of the internal power struggles among the various Tuareg clans, played one against another. The result was the gradual development of a state of anarchy throughout the North. This anarchy in turn favoured illegal and criminal economic activities. These later culminated in certain groups emerging who began to dominate the affairs of the region in the absence of state authority.[189] For instance, one Hadj Bettou was known to dominate contraband and weapons smuggling in southern Algeria in the 80's and 90's. Mokhtar Belmokhtar, the leader of al-Qaeda in the Maghreb (AQIM) ran a cigarette smuggling racket for a long time across the Sahara. He is said to have master-minded the capture and kidnapping of western hostages at the Amena gas facility in Algeria in January, 2013.

Given the wide dispersal of the Tuaregs as a group, events taking place in the Sahel region as a whole also impacted on developments in Mali. We recall that after the 1963 war, many Tuaregs became involved in trafficking as a result of the drought that hit Mali and affected their means of livelihood. However, at that time, they engaged mainly in the trafficking of consumer goods such as clothes, petrol, and household products. However, over time, things changed particularly after the 1990 war. Cross border trading became smuggling as the goods being trafficked bypassed official customs system and was replaced by informal arrangements between traders and officials. Exports from Mali and Niger to Algeria and Libya grew overtime and such activity relied heavily on informal established networks to thrive. Many Malians became involved in these trafficking networks.

In the 1990s, Algeria cut its subsidy budget[190]and this led to a deterioration of the economy. An embargo was imposed on the Gaddafi regime in Libya. Then too conflicts broke out in Algeria, northern Niger in addition to that in Mali. This began to turn the entire region into a major arms-trafficking market. Contraband weapons were smuggled across the region by networks working hand in hand with senior government officials[191].

The introduction of cigarette smuggling paved the way for the introduction of other illicit commodities and drugs. Cigarettes were usually smuggled from Mauritania to the North African markets, mainly Algeria and Morocco. They were also imported through Benin and Togo and passed through Niger and Burkina Faso to Libya and Algeria. In 2009, it was estimated that about 60% of the Libyan tobacco market consisted of smuggled tobacco, with proceeds in retail amounting to about $228 million. Those involved in such business came to be identified as legal cigarettes importers and distributors, who usually imported their goods from free trade zones such as Dubai. Generally, the cigarettes smuggling business came to be explained as a deliberate strategy by tobacco companies to avoid taxes as well as to break the North African states' monopolies on cigarette distribution[192]. This resulted in the breakdown of official customs services owing to corrupt collusion between the smugglers and state officials. In Libya, it was reported that the business was dominated and controlled by networks within the security forces, who were mostly members of President Ghaddafi's tribe.

Between Mauritania, Mali, and Algeria, the Sahrawi networked in collaboration with officials in the POLISARIO movement, which sought the independence of the Western Sahara. Subsidised Algerian goods and humanitarian aid were traded southwards and cigarettes northwards to Algeria and Morocco. Mokhtar Belmokhtar, later emerged as leading figure in AQIM, was known to have run a cigarette smuggling racket across the Sahara[193].

Like the smuggling in licit [legal items] goods and cigarettes, a new business developed in the region, namely the transporting of migrants and the facilitation of their illegal passage to other countries. This led to the emergence of carriers in the region who specialised in off-road transport and arrangements with corrupt officials. The major migration flow was from sub-Saharan Africa to Europe via North Africa. The business of illegal migration dated back to the 1990s and was later to become a source of concern to many European states. The cities of Gao and Agadez came to be known as important centres of migrant movement to Morocco, through Algeria or Libya, and then from Morocco to Europe through Spain. In Libya many militias emerged to control the migration business and the profits that came with it. At one time, Libyan territory became very dangerous to approach due to the presence of these militias along the borders, who intercepted travellers at many different locations.

Apart from cigarettes and illegal migration, smuggling in illicit drugs flourished. The two main flows that came to be identified and which have expanded overtime since 2005 include South American cocaine to Europe, via Libya and Egypt, and Moroccan cannabis to Libya, Egypt, and the Arabian peninsula. The growth in the smuggling of illicit drugs expanded rapidly owing to the rising demand for such drugs in Europe. It was estimated that about 14% of Europe's cocaine, with a total estimated value of about $1 billion, transited annually through West Africa. Most of the cocaine passing through West Africa usually arrives in one of the coastal states such as Guinea, Guinea Bissau, Togo, Benin, or Ghana and is then moved on by boat or air. It is sometimes also sent by couriers to Europe, including through airports in West Africa. Airports such as those of Bamako, Ouagadougou, and Niamey are well-known hubs for air couriers; and at times cocaine transits via Algiers airport.[194]

Overland routes across the Sahel and Sahara are diverse; and sometimes cocaine is transported from the coastal hubs of Guinea or Mauritania, overland to Mali, and then to Morocco, Algeria, or Libya. In 2009, a Boeing 727 containing ten tonnes of cocaine crashed in the desert, north of Gao City in Mali. The plane came to be named 'air cocaine' by the media and was reported to have taken off from Venezuela but registered in Guinea. According to investigations, cocaine was smuggled overland to Morocco by networks of Spanish, French, Moroccan, Malian, and Senegalese nationals. Apart from this, there have been many reports of smaller types of aircraft being used to carry cocaine from the coastal hubs to the north of Mali[195]. It was reported by the UN Office on Drugs and Crime that approximately 60 tonnes of cocaine and about 400 kilograms of heroin are smuggled through West Africa every year, generating over $900 million annually for the various groups involved in the business[196]. It is estimated that of the about $1 billion worth of cocaine transported to Europe from West Africa, $500 million remained in West Africa. The fact that Mali's entire defence budget was only $180 million provides an indication of the problem. In 2010 it was estimated that about $1.25 billion worth of cocaine was transported to Europe from West Africa[197].

Here, it is important to note that some of the groups that participated in the 2012 revolt in Mali have been accused of involvement in the drug trade. However, no evidence has been found of their direct involvement. But there is evidence that among these groups al-Qaeda in the Islamic Magreb [AQIM], for example, may have tried or imposed transit fees on drug smugglers or lent its protection to smuggling convoys and is therefore indirectly involved and is benefiting from the income of the trade in drugs[198].

Kidnapping for ransom also emerged as another profitable business venture in the region side by side with all the other rackets. Kidnapping for ransom came to be linked to and explained as part the main reasons behind the presence of AQIM in the Sahel region. Kidnapping foreign nationals for political and financial ends began to flourish in the wake of the Tuareg rebellions in Mali and Niger in the 1990s. In 2003, thirty-two European tourists were kidnapped in southern Algeria. Seventeen were subsequently released in Algeria, while fifteen remained hostages. They were later released in northern Mali after six months of captivity. These kidnappings were mainly carried out by the Algerian Salafi group, which changed its name in 2007 to al-Qaeda in the Islamic Maghreb [AQIM]. The involvement of AQIM was initially disputed but, by December 2007, it became clear after four French nationals were kidnapped and killed by AQIM members in Mauritania. In April 2012, forty-two foreign nationals were abducted. Twenty-four were released while five were killed, and the remaining 14 remained in captivity until August 2012.

These kidnappings usually take place in areas such as southern Algeria, Tunisia, Mauritania, Niger, and northern Mali by AQIM and later a splinter group from AQIM known as Movement for Tawhid and Jihad in West Africa [MUJWA]. Such kidnappings were seen to focus on foreign nationals of countries that are known to be willing to negotiate[199]. Political motives are sometimes behind AQIM's role in hostage-taking, the idea being to spread terror. Political demands were sometimes made in messages posted on the internet, and most releases were usually made after ransom was paid. Generally, kidnapping for ransom grew into a highly profitable industry that paved the way for AQIM and MUJWA to emerge as important political and military forces in the Sahel and the Saharan regions, respectively. It was reported that ransoms ranging between $1.4 million and $4 million were paid for hostage taking, and it was estimated that between $40 million and $65 million accrued to these groups from ransoms paid in order to release kidnapped foreign nationals since 2008, and such payments were made by Western governments[200].

At some point, it became very clear that there was a link between the organised crime that was taking place in the region and nations such as Mali, Mauritania, and other Sahel states. The complicity became more and more obvious as the rate of such kidnappings continued to rise. The business was dominated by AQIM and MUJWA. Tensions related to the growing drug business and the absence of state authority due to complicity with organised crime played significant roles in the developments that led to the outbreak of the conflict or revolt in northern Mali in January 2012.

In Mauritania, the involvement of security officials and businessmen in the contraband and weapons smuggling is well known. In 2007, a major cocaine seizure was made that exposed the linkages between influential figures and the growing drug trade. The nephew of the former president of Mauritania Sidi Ahmed OuldTaya and Sidi Mohamed OuldHaidallah, the son of another former president, were arrested for cocaine smuggling transactions at Nouadhibou airport. The decision of serving president Ould Abdel Aziz to reduce the prison sentences of cocaine smugglers in 2011 raised eyebrows in many quarters. Not only that, the appeal court's decision to release thirty convicted cocaine smugglers in July 2011 was widely seen to result from pressure on the judiciary after high-level players had fled the country[201,202]. Again, special permits were issued to certain individuals by the former head of police to avoid check points just as retired military officers came to be linked to a cannabis seizure on May 2012. The borders of Niger republic also appeared uncontrollable. Contraband goods and irregular migration became the order of the day and were carried on with the full connivance of state authorities. Weapons or drugs were freely traded on the northern side of the Niger border as the state authorities simply overlook the smuggling of these items. In 2011, an Arab rebel leader Abta Hamdine was arrested after a clash between the Niger army and a convoy carrying explosives and other weapons from Libya, clearly to be delivered to AQIM in northern Mali. Abta was subsequently released. Aghali Alambo, who served as adviser to the president of the Niger Legislative Assembly was also implicated in the matter. He was arrested briefly along with Abta and then also released.

The collusion in such crimes stretched as far as Algeria and Libya. In Libya, smuggling was managed by senior government officials until the overthrow of Gaddafi; and since then arms smuggling out of Libya to Egypt, Tunisia, Algeria, and the entire region has become rampant. It has succeeded in creating vested interests that would be difficult to dismantle by any future Libyan government. These instances of open collusion among government officials of the different states in the Sahel, including Mali, largely contributed to the rise of transnational Islamist groups who were later to launch the 2012 Tuareg war in Mali.

In Mali, organised crime is traceable to the 2006 rebellion, which was led by many Tuareg officers from Kidal City. It was certain that though the revolt started due to political grievances, rivalry and struggle for influence over smuggling was more prominent in the conflict than the politics of autonomy or implementation of the National Pact. The struggle by different smuggling networks to control routes or impose transit fees on smugglers from other groups became the main preoccupation due to the growing profits. The complicity of the Malian government was clear as they chose to give their support to leaders of the Arab clan and the Lamhar tribes of the north in order to counter the Ifoghas and the IdnanTuareg rebels. And from then on, a small group of Tuareg rebels from among the Ifoghas continued to attack many of the Merabuche and Lamhar drug smuggling convoys in the north.

Clashes related to cocaine smuggling became rampant[203] and, in certain instances, state officials intervened. Lieutenant Colonel Lamema OuldBou, an officer of the Malian army close to the head of state security, interfered in a cocaine clash in 2007 and was reported to have arranged a cocaine shipment in exchange for a substantial payment[204]. In November 2009, the discovery of a cocaine shipment by plane made the relationship between the Malian authorities, local notables, and businessmen in the drug trade very clearer. The shipment landed in Tarkint City, north of Gao, and was organised by Lamhar notables, including the Mayor of Tarkint, Baba Ould Cheick, who was said to be very close to the Malian government.

Many prominent Arab leaders in the provinces of Timbuktu and Gao tried to protect their business interests by establishing militias. This seemed to be welcomed by the Malian government, whose main interest and aim was to continue to mobilise Arab leaders to fight the rebel Tuaregs. Therefore, the militias created by businessmen such as Dina Ould Daya and Oumar Ould Ahmad were actually headed for some time by members of the Malian army such as Colonel Mohamed Ould Meydou and Lieutenant Colonel Bou[205].

The Malian government's alliance with certain groups among the Arab population, based on organised crime, also extended to AQIM and its kidnapping for ransom business[206]. In 2003, some European tourists were abducted and the Malian government and Western European governments relied on Iyad ag Ghaly, a former Tuareg rebel leader and head of the Ansardine organisation, and the mayor of Tarkint to act as intermediaries in ransom negotiations. It was alleged that successful negotiations implied that the intermediaries took a large part of the ransom negotiated, which they shared with their political protectors in the Malian government. The many instances of open complicity in organised crime between the Malian government and organisations such as AQIM and other drug trafficking networks led to the Malian authorities losing credibility and their corrupt actions undermined regional security arrangements. Attempts by neighbouring countries such as Mauritania and Algeria, to curb the excesses of AQIM and other organisations in the region were frustrated by the Malian government, which protected certain individuals from within these groups[207].

Though the 2012 war could not be said to be simply a clash between competing drug-smuggling-related groups such as AQIM, MUJAO, and other networks, it cannot be denied that the actors and organisations or groups involved in organised crime in the Sahel region played significant roles in the conflict as a result of the political and military influence they wielded across the region as a result of their illegal and criminal activities.

Thus the 2012 war was clearly contributed to by a combination of these interlinked factors - organised crime such as the trade in drugs, kidnapping for ransom and smuggling in goods such as cigarettes and weapons, as well as the political, social, economic, and environmental conditions described above, which to a large extent resulted from the general atmosphere of lawlessness and corruption. This is not to say that the nationalist and cultural aspirations of the Tuareg no longer played a part. The 2006–2009 rebellion, led by Ibrahim Bahanga, Iyad ag Ghaly, and other former Tuareg leaders, may not have been a revolution on the same scale as the 1963 or 1990 wars but was a revolt all the same. As we have seen, Ibrahim Bahanga never gave up his hopes. Before he died, he had formed a separate rebel group and was planning to launch a new Tuareg revolt. His group, based in Libya, was simply waiting for a favourable opportunity to do so.

## CHAPTER NINE

# Outbreak of the 2012 Tuareg War

*The revolution is a long thread Easily twisted Hard to stretch.* Tenalle Chegret [The Long Thread] song.

– Ibrahim Ag Alhabib
Tinariwen Musical Band
[Rebel Songs,The New Yorker]

The destruction by NATO of the Libyan government headed by President Muammar Gaddafi in 2011 had catastrophic results not only for Libya but it also led to the dramatic deterioration of the situation described in the previous chapter in the Sahel region and in Mali in particular. First, it resulted in a dangerous proliferation of weapons across the region, most of which fell into the hands of the smugglers, drug dealers, kidnappers and the many armed groups such as Al Qaeda, AQIM, MUJWA, and Ansardine. The situation that existed before the collapse of Libya had already rendered the region and northern Mali, in particular, dangerous and volatile. Now the flood of weapons emanating from Libya greatly exacerbated the already existing volatile and dangerous situation.

Another consequence of Libya's destruction, was the return of a large number of former Tuareg rebels who had been part of the Libyan army since the 1963 or 1990 revolts and many others who had emigrated to Libya as a result of Gaddafi's declaration that Libya was the original home of the Tuareg. Many of them may have been part of Bahanga's group and have been planning for a new Tuareg revolution in Mali. Some commentators maintain that the Tuareg group specifically returned with the intention of creating an Azawad country in Mali[208]. This contention would appear to have been tenable especially in the light of the developments that followed from their return.

The MNLA [National Movement for the Liberation of Azawad] was formed in October, 2011, with the express aim of independence for the Tuaregs of Mali. Its membership came to be dominated mostly by those Tuaregs that had returned from Libya after the fall of Gaddafi. Another Tuareg organisation, Ansardine, was formed by Iyad ag Ghaly after it became clear that Amenokal Intalla ag Attaher, a Tuareg chief, was opposed to his leadership of the MNLA. The MNLA in turn subsequently fell under the leadership of Bilal ag Acherif.

Iyad ag Ghaly was a former Tuareg rebel leader, and many of his former officers joined the MNLA. Thus the two organisations, MNLA and Ansardine, were able to form an alliance. The return of the Tuaregs from Libya had altered the balance of power among the various competing groups in favour of the Tuaregs, which made it possible for the Tuareg under the MNLA leadership to form an alliance with the Islamist groups, AQIM and MUJWA, in order to launch their attack on the Malian government. This they did in March, 2012, and simultaneously declared their independence as the state of Azawad[209].

The Malian army appeared ill-equipped to withstand the fire power of the rebels and the attack launched by the rebel groups of MNLA, Ansardine, AQIM and MUJWA, recorded substantial successes.[210]Between January 17th and April 1st, the rebels had captured not only the key town of Menaka but also Kidal on 30th March, Gao on 31st March, and Timbuktu on 1st April 2012[211]. This meant they had effectively taken control over northern Mali.

However, then the rebel group's alliances began to fall apart. A rift now yawned wide between the MNLA, on the one hand, and Ansardine and the two Islamist groups of AQIM and MUJWA, on the other. It wasn't long before the MNLA was driven out of the region by the Ansardine, led by Iyad ag Ghaly and his allies, AQIM and MUJWA. Ansardine, thought Tuareg was Islamist and Jihadist in character. These three organisations proceeded to impose Islamic law in the various cities they had captured in the North.[212]Ghaly's introduction of Sharia was seen as a move to consolidate his control in the area and to gain the support of the population by exploiting religious sentiments. With the help of AQIM and MUJWA, Ansardine was able to restore order, which had been absent since the outbreak of the conflict and which formed part of the reasons why the MNLA came to be despised by the population in the north. The MNLA was accused of arrogance, the robbery of civilians and rape. The disorder they introduced had led to the civilian population being forced to flee. After driving out the MNLA, Ansardine embarked on humanitarian assistance and distributed food and other relief items, further making its impact felt by the people in the North whose support for the group increased,[213]

The situation was obviously critical for Mali and the crisis led to a military coup on 22nd March, 2012, shortly before the scheduled presidential election that would have marked the end of Touré's second tenure as president. The coup was explained to have been caused by the growing dissatisfaction with the manner in which the Touré government had handled the crisis in the north of the country. It started with a mutiny sparked off by the conditions in which the Malian soldiers were expected to fight against the armed rebel groups.[214] But it soon exposed the many years of corruption and general maladministration of the Mali government under Touré. Captain Amadou Sanogo emerged as the new military ruler in Mali and gradually tried to consolidate his position within the military. Units considered loyal to President Touré were dissolved while leading officers of those units were arrested and subsequently imprisoned.

## CHAPTER TEN

# International Response to the War

> The fight against terrorist groups and the defense of democracy and the rule of law are inseparable.
>
> – Emmanuel Macron [BBC].

The military coup in Mali attracted widespread condemnation from the international community. In separate communiqués the United Nations, African Union[215], ECOWAS[216], and the European Union, all called for the immediate restoration of constitutional order in Mali. The African Union and ECOWAS made reference to the provisions of the African charter on democracy, elections, and governance, which reject any unconstitutional change of government, including seizure of power by force.[217] The ECOWAS first responded by refusing to recognise the new military junta and requested for the establishment of a transitional civilian administration to be headed by the Speaker of the Malian National Assembly, Dioncounda Traoré. In the event of any failure by the Malian military junta to comply with its demands, the ECOWAS threatened sanctions. As the junta did not comply,

ECOWAS imposed sanctions on 27th March, 2012. These included, among others, the suspension of Mali's membership of ECOWAS, a travel ban on the members of the junta and their associates, the recall of all ECOWAS ambassadors from Mali, as well as the closure of borders with all member states. In consideration of the weight and implications of these sanctions, the new military regime had no alternative but to cooperate and hand over power to a transitional administration, which came to be headed by DioncoundaTraoré, as requested by ECOWAS. Traoré, who had been the Speaker of the National Assembly under Touré, took over as Mali's interim president on 6 April 2012, which resulted in ECOWAS lifting the sanctions.[218]

The transitional government had taken over power but faced many problems, particularly since the rôle of the military junta under the transition administration was not clearly defined. This created confusion as the junta continued to occupy the political space, further complicating the already existing poor security situation in the country. ECOWAS appointed the president of Burkina Faso, Blaise Compaoré, to mediate in the conflict in Mali but because of the interference by the military junta ECOWAS, at some point, contemplated the reinstatement of the sanctions it had earlier lifted as the junta's interference contravened Article 1 of the ECOWAS Protocol on Democracy and Good Governance, which bars serving members of armed forces from engaging in politics. Compaoré failed in his attempt to broker a peace deal and this prompted the regional body to consider military action in Mali. This was due to the fact that the political instability in Mali as a whole was obviously affecting the security situation in the North - as correctly observed by Victoria Nuland of the US State Department in the following words:

> We thought we had a deal brokered by ECOWAS to return
> Mali to civilian rule so that we could get to the elections. We
> have concerns that the deal appears to be breaking down, it

*is not being honoured, of course, that's just providing space
for more mischief in the north of Mali.*[219]

Despite efforts made by ECOWAS, numerous problems were identified as being responsible for the failure of its efforts in the Mali conflict. Expectations that ECOWAS would exert some influence were seen to be based on the principle of solidarity and the fact that international and regional organisations were usually effective in putting in place measures to avoid, resolve, and manage crises, particularly within their sphere of influence. But the situation in Mali was complicated and confusing. It soon became apparent that ECOWAS did not have a clear strategy as to how to handle the crisis. ECOWAS was also blamed for delaying in taking action until 3rd September, 2012, when it was felt it could have done so long before then. It was reported that a number of high-level meetings had taken place among the ECOWAS states regarding the crisis, but those meetings did not seem to yield meaningful results. It was because of this lack of a clear strategy in Mali that the United Nations initially declined an ECOWAS request for military action in Mali. The organisation observed that for any meaningful action to be taken in Mali, it required the support of certain non-member countries, especially those that had observer status, such as Chad and Algeria. The Chadian army was well familiar with desert combat but was not involved in any of ECOWAS's negotiations and meetings. The same could be said for Algeria, whose logistical support would have been of inestimable value in handling the situation in the North. But it was not consulted. It soon became clear that ECOWAS could not go it alone and needed the help and support of other strategic partners such as the UN, AU, EU and countries like the United States, France, and United Kingdom.[220]

Meanwhile the rebels continued unabated. In September, 2012, the interim administration in Mali sought the assistance of ECOWAS in suppressing the offensive of the rebel groups. Following this request from the interim president, Traoré, ECOWAS forwarded the request to the African Union in order to facilitate the mobilisation of the required international support and authority for any planned mission. The AU and ECOWAS jointly prepared documents required by the Security Council of the UN to pass resolutions 2056 [2012] and resolution 2071 [2012] on 5th July and 12th October, respectively.[221] The two resolutions gave authority to ECOWAS and the African Union to develop a plan for military action in Mali and to report to the UN within 45 days.[222] It was on this basis that the AU Commission—in close collaboration with ECOWAS, concerned nations, the UN, and other partners—became actively involved in the preparation of a harmonised concept of operations [CONOPS] for the deployment of a military force in to Mali. The said concept of operations was endorsed first of all by the ECOWAS Summit of Heads of States and the Peace and Security Council of the African Union on 11th and 13th November, 2012, respectively. The document was said to have been the result of in-depth consultations with various stakeholders and outlined the measures or actions to be taken to bring a quick end to the war in Mali.

Consequently, on 20th December, 2012, the United Nations Security Council adopted resolution 2085 [2012] authorising the deployment of a 3,300-strong African-led international support mission to Mali, known as AFISMA, for an initial period of one year.[223] The approval by the UN Security Council did not go so far as to approve the request by the AU for the UN to establish a support package to be funded by contributions by the United Nations. Instead it recommended the establishment of a special trust fund to receive voluntary contributions for AFISMA and another fund for the Defence and Security Forces of Mali [MDSF]. The authorisation for the military action by the UN was also based on certain political and technical conditions.[224]

While efforts were being made for the deployment of the African-led mission to Mali, mediation efforts were also ongoing. On 8ᵗʰJanuary, 2013, the rebel groups were reported to have taken control of the strategic town of Konna, about 70 kilometres north of the Malian government's stronghold in Sevare. This was viewed as a clear threat to Bamako, the Malian capital; and as such, something needed to be done. The attack on cities such as Konna and Lere were seen as a strategic move to seize key infrastructure in the north, which included an airport. It was as a result of the offensive on these cities that the Malian authorities became afraid and thought that the Malian army might not be able to repel the combined offensive of Ansardine, AQIM and MUJWA. The result was that the interim president of Mali DioncoundaTraoré, on 10 January, 2013, called on France for a quick military action before the rebels could reach Bamako[225]. France responded positively with what came to be called Operation Serval.

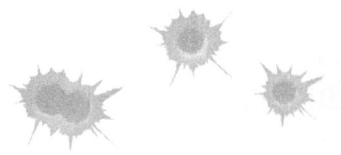

## CHAPTER ELEVEN

# French Policies towards Africa

*Oh, Lord, take away from my memory France that is not France. This mask of meanness and hate on the face of France.... For I have a great weakness for France.*

– Leopold Senghor.

Since his election into office on 15th May, 2012, the ex-president of France, Francois Hollande, had felt the need to give special attention to Africa as a result of the crisis in Mali. He was said to have reached a conclusion that the crisis posed a fundamental threat to French national interest and that it might enhance the capacity of the rebels and terrorists to stage attacks on France itself. The disintegration of Mali, he believed, could lead to instability in the entire West African sub-region. Thus, from the start, the French president publicly gave priority to the conflict in Mali. He hosted members of the Malian community, including the interim president, DioncoundaTraoré, at the Elysée Palace. Hollande continued his predecessor, Nicolas Sarkozy's, position by aligning with ECOWAS on the need to restore constitutional order as well as with the proposal to send a military mission to Mali to rescue the North from the rebels, whom the West saw as terrorists. Paris lobbied seriously during the summer and autumn of 2012 for the United Nations Security Council to support the ECOWAS proposal for the deployment of African troops to Mali[226]. Initially, the United States had opposed the proposal on the grounds that the plans by ECOWAS were not comprehensive enough, and this led to the Security Council's initial reluctance to accept the proposal. It was the sustained diplomatic efforts of Paris that finally convinced the UK and other EU partners of the need not only to send troops to Mali but also to train the African-led international mission and provide all the necessary support.

Unlike in the past, the Foreign Affairs Ministry in Paris under Hollande had become very active in shaping French policy towards Africa. The ministry did not just rely on instructions from the presidency. Hollande had appointed professional experts to deal with African issues and for this reason the ministry came to be fully involved in all issues related to French policy in Africa. The constitution of France vests all powers relating to foreign affairs and defence on the President rather than the Prime Minister and his government, which needed a parliamentary majority before they took any major decision. The French president however needed only to inform the parliament about his decisions relating to foreign affairs and defence as such issues were his prerogative and did not require parliamentary approval before taking any action[227]. The French National Assembly only debated issues relating to operations in Mali after the President had taken a decision. However, the French president at that time appeared to have relied on a circle of colleagues that advised him on how to handle the Malian crisis, including General Benoit Puga, Chief of Staff of the Republic, who was known to be a veteran of African interventions, and Defence Minister Jean-Yves Le Drian, who was a close confidant of the president and supported a strong military response to the crisis[228]. Hollande also relied on the African advisory unit at the Elysée Palace, which he created and which was headed by Héléne Le Gal, who had been a career diplomat. It was also reported that President Hollande and his ministers personally sought the opinion of many African presidents regarding the Mali issue, both within and outside West Africa, including Jacob Zuma of South Africa, as well as the president of Algeria Abdelaziz Bouteflika. Many African governments expressed their appreciation for Paris's consultations on the Mali crisis. Many African states became convinced of the need for military action and the quick stabilisation of the situation in Mali as a result of French diplomatic efforts. The Hollande government worked in close collaboration with the African Union and other regional power blocs with regard to French policy in Africa and the Mali conflict, in particular[229].

Many commentators have debated the arguments relating to the public support for Operation Serval within France and in Mali. According to a report of the Voice of America on 14th January, 2014,[230] polls conducted in France showed that a hefty majority of the French people supported the operation. The clarity of French goal, namely; to drive the Islamist fundamentalists and the fact that the French forces produced rapid results, contributed to such public support in France. There was a general feeling, as reported among the French public, that Operation Serval was the right thing to do.[231] The Parliamentary Oversight of Armed Forces blog, on 28thJanuary, 2013, was quoted as saying that 'the French public is usually known for its support to the President who is seen to always help France maintain its international position'.

Following the request by the Malian president for Paris to intervene militarily, and in pursuance of UN resolution 2085 [2012], Paris launched Operation Serval to put a stop to rebel advances, as well as all activities of the various armed groups in Mali, and the restoration of the territorial integrity of the country. Several reasons were advanced to support the French intervention. The first was that there was considerable delay, attributed to logistical and financial constraints, in the operational readiness, logistical preparation, as well as the build-up of units placed at the disposal of AFISMA. Secondly, lack of political commitment among African states regarding the Mali crisis and the UN resolution authorising the deployment of the African-led force were another reason for Malian support of the operation. The African states did not have the capacity to respond to the emergency situation, which the offensive of the rebel terrorist groups had created, swiftly enough and this had prompted Bamako to seek emergency assistance from Paris. Mali's geographical location also made co-ordinating the African mission complicated. The Sahel region is at the crossroads of west, north, and the central regions of Africa, which belong to different regional bodies and as such made coordination challenging[232]. At first the Malian public gave the French force enthusiastic welcome when they arrived to rescue them from the Islamist incursion. However, according to some sources, opinion in Mali may have subsequently shifted. There was the fear that the ex-colonial power might wish to maintain a permanent military presence in Mali. This fear was expressed in a recently published book by a Malian activist, Aminata Dramane Traoré, and a Senegalese novelist, Boubacar Boris Diop, entitled *La Gloire des Imposteurs*. In that book, the authors outlined the fears of the Malian people, who they claimed were confused by a situation in which they had to choose to fight the jihadists for a very long time or have their sovereignty challenged and their territory occupied by the former colonialist power- or possibly even partitioned to satisfy a group, namely the Tuareg, which had traditionally been allied to it.[233].

Operation Serval was launched by Paris on 11th January, 2013, when the Special Forces Aviation Unit stationed in Burkina Faso destroyed pick-up vans belonging to the rebel forces. French detachment were sent from Chad, Ivory Coast and Senegal in a contingency effort to rescue Mali from the rebels. After three weeks of fighting, certain cities were recovered, including the cities Timbuktu and Gao on 26th and 28th January, respectively. Both were considered highly important and strategically necessary in order to defeat the rebels.

The rebel groups then moved into the countryside to be able to regroup and re-strategise. By March, the Chadian troops[234], French Airborne, and armoured troops had begun clearing the positions of the terrorists in the Ifogha Mountains, making sure that important cities and infrastructures would be able to withstand the offensive of the rebel groups. French forces led the operations while integrating the Malian soldiers into their ranks. It was reported that resistance in both the recaptured cities was weak from the rebel side, in the case of Timbuktu it was almost non-existent. The administrative region of Kidal, which covers a wide strip of desert, is sparsely populated and located on the Algerian border, proved rather more difficult to deal with for humanitarian and geographical reasons. The region is entirely different from Timbuktu and Gao for a number of important reasons. The most important military commanders from among the Tuaregs since the 1990 war and the newly formed MNLA and Ansardine, including Iyad ag Ghaly, Ibrahim Bahanga, and Hasanag Fagaga, all come from there. Among the three regions in the North, Kidal had a Tuareg majority. The Ifogha mountains, located in the region, had traditionally been a refuge for many armed movements. Strangely, the rebels fled Kidal even before the arrival of the French troops. When the French arrived in Kidal on 28th January, they found the city under the control of the MNLA, who had indicated that they would welcome the coming of the French on condition that Malian army stayed away. For this reason, the Malian army was not involved in the Kidal offensive, which was launched on18[th] February, 2013, and came to be known as Operation Panther. Operation Panther started with destruction of all terrorist bases around the small town of Tessalit. In the region of about thirty Chadian soldiers were said to have been lost in the operation. After a successful collaboration between the French army and the MNLA, Kidal was stabilised and the MNLA[235] consolidated its position in the city[236].

In general, Operation Serval was highly successful in terms of organisation, operation, and planning despite the many challenges it faced. The French had deployed 4,000 soldiers to Mali, and its army had vast experience in combat operations, having taken part in actions in volunteer operations in Africa, Afghanistan, the Middle East, and the Balkans. In terms of intelligence, the French and other allied intelligence details had been tracking the activities of terrorist groups in the Sahel region for quite some time. Joint intelligent operations such as satellite observation, naval patrol aircraft, U.S. Air Force unmanned aerial vehicles, as well as U.S. Army human intelligence, had for long focused on Mali and proved crucial during the operation[237]. They helped in providing targets for air strikes that paved the way for ground troops to advance. They further helped identify positions in the Ifogha Mountains.

The operation in its entirety was seen to have consisted of three main phases: block, drive back, and clear. In terms of supplies, allied contributions helped bridge French gaps in strategic and tactical transport at the start of the operations. With regard to planning, a contingency plan in support of AFISMA had been drafted but was not implemented, and the G5 of the French armed forces was revised and deployed and came to be known as Guépardor Cheetah. It generally consisted of a mechanised brigade on high readiness, backed by an airborne emergency element. The three phases of the operation had been clear to the French right from the start and provided enough latitude to the tactical commanders. The broadband global area network and other satellite communications systems provided signals for the operation, though they were found not in the standard of army inventory and could not be used on the move. Serval was described as unprecedented in speed, number of troops, and distances involved. According to certain sources, the operation revealed the determination, ruggedness and resourcefulness of the French troops who were fighting in such austere conditions[238].

France's intervention in Mali was viewed positively by numerous organisations such as the UN, AU, EU, NATO, and ECOWAS. The

EU established a training mission in Mali to boost the operational capacity of both AFISMA and the Malian forces. The EU High Representative, Catherine Ashton, speaking after a meeting of EU foreign ministers that took place on 17th January,2013, to accelerate the deployment of the Mali EU mission, said: *"The situation highlights the need for enhanced and accelerated international engagement in support of the restoration of stability and state authority throughout Mali, in line with UN resolution 2085".*[239]ECOWAS—in a communiqué issued at the end of its third extraordinary meeting of the Mediation and Security Council on 15thJuly, 2013, held in Abuja, Nigeria— reiterated its gratitude to France and Chad for the sacrifices made to assist Mali in her time of needs. ECOWAS also welcomed the deployment of the AFISMA mission to Mali and later supported the transition of AFISMA to MINUSMA, following a request to the United Nations and subsequent approval as will be seen in the next chapter.

Western countries such as Italy, Denmark, Belgium, Canada and Germany in one way or the other supplemented the French effort by providing logistics. The UN secretary general Ban Ki-moon was quoted during a press conference on 22 January 2013 as saying: *'I applaud France for its courageous decision to deploy troops following the troubling move southward by extremist groups'*[240]. David Cameron, the British Prime Minister at that time, was also quoted on 12thJanuary, 2012, as saying: *'I welcome the military assistance France has provided to the Malian government, at their request, to halt, this progress in implementing UN Security Council resolution on Mali, and ensuring that military intervention is reinforced by an inclusive political process leading to election and a return to civil rule'*[241]. Again on 25 January, 2013, the British Ministry of Defence, in a speech by the Secretary for Defence, Philip Hammond, said: *'Following discussion with the French, we have now decided to deploy Sentinel*[242], *a surveillance capability that proved its worth in Libya and an ongoing basis for counter insurgency operations in Afghanistan'.*[243] London deployed about twenty personnel to support the French air transport liaisons and seventy supporting ground crew for the Sentinel aircraft. Canada, on its part, chipped in by providing a single CC-177 Globemaster III military transport plane and deploying a special joint task force to Mali to provide protection for Canadian assets and the embassy at Bamako[244].

The United States was initially expected to oppose the French action. However, a testimony by its Assistant Secretary of the Bureau of African Affairs, Johnnie Carson, attached to a memo sent to the US president of that time, Barack Obama, by the National Security Adviser entitled: 'The need for a stronger U.S. policy towards the Mali crisis' dated 15th February, 2013 both expressed support for the French intervention in Mali. Johnnie Carson wrote: '*We commend and strongly support the ongoing French and African military operation in northern Mali. On 20 December, 2012 the UN adopted resolution 2085, co-sponsored by the U.S, which recognised Mali's overlapping challenges; underscored the international community's support for restoring peace.*' In yet another testimony before the Foreign Affairs committee, Amanda Dor, the Deputy Assistant Secretary of Defence for Africa in the Office of the Secretary for Defence, was quoted as saying: '*We are supporting the French by providing intelligence, aerial refuelling services, and airlift, and are pursuing a range of funding options for our contributions. The counter terrorism effort in Mali complements the parallel U.S. strategic objectives to support a sustainable solution to northern grievances, help Mali's transition back to democracy, and ameliorate the humanitarian situation*'[245].

## CHAPTER TWELVE

# AFISMA and MINUSMA Forces in the Mali War

*Going forward, the AU and ECOWAS will maintain a strong presence in Mali and accompany the country in its efforts to resolve the crisis.*

– Pierre Buyoya [African Union].

Shortly after Operation Serval ended, starting on 17th January, 2013, AFISMA forces were deployed to Mali to help further stabilise the country, in accordance with UN resolution 2085 [2012]. Nigerian troops were the first to arrive. African nations[246] moved swiftly to expedite their troop contributions, especially following the action of the French. Planning and coordination initially presented challenges but international partners provided support through strategic airlifts as well as ground transportation. On 25th January, 2013, the AU Peace and Security Council requested all commissioners, ECOWAS, UN, EU, and other partners, to revise the joint strategic concept of operations and increase the troop strength of AFISMA. According to Major General Shehu Abdulkadir, the AFISMA force commander, 6,288 military personnel were deployed to Mali, including 84 officers at the AFISMA headquarters. It was expected that the AFISMA contingents would be self-sufficient for 90 days after deployment[247] but they soon came to face serious logistical problems, including shortage of food, fuel, and water. Obviously adequate provision of logistical support remained crucial for the timely completion of deployment, for sustainability, as well as for the effectiveness of operations[248]. UN military planners had provided or helped to establish coordination mechanisms and identified priority needs for AFISMA, including increased awareness in terms of situations at the AFISMA headquarters. The planners helped in the development of key documents for the operation, which included, among others, operational directives, guidelines for the protection of civilians, rules of engagement and a code of conduct[249].

AFISMA was charged by the UN to contribute to the rebuilding of the capacity of the Malian Defence and Security Forces in close coordination with other international partners involved in the process, including the European Union and other member states. The mission was also intended to support the Malian authorities in recovering the areas in the north of its territory under the control of terrorist, extremist, and armed groups and in reducing the threat posed by terrorist organisations such as AQIM and MUJWA, while taking appropriate measures to reduce the impact of military actions on the civilian population. AFISMA was further expected to help in transition and stabilisation activities and support the Malian authorities in maintaining security and consolidating state authority through appropriate capacities. It was also expected to support the Malian authorities in their primary responsibility to protect the population and again help support the Malian authorities to create a secure environment for the civilian-led delivery of humanitarian assistance and the voluntary return of internally displaced persons and refugees, as requested, within its capabilities and in close coordination with humanitarian actors. The mission was also expected to protect its personnel, facilities, premises, equipment, and mission and to ensure the security and movement of its personnel[250].

Despite the deployment of the AFISMA forces and the presence of French troops in Mali, the mission still faced a lot of challenges in terms of capacity, training, and logistical support. AFISMA force commander, Major General Shehu Abdulkadir, while briefing the ECOWAS Mediation and Security Council during the forty-third ordinary session of ECOWAS Authority of Heads of States and Governments, informed the council that AFISMA had covered the entire battleground in Mali and performed professionally and effectively since deployment. He, however, noted in his briefing that the mission faced challenges that complicated the operation of the troops in terms of logistics, intelligence, and lack of air assets, improvised explosive devices, communication equipment, and accommodation. The commander affirmed that the mission had fulfilled its mandate as set out under UN resolution 2085 and recommended an after-action programme and a review of the regional peace and security architecture with regard to rapid response capabilities and strategic lift, as well as a harmonised pre-deployment training exercise – in other words a combined training of all troops that would be contributed by ECOWAS member states, UN troops or any other troops that would participate in the Mali operation – as well as the strengthening of the ECOWAS standby force[251].

As a result of the continued security threat posed by the rebel terrorist groups in the north of Mali, as well as the challenges facing AFISMA and the need to stabilise Mali due to the humanitarian situation created by the conflict, there was urgent need to mobilise donor support to help address certain priority needs: re-building rule of law institutions; reconstruction of offices; vehicles; communications equipment; and basic supplies. It became clear that the operation required a larger commitment than that provided by the AU or ECOWAS.

It was against this background that interim president of the transitional government in Mali, in collaboration with ECOWAS and AU, sent a letter to the United Nation's Security Council. The Malian government, ECOWAS, and the AU requested the transformation of AFISMA into a United Nations stabilisation and peacekeeping operation. Following this, the Assistant Secretary General for peacekeeping operations at the UN, Edmond Mulet, led a delegation to Mali in order to develop recommendations for the Security Council's consideration on options for the establishment of a United Nations peacekeeping operation in Mali[252]. The UN delegation visited Mali from 10th to 16th March, 2013, and reported its findings to the Council.

Upon assessment of the political and security situation in Mali by the UN delegation, the UN reaffirmed its strong commitment to the sovereignty, unity, and territorial integrity of Mali. The UN, in consideration of the offensive of the rebel groups, welcomed the swift action of the French forces and also commended the efforts of the Malian and AFISMA forces in Mali. Acting on on the recommendations of the UN delegation to Mali, the UN took the decision to accept the request of the transitional government, ECOWAS and the AU and consequently established the United Nations Multi-dimensional Integrated Stabilization Mission in Mali [MINUSMA]. ECOWAS welcomed the smooth transition of AFISMA to MINUSMA and called on the UN to further strengthen co-operation and collaboration among African partners in the stabilisation of the security and political situation in Mali. In its communiqué, ECOWAS expressed gratitude to all partners - the UN, the EU, the United States, France, and all neighbouring states for their cooperation on intelligence, finance, logistics, and political support in Mali and appealed to the donor community to provide urgent financial support and relief supplies in response to the humanitarian situation in Mali[253].

MINUSMA came into force on 1st July, 2013, in accordance with UN Security Council Resolution 2100 [2013] on 25th April, 2013. The mandate of MINUSMA, as outlined by the United Nations Security Council Resolution 2100, was mainly the stabilisation of Mali; and this included, among others, the re-establishing of state authority throughout the country[254]. It was also charged with the responsibility of supporting the rebuilding of the entire Malian society by supporting the Malian forces and by helping in the disarmament and demobilisation process already begun, as well as by supporting reintegration programmes. The mission was to support in the general implementation of the transitional roadmap, as well as to facilitate progress towards national dialogue and reconciliation. Further it was to supervise the organisation and conduct of a free, fair and transparent general election throughout the country. The mission was to provide protection to some of the areas that were under the threat of violence during the election. MINUSMA was also charged with the responsibility of supporting humanitarian assistance and the preservation of Malian and world culture in Mali in collaboration with other UN agencies, including UNESCO[255].

The deployment of MINUSMA encountered several problems or difficulties as a result of the security situation in Mali at that time. The absence of a central authority as well as harsh weather conditions made things very difficult for the mission, particularly in the north of Mali, which had been occupied by the rebel groups. MINUSMA deployed its logistical equipment to Kidal on 28th July, 2013, and its representatives made contact with Malian authorities, journalists, civil society organisations and other UN specialised agencies resident in Mali. The first and immediate task facing the mission remained the conversion of the 6,000 strong AFISMA force to MINUSMA. The United Nations had given the mission a time frame of months to convert the forces but it faced challenges in making the conversion. One of the reasons was that certain countries did not meet the stipulated number of troops requested. Countries such as Burkina

Faso sent a contingent of between 500 and 600 as against the 850 requested by the United Nations. There was also a problem of child soldiers as certain contingents from countries like Chad included soldiers who were under age.

The mission's second immediate task was the supervision of general elections in the country, including the presidential elections. MINUSMA successfully supervised the conduct of the said elections, which took place on 28th July, 2013, as well as the run-off that took place on 11th August the same year. The elections went ahead in what was generally agreed to be a conduicive atmosphere devoid of violence or disorganisation. About twenty-seven candidates presented themselves to contest the presidency of Mali. However, the main contenders were Ibrahim Boubacar Keita and Soumaïla Cissé.

Prior to the elections, MINUSMA, in collaboration with the UN and other agencies such as the UNDP, had tried to support the establishment of a biometric electoral register and provided finger prints and photographic equipment to produce voting cards. The mission and other partners organised and supervised workshops aimed at training civil society on the conduct of peaceful elections. Flights were organised to Mauritania to distribute voters' cards to Malian refugees as diaspora voting had been agreed by the Malian government. Malians in diaspora registered at the various Malian embassies and consulates of their respective countries of residence and voted at the embassies and consulates on the day of the election. All in all, a total of about 6.83 million people registered to vote in the election. A three-week campaign period throughout the country had been approved before the election for all office seekers, beginning from 9th to 26th July 2013. In the first round of the elections, popular participation was recorded at over 48% and in the run-off election for the president, Ibrahim Boubacar Keita emerged victorious with an estimated 77% of the total votes cast[256].

The elections were observed by both domestic and international observer teams. The United States sent about 70 observers into areas such as Bamako, Segou, Sikasso, Koutiala, Selingue, and Koulikoro. The EU also sent about 50 observers to the southern part of the country while the African Union on its part also sent about 60 observers to the south of Mali. ECOWAS sent about 300 observers to different cities across Mali. The British embassy sent 6 observers. The International Republican Institute also sent 12 observers to Bamako, Kayes, Segou, and Sikasso.

Despite the successes recorded in the various areas, including the supervision of the conduct of the general elections, the mission appeared to have been hit by leadership crisis right from the start and that was seen to have affected the general coordination of its activities, as well as its capacity to function fully. From its inception, Resolution 2100 had authorized the deployment of an African led force and charged it with with the responsibility of stabilisation. Practically, it became difficult to define and differentiate the responsibilities and roles of MINUSMA AFISMA and Serval. The role of AFISMA and Serval, according to the UN resolution, was the 'enforcement of peace activities', and MINUSMA was to 'deter threats'. The two roles appeared confusing and complicated and often brought about dispute and confusion in terms of command. Leadership came to be contended between the French mission, AFISMA and MINUSMA. A Dutch citizen, Bert Koenders, had been appointed head of the UN mission while Pierre Buyoya, the former president of Burundi, headed AFISMA forces in Mali. Meanwhile, the UN had appointed Major General Jean Bosco Kazura force commander of MINUSMA, thus seeming to sideline Major General Shehu Abdulkadir, a Nigerian who had been appointed AFISMA forces commander since January 2013. Despite all this, the commander of the French forces, General Vianney Pillet, appeared to be in control of the entire operation even though Operation Serval was meant to have ended[257].

## CHAPTER THIRTEEN

# The Strategic Interest of France in Mali

*The third world faces Europe like a colossal mass whose aim should be to try to resolve the problems to which Europe has not been able to find answers.*

– Frantz Fanon [Wretched of the Earth].

D espite the glaring security situation in Mali and in consideration of the fact that there had been a request from the interim president of Mali for Paris to intervene, the intervention by Paris has come under strong scrutiny in many quarters. Many queried the motives for the intervention, and the actions of France were subjected to various interpretations. Though many believed that France had actually intervened to rescue Bamako from the rebel terrorist adavance and to block the emergence of a terrorist state in the Sahel region that could pose a threat to Europe in the future if not taken care of, others suspected that certain economic factors may have motivated the French intervention.

Mali, like other African states, had attracted a lot of foreign capital in various sectors of its economy. The influx of this foreign capital and permits for the repatriation of dividends and proceeds from sales and liquidations were not limited by any restrictions under Malian law. About 2.4 million hectares of land in Mali had been allocated to foreign nationals and companies engaged in the production of biofuels and cotton. It was well known that Mali possessed many mineral resources, some of which were yet to be exploited. It was already the sixteenth largest producer of gold worldwide and it had various other mineral resources such as precious stones, bauxite, and uranium, which were equally valuable and in high demand in the international market. There were speculations that petroleum may have been found in the Taoudeni region in the north of the country. Although oil exploration had posed challenges due to the huge amount of capital involved, and partly as a result of the security situation in the north where it was located, nevertheless, it had attracted the attention of many foreign nations and companies[258].

France was known to have energy interests in Mali; and one of its companies, Areva Nuclear Energy Company, was said to have monopolised the exploration of uranium deposits in Niger republic, located 300 kilometres east of the Malian border. Much of the fuel consumed by French nuclear plants came from Niger, and France had signed an agreement for the exploration of the second largest uranium reserve in the world. It was located 80 kilometres south of Arlit. The contract was signed with Areva, and about 1.2 billion euros would be invested in the exploration.

France was not economically privileged in Mali, despite being the former colonial power, as it was in other countries. Even though it was estimated that imports from France into Mali including refined petroleum, cement, and packaged medicaments are totalling about $423.04 million in 2012, they constitute only about 12% of Mali's total imports. Exports to France from Mali of commodities such as gold, cotton and other minerals totalled about $57.86 million in 2012 and constituted about 20% of Mali's total exports. In terms of imports, France remained Mali's second most important partner after Senegal while in terms of exports it was the eighth, South Africa being number one. With this in mind, the intervention in Mali came to be explained as being motivated by both France's economic and strategic/political concerns with regard to Mali and Africa as a whole. Even as it was, it was also reported that France had achieved a trade surplus with Mali of over 300 million euros, five times its foreign aid to Mali. As such, many tended to see the intervention as a kind of military investment for economic returns[259].

France had reformed its armed forces after the end of the cold war to be able to meet the challenges of the emerging security environment. A 1994 French government's White Paper had created a plan for the military that no longer focused on the threat of the Soviet Union but was directed at dealing with pockets of instability around the globe. This was due to the risk associated with the proliferation of weapons of mass destruction, as well the emergence of threats associated with terrorism. The coming of Jacques Chirac to power in 1995 saw the French armed forces transformed into an all-professional armed force that was readily deployable and capable of operating within an international coalition[260]. Since then, for over 20 years, the French military had been involved in different operations overseas for a variety of reasons, ranging from war against terrorism, humanitarian crises and missions related to peacekeeping. However, a quick review of those interventions would reveal that the majority of French interventions had been in countries in Africa. These included Rwanda, Somalia, Zaire, Comoros, Congo, Cote D'Ivoire, Chad, Gulf of Aden, Libya, and then Mali. Another characteristic of French military operations was that most of the countries they took place in were former French colonies.

The costs of such military interventions forced Paris to identify priority areas and zones for involvement. These were identified by the French government as the European periphery, the Mediterranean

Basin, the Persian Gulf, the Indian Ocean, North Africa and the Sahel to equatorial Africa. The Sahel region was seen and identified by Paris as a zone of vital interest that it believed should be defended[261]. Mali was among the Sahel states that had historic ties with France. It is estimated that up to 210,000 French expatriates were scattered across Africa; and certain countries like Gabon, Senegal, Djibouti and Chad had special defence agreements with France, which has given the French legitimacy and operational advantage in terms of military interventions in the continent[262].

Many of the African leaders who had been loyal to French interests in Africa during the cold war period were no longer in power. As a result, the influence of France was seen to be waning. The United States had recently developed a strategic interest in the African continent and it began to expand its legal framework for economic relations with African states. The African Growth and Opportunity Act of 2000, which was adopted by the US Congress, was specifically intended to ensure the eradication of customs restrictions on African goods. Many trade negotiations and bilateral investment treaties were signed between the United States and several African states, including Nigeria, South Africa, Angola, Cameroun, and Senegal. The United States, in its effort to reach out to African states, initiated the Millennium Change Corporation with the aim of providing support for various economic projects across the African continent. It was observed that many such agreements and treaties between the United States and the African states fell under or were considered to be traditionally France's sphere of influence as former colonial power and this was seen to be a major source of concern for Paris[263].

Increased U.S. military presence in the African continent had also led to the expansion of economic relations with African states. The U.S. State Department launched the Pan-Sahel initiative in 2002, which later evolved into what came to be known as the Trans-Saharan Counterterrorism Partnership Program [TSCTP][264]. In the first year, about $6.25 million was spent on training and capacity building in Niger, Mali, Chad, and Mauritania. The programme was born out of concerns for post-9/11 attacks as the Sahel region was viewed as a potential theatre for the operations of the transnational al-Qaeda network[265]. The Trans-Sahara Counterterrorism programme was allocated about $230 million between 2005 and 2007, with Mali, Niger, Chad, and Mauritania receiving the bulk of the funds.

Another significant development regarding United States policy towards Africa was the establishment of the new Africa Command [Africom]. The Command had been set up to counteract threats posed by terrorism, as well as to reinforce the United States strategic presence in Africa as well as to secure access to African resources regarding U.S. energy demands[266]. The U.S. military presence in the Sahel region was believed to be a major source for concern for Paris, especially considering the fact that almost all the countries that had security and military relations with the French had joined the U.S. initiative. A report submitted to the French National Assembly on 6th March, 2012, noted with concern increased American presence in the Sahel region since 2005[267].

Additionally, the involvement of the BRICS states in the affairs of the African continent became a major source of concern for Paris.[268] Including Russia, India, China, Brazil and South Africa, the BRICS states formed an axis that had the potential systematically to oppose the views [and interests] of France, the United States, and the UK, particularly on issues related to the African continent. The 2011 NATO intervention in Libya and involvement in Cote D'Ivoire was a case in point where the BRICS states opposed the interventions. As such, Paris feared that the BRICS may transform into a politicised and institutionalised group speaking with one voice. France was particularly concerned that the grouping included South Africa, which it saw as adding a new dimension to the alliance and its influence on African states. It was for this reason that Paris began to advocate a proposal to enlarge the UN Security Council on the basis that it should reflect the shifts in global balance of power[269].

The Mali conflict has been seen by some as an expression of the competition that exists between China, Russia and Brazil, on the one hand, and the USA and Europe on the other. This competition affects areas such as biofuel, garment and textile manufacturing, as well as agriculture. Cotton plays a significant role in the Chinese economy, where about 40 million people are employed in the industry. Cotton represented 11% of China's GDP, and West Africa was seen as one of China's main sources of cotton imports. Between January and July 2011, Mali produced about 7% of China's cotton imports from the African continent. As a result of the expansion and growth of China's textile market, the United States enacted an act that was intended specifically to prevent China from entering the U.S. The act states that textile products must be produced indigenous as laid out by the rules-of-origin framework[270].

Brazil was also seen to have a cotton project that was expected to cover the countries of Mali, Burkina Faso, Benin, and Chad. The project aimed to increase the competitiveness of cotton in those countries. The Brazilian foreign minister visited Mali in 2009 to discuss with its agricultural minister regarding the project, which was expected to put Brazil into the production stages of contemporary technologies and was seen to be supported by the Brazilian Development Agency. Brazil and Mali reached a joint decision to expand co-operation in the field of cotton production, as well as the production of rice. France continued to view such activities in many of the French-speaking African states that were in the past considered exclusively France's sphere of influence with a lot of concern.

The maritime strategy of countries like China and Brazil has witnessed a transformation. This transformation also involved African states, which were not in the interest of France. Since the 1980s, China adopted the comprehensive defence theory, which meant preparing Chinese naval forces to be able to move freely in the waters to the west, south, and north of China. This change came hand in hand with her focus on economic developments with regard to increase in the need for marine and energy resources. Between 1995 and 1996, Sino-American relations began to turn sour and consequently led to an accelleration in China's plans to expand her naval forces. A new policy was adopted to replace the previous one, one of active maritime defence. The new policy saw the widening of China's geographical areas of operation, which was meant to give China access to the international markets. As contained in its National Defence White Paper of 2006, China felt compelled to modernise its naval forces, as well as to enlarge its area of operations. This process was put into effect in three different phases. The first stage was meant to develop capabilities for responding to Taiwanese potential threats – and for this, a line had to be formed, connecting the islands that extended from southern Japan through the Philippines and Malaysia to Vietnam. Under the second phase, between 2010 and 2020, China envisioned a connection between the islands of Japan to Indonesia with further penetration into the Asia-Pacific region. And in the last phase, which was expected to start from 2020, China hoped to be able to close the technological gap between its navy and that of the United States[271].

In the course of implementing the new policy, China had to make a series of military agreements and commitments with many of its neighbouring states. It signed agreements with Cambodia in 2003 and provided military equipment to Bangladesh to ward off threats from India. In 2007, it also signed an agreement to construct a port in Sri Lanka and it has also erected a surveillance station in the Gwardar region of Pakistan. The Indian Ocean has come to occupy an important position for China, owing to the fact that the coast faced the Strait of Malacca and linked it to the Persian Gulf and the Horn of Africa. Hence, the majority of goods transported between China, the Middle East, and Africa had to pass through this region. As a result, China found itself developing relations politically, economically, and militarily with relevant African states on the Indian Ocean literal, particularly in Eastern Africa, with states like Kenya, Tanzania and Egypt. Naval exercises were reported to have taken place with the participation of African states including Egypt and South Africa. China was planning a naval base in East Africa as a result of the piracy that began to emerge off the coast of Somalia which was forcing China to deploy war ships to Djibouti. The base was expected to ease problems for Chinese fleets on long-distance journeys. China considered the East African states highly important as a result of their strategic locations on the Indian Ocean. Many have tried to see a connection between China's advances towards Africa's Indian and Atlantic Ocean coasts and its relations with East African states as a counter to U.S. geo-strategic interests as China believed, with good reason, that the United States was pursuing a policy to contain it and prevent it from becoming a global power. As a result she planned to establish military bases in Seychelles, Maldives, Singapore, and Vietnam. It is also believed that she is attempting to increase her presence in the Horn of Africa and the Indian Ocean through the establishment of military bases and agreements[272].

Brazil, on the other hand, was seen to be drifting towards West Africa, a move that was being viewed with great concern by many countries, including France and the United States. Brazil began to make its presence felt in West Africa in 1980. In 1986, it succeeded in convincing the UN General Assembly to issue a decree that would proclaim the area between South America and Africa as the South Atlantic Peace and Cooperation Zone. Again, in 1996, a community of Portuguese-speaking or Lusophone countries came into place, consisting of Angola, Mozambique, Cape Verde, Guinea Bissau, and Sao Tome and Principe. Brazil assumed a new role in West Africa through the new organisation. Its success in convincing the United Nations to issue decree 41/11[273] that proclaimed the South Atlantic Cooperation Zone gave her further advantages. Under international law, Brazil enjoyed exclusive economic rights up to 200 nautical miles off its coastline. Brazil's vision recognised the need to develop cooperation with geo-strategic regions in the south Atlantic, which included the Southern Cone of South America, the Amazon Basin, and the Portuguese-speaking African states[274].

As a result, Brazil's relations with African states began to develop gradually, not only with the Portuguese-speaking states but with other African states also. These states included many which are considered to fall under the influence of France. The coming to power of Luiz Inacio Lula da Silva in Brazil led to Brazil's foreign policy focussing even more on Africa. About seventeen out of Brazil's thirty-five diplomatic missions scattered across the African continent were opened after 2003. Brazil also entered into strategic partnerships with several African states. The Brazilian national defence strategy, published in 2008, came to include West Africa in the strategic and technical line of its navy. The Brazilian navy outlined about four major areas of concern, which included proactive defence for offshore oil drilling; defence of marine facilities, harbours, and islands within Brazilian territorial waters; as well as rapid response to any threat directed against maritime trade routes from other countries. Brazil also aims to be able to participate in international peacekeeping operations outside the Brazilian territory. A study published by a strategic research institute affiliated to the French Military Academy reported that Brazil was highly keen to assume a role of maintaining international balances. The report stated that Brazil was relying on its 'cultural fraternity' mission to assume this role. It further stated that Brazil desired to win a permanent seat on the UN Security Council. Her involvement in the BRICS led to a partnership with South Africa, India, and China and is aimed at playing a bigger role in international politics[275].

In a rapidly developing international situation of this kind, a traditional power like France, which had for a long time been used to maintaining and benefitting from what it considered its spheres of influence, had a lot to feel threatened by. Accordingly, a white paper published by the French Ministry of Defence in 2008 stated that France needed to make its forces visible once more on the 'strategic belt' axis. This axis was explained to extend from the Atlantic Ocean to the Indian Ocean[276]. The report was said to have been made in reaction to French concerns about the increasing roles of powers such as China, India, Brazil, and the United States on the African continent as described above. French interests in the Indian Ocean were identified to be based on two axes; one extends from Djibouti to the Persian Gulf while the other falls on the south of the Indian Ocean near Madagascar – both of which are also seen to be areas of strategic interest to the Chinese. The Chinese presence in areas of critical interest to Paris no doubt pushed her to adopt new policies and measures in certain places. These included playing the leading rôle in European anti-piracy operations in the 1990s and the construction of a naval base in Abu Dhabi.

France's main goal was to prevent China from entering the Gulf of Guinea. Paris was concerned that economic relations between the Chinese and African states were invariably followed by military relations. As such, relations between Paris and China came to be defined by geo-strategic and geo-economic concerns; and relations between the two became confrontational, though their confrontation was not expressed militarily. Paris was determined not to lose her influence in areas it considered under its sphere of influence in the past as a colonial power.

Another driver of the conflict in Mali was international competition over mineral resources, particularly over uranium deposits in the Sahel region. Northern Mali and Niger were known to be rich in various mineral resources and French companies such as Areva had enjoyed a monopoly on uranium exploration in the region. The demand for uranium was steadily increasing in the international market as a result of the construction of new nuclear plants in India, China, Russia, and the United States. A report from the International Atomic Agency revealed that about 450 new nuclear reactors would be constructed by 2030. Paris had already expressed its concern that the Tuareg uprising could hinder Areva's ability to export uranium.[277] France became particularly worried after the kidnapping of French workers in one of the new uranium operational zones on the eve of the war. Therefore, Paris's concerns about the Tuareg war need to be seen also in this context - the safety of its investments in the Sahel; the competition in the uranium industry, likely to affect projects that French firms were involved in; French company, Areva's, nuclear power plant for the United Arab Emirates, touted as 'the deal of the century'; and the new negotiations between China and Niger over uranium exploration.[278].

Russia also appeared to have shown an interest in Mali's mineral resources. Statements in certain newspapers quoted the special representative of the Russian president as saying: "Given its rich reserves and resources, Mali is considered a likely field for future wars." And Russia was reported to have responded to the Malian crisis with security and military support, which it said was in its interest to see that order was restored in northern Mali. Russia possibly saw the conflict in Mali as an opportunity to become engaged in the country. Since the end of the cold war, Russia's relations with African states have usually been defined by geo-economic concerns[279].

Another factor affecting France's decision to intervene may have been the oil reserves in the Sahel region and the Gulf of Guinea. Since the discovery of oil in the region, drilling activities have steadily increased, especially with the rise in the price of oil on the international market. Companies from Algeria, France, Qatar, Tunisia, and Italy became seriously engaged in oil exploration in Mauritania, Mali, Niger, Chad, and Sudan. China was also reported to have indicated interest in the oil resources of the region and a Chinese firm began exploration in

Niger and Chad since 2003. In 2004, China's Sinopec obtained two licences to drill in five different zones in Mali, around the cities of Timbuktu and Gao. The French oil giant, Total, was given a licence to drill in Mauritania while Sipex, a British firm, was also drilling in Niger. France had not acquired a licence to explore oil in Mali despite its long relations with the country and it was reported that Paris had been making efforts to acquire one.

Previously a Western monopoly, China and Russia's increasing involvement in the energy sector also became a source of some concern to the West. However, even some African states have resented China's dominance of their energy sector. Chad and China became engaged in a conflict over the management of Chad's oil refinery. Many African states had initially looked up to China to play a balancing role with regard to the rôle of Western European nations in the African continent, which were viewed as purely imperialistic. However, when an armed rebellion started in Chad around 2012, China was quick to show support for the rebels against the Chadian government in order to maintain its investments in the country. China maintains three light-arms production plants in Mali, Sudan, and the DRC. Mali, in particular, was seen as a potential source of Chinese weapons, especially if the security situation was taken into consideration. So also was Sudan, where China was initially seen to have developed Sudanese channels to support the Chadian rebels against their government.

France naturally was worried about China's involvement in the oil and pipeline projects that were springing up, as well as in the discovery of new oil wells. She was also disturbed about Chinese investment in large infrastructural developments, an oil storage facility in Mauritania, for instance. The new trans-Saharan gas pipeline, which was planned to transport natural gas from Nigeria through Niger to Algeria and then to Europe, was also seen as a source of concern for Paris. Then Mali had given a Canadian the consultancy, a contract to draw up a feasibility report on its potential participation in the trans-Saharan project, and Mali had officially applied to join the project[280]. Many European companies had indicated interest in the project, including France's Total, Italy's Eni, and Spain's Gas Natural Fenosa. Russia, fearing that the pipeline may threaten its exports to Europe, was reported to have proposed a partnership on the project and as a result the Nigerian National Petroleum Company [NNPC] went into a joint venture with the Russian giant, Gazprom.

The secession of Northern Mali and interests in Africa, the 2013 white paper that outlined France's new defence strategy, focussed on Africa geo-strategically and tried to map out a way for France to adapt to the new strategic environment resulting from the so-called 'Arab Spring' and the situation in the Sahel region. The White Paper highlighted the need for France to maintain the five main strategic functions set out in 2008; strategy of protection, awareness, prevention, deterrence, and intervention. The paper observed that the operations in Mali had demonstrated the need for Paris to be prepared for short-notice interventions, as well as the need to sustain interventions over vast distances, both within the theatre and between the theatre and the main military bases. It further emphasised the need to develop the capability to carry out multidimensional operations. Operation Serval exposed the gaps in French capabilities, particularly, the lack of aircraft to transport troops and equipment such as new air-to-air refuelling systems to allow planes to fly long distances, as well as gaps in areas such as intelligence and surveillance. The paper clearly indicated the willingness of Paris to intervene in areas where its interest was most acute, namely as already mentioned the periphery of Europe, the Mediterranean Basin, Africa, and the Persian Gulf[281].

In this analysis of France's national objectives as they relate to Mali and others of its erstwhile colonies, the question may be posed: "But is not France a key member of the European Union? How did France's national objectives relate to those of the European Community?" In this respect it might be useful to examine briefly how the EU saw the conflict in Mali and in general the situation in North and West Africa.

EU-Mali relations go back to 1958 when the EU began carrying out projects in Mali that included rural development, road infrastructure, and humanitarian aid[282]. Over the years, cooperation between EU and Mali expanded to cover many areas including political dialogue, security, and trade. Generally, the EU had for a long time maintained relations with the Sahel states and become involved in the development and security of the region, which the EU considered vital to its own security. The EU viewed the Sahel region as one of the poorest in the world, facing challenges of poverty, climate change, food crisis, high population growth, fragile governance, corruption, unresolved internal tensions, risks of violent extremism and radicalisation, illicit trafficking, as well as other terrorist-linked security threats. The EU was worried about the activities of groups such as al-Qaeda in the Maghreb [AQIM] in the north of Mali whose activities were seen to be focused on Western targets. The EU viewed the activities of those groups in the north of Mali with deep concern, especially with regard to the development cooperation and the restriction of humanitarian assistance and development aid, which further made the population of the region and Mali, in particular, vulnerable.

The EU had since 2008 advocated for a comprehensive security and development approach in order to respond to the complexity of challenges facing the Sahel region and Mali, in particular. In April 2009, the EU sent fact-finding missions to Mali, Mauritania, and Niger at the political and technical levels after the security situation in the region had rapidly deteriorated, resulting in the kidnapping of several European nationals. Consequent upon the findings of these missions the Foreign Affairs Council of the European Union invited the High Representative to draw up, in close collaboration with the commission, a strategy on the Sahel and a joint communication by the commission and the High Representative's plans were presented in March, 2011.

The European Union then drew up a development policy in partnership with concerned states in the Sahel, including Mali, which was directed towards dealing with the root causes of the challenges identified in the region[283]. The policy tried to look into ways by which the EU could create grassroots conditions for economic opportunity and human development to flourish. However, it was convinced that achieving such objectives would be difficult as long as security challenges remained unchecked. It also viewed the security challenges facing the region as cross-border and closely intertwined and, as such, considered a regional integrated strategy as the only approach likely to succeed in overcoming the security challenges facing the region. The strategy encouraged EU member states and other partners to play an integrated part in the region with all the instruments at their disposal. The EU strategy proposed a framework that would see the co-ordination of its current and future engagement in the Sahel region with a common objective of security and development in the region. Some of the challenges identified by the EU included governance, development and conflict resolution, regional level political challenges and policy coordination, security, the rule of law and the fight against violent extremism. The EU concluded that if the challenges were overcome, the Sahel region would be free for investment and other economic activities and safe from terrorism and insecurity.

The EU viewed the challenges of governance in the region as partly responsible for the situation in many of the Sahel states, including Mali. Many governments in the region could not provide security and public services to their population. Lack of education and uneven distribution of resources in many of the states were seen as another challenge, which coupled with a poor level of education and unemployment led the youth population to be attracted by and get involved with transnational groups such as AQIM and Ansardine.

Again, at the regional political level there did not seem to exist a desire to take finding a solution to the security issues in the region, which were viewed as 'transnational' in nature though differing in intensity from one country to another. The divergence of perception by some of the Sahel countries, including Mali and some of the North African states like Algeria, Libya, and Morocco, and the absence of a sub-regional organisation encompassing the Sahel and the Maghreb had led to unilateral and poorly coordinated action instead of a more effective regional approach. What is more, most of the Sahel states lacked sufficient strategic capacity in terms of the security, law enforcement, and judicial sectors, which included the police, military, customs, and immigrations, to control territory, provide human security, and respond to various security threats. Factors such as poverty, social exclusion, and other economic needs, as well as radicalised Islamist ideologies, pose the threat of extremism and the recruitment of youths by groups such as AQIM in the region[284].

It was in realisation of these challenges that the EU considered the four areas highlighted above its strategic lines of action in the region. It focused on finding solution to the problems in the Sahel by improving upon governance, development, internal conflict resolution and the promotion of a common political and diplomatic vision or strategy by the relevant countries in the region to handle cross-border threats, as well as addressing development challenges. The EU further focused on the need to strengthen the capacity of security, law enforcement and the rule of law within the Sahel states to fight threats of terrorism and organised crime. In addition, the EU also considered the provision of basic social services important just as it considered the stimulation of economic activities and the provision of employment opportunities necessary in order to prevent the radicalisation of the youth population and recruitment by transnational groups such as AQIM.

## CHAPTER FOURTEEN

# Impact and Consequences of the Tuareg War

*Never think that war, no matter how necessary, nor how justified, is not a crime.*

– Ernest Hemingway, 1946.

The war in Mali and the French intervention in that conflict had deep regional and international implications. Its consequences were devastating for neighbouring states and the continent at large. Mali came to be considered a threat to international peace and security, and as a result, measures had to be taken to control the conflict and the emerging threats. The conflict was seen by France as a potential threat to peace and security in the whole of West Africa, including the Gulf of Guinea, North Africa, and the Sahel and Sahara regions, as well as Mali's immediate neighbouring states. It was feared that Mali could become another failed state like Somalia and Libya, that it could be taken over by Islamist extremist groups and that the conflict could explode into a regional and global threat to peace and security. Many years of poor governance, poverty, neglect, as well as marginalisation had turned Mali into a recruiting ground for radical extremists.

The Sahel and Sahara regions seemed to be gradually being occupied and dominated by elements whose motives ranged from criminal enterprise to secession and global jihad with linkages to al-Qaeda. It seemed as if international terrorism had successfully migrated from its 'traditional' zones of operations in South Asia, Yemen, and Somalia into the Sahel region – a phenomenon which had been facilitated by the NATO intervention in Libya which led to the overthrow of Muammar Gaddafi in 2011.[285] Now Mali and its neighbouring states were considered the new zones of instability as a result of the regionalisation effect of the Malian civil war. The influx of refugees fleeing armed rebels and Islamist extremists into neighbouring countries had threatened the national security of those states and they too suffered the effects and impact of the fallout of the crisis and the intervention in Mali by the French.

For instance, Islamist extremist groups operating in Mali posed a serious threat to Algeria's security and stability. Most of the people in these organisations had been involved in the Algerian civil war in the 1990s. It was as a result of this experience that Algeria was initially opposed to a military action in Mali. Algeria may have feared escalation. She may have feared that heavily armed rebels and Islamist militants would retreat into Algeria itself across its long border with Mali. For that reason, Algeria closed its borders to avoid such unwelcome consequences of the conflict in Mali. Many rebels fleeing Timbuktu and Gao as a result of French air strikes retreated into the mountain ranges near Kidal, very close to the Algerian border. The rebels attacked the Amenas gas plant in Algeria and kidnapped and killed certain foreign nationals in retaliation for the French air strikes in Mali during Operation Serval. The kidnapping of the foreign officials at the gas plant led to an intensification in the fight against terrorism by many western nations in the region, including Britain and the United States.

Niger, like Algeria, also witnessed the influx of armed Tuareg and Islamist rebels. The efforts of Niger and its involvement in ECOWAS and AFISMA activities were to help stabilise Mali and to prevent the spill-over of the crisis into its territory. Niger feared its own Tuareg community may easily be influenced to start an uprising and could use Niger as a base to regroup and launch guerrilla attacks against the French and African forces in Mali. There was a great danger that the Mali conflict would spill over into Niger as the two countries shared a common experience of Tuareg uprisings, a problem that had remained largely unsolved in both countries.

The conflict in Mali was considered by many to be a casualty of the Libyan conflict.[286] The NATO intervention in Libya and the overthrow of Gaddafi were the immediate cause of the 2012 Tuareg war in Mali. As mentioned, hundreds of heavily armed and battle-hardened Tuareg rebels who had been trained in Gaddafi's Army, returned to Mali after his assassination in 2011 and formed the MNLA with the intention of starting a war in Mali. It was therefore to be expected that the French intervention could lead to the armed groups moving back again into Libya, further destabilising an already unstable situation in that country.

Nigeria does not share a border with Mali but the country was among the states that suffered from the effects of the Malian conflict. The government of Nigeria viewed the Mali conflict as a threat to its national security. Nigeria was already fighting a war with a violent Islamist terror organisation of its own, known as Boko Haram. Many intelligence reports indicated that AQIM had continued to provide insurgency training to Boko Haram members just as another AQIM affiliate in Somalia, al-Shabaab, was also providing similar training to the group. Nigeria's involvement and commitment in the ECOWAS effort to stabilise Mali was seen as aimed primarily to prevent the collapse of Mali and the emergence of a terrorist state that would threaten stability within Nigeria. This fear was confirmed when a Nigerian-based terrorist group known as Ansaru kidnapped a French family in northern Cameroon along the Nigerian border - and again on 10th March, 2013, when the same group announced the killing of seven foreign hostages it had kidnapped in the north-eastern state of Bauchi in Nigeria[287].

The intervention by Paris in Mali heightened fears of reprisal attacks on French citizens or interests both within and outside France. Since the intervention by France, attacks against French citizens in the Sahel and other parts of Africa escalated.[288] About fifteen hostages were taken by Islamist extremists in the Sahel region and claimed to be retaliatory attacks for the French intervention in the Mali conflict. The intervention put at risk the lives of up to 30,000 French citizens residing within the West African sub-region.

The intervention was also seen to have further raised concerns of possible attacks within France, from among its about five million Muslims, mostly from north and West Africa, as well as others entering France to commit terrorist attacks. It was thought that there was a possibility that they could be motivated by the French intervention to carry out attacks within France. These concerns were based on the fact that France had in the 1990's battled terrorism within its territory. Not long ago three off-duty French soldiers, three Jewish children and a rabbi were attacked by a French citizen who was trained in Pakistan and was said to have links with the al-Qaeda in the Maghreb. Then there was the bombing of the offices of *Charlie Hebdo*, a satirical newspaper that published cartoons of the Prophet Mohammed, and a grenade attack on a Jewish supermarket in Paris in September 2012. A bomb-making outfit was discovered by the police in Paris and it was alleged that an Islamist terror cell was behind it and planning a bomb attack in Paris. A French citizen was arrested while trying to join a rebel Islamic group in Mali. Thus the French intervention raised the level of threat of domestic terror in France itself.[289] Others feared that France's involvement could eventually involve the country in a long drawn out insurgency war with terrorist and Islamist extremist groups, similar to that in Afghanistan, with many French casualties. The intervention was seen as capable of creating a very volatile situation for France in the Sahel region that would make it difficult for the French troops to make a quick exit from the region. It was also feared that the killing of French citizens and soldiers could provoke a negative reaction domestically and result in the withdrawal of French troops from Mali before they had completed their mission.

The Mali conflict attracted foreign fighters and other Islamist extremists and jihadist groups that were committed to the spread of global jihad. The emergence of certain groups such as AQIM, Boko Haram, al-Shabaab, and Ansaru, which were interlinked with one another and based in different countries, posed a serious international security threat, adding another dimension to the conflict. Mali served as a new centre for the recruitment of terrorist and Islamic jihadists. Foreign Islamic militants, including Europeans, fighting in Syria alongside the Syrian rebels against the Assad regime, were reported to have gone to Mali to fight on the side of the rebels. A French citizen was captured fighting on the rebel's side in March 2013.

The French military action appeared to have paved the way for the expansion of U.S. drone warfare in the Sahel region. It demonstrated that U.S. drones could henceforth be used in Central and East Africa against any army that was inimical to U.S, interests.[290] The conflict might have dragged on with the U.S. making increasing use of drones against terrorists and militants and in the process raising the numbers of civilian casualties as is the case in Afghanistan, Somalia, Pakistan, and Yemen.

There was too the fear that the situation in Mali could turn out to be similar to what happened in the war with the Taliban in Afghanistan. It was thought that superior French fire power could force the rebels to simply disappear into the civilian population or tactically withdraw into the mountains and inaccessible desert areas where they could regroup and launch renewed attacks on the French forces. The rebels did adopt new tactics in the form of suicide attacks in the areas around Gao while firing rockets at the French troops. Such scenes were reminiscent of the al-Qaeda-Taliban insurgency attacks on the US-led coalition forces in Afghanistan. With Mali already considered a dysfunctional state, with ill equipped and ineffective armed forces, this presented a danger that the Malian situation may turn into that of an Afghanistan in the Sahel region, with devastating consequences for the French and Western nationals and their strategic interests in the region. Most of the rebel fighters were seen to be battle-hardened, having fought in insurgency wars in Afghanistan, Pakistan, Yemen, Syria, and Somalia as well as for Gaddafi during the NATO-assisted insurrection. They had brought their experience and expertise to Mali with what could have been dire consequences for the French forces in Mali[291].

# PART FOUR

## Post-War Mali

*"I know where the desert is located I urge you my soul to stay alive Love is a field if it is not watered It dies It is a religion When you stop to pray You perish"*. Songs of Love and Exile.

– Hamma Ag Awaissoune
[Songs of Love and Exile]

## CHAPTER FIFTEEN

# Mass Exodus and Food Insecurity

*No one leaves home unless home is the mouth of a shark.*

— Warsan Shire

The military intervention in Mali was generally described as successful and much territory was recovered from the rebels, who had now been driven into the mountains in the North. However, this had been achieved at the cost of large-scale displacement of the population, which varied according to ethnic origin. Black people who derived from the South fled to the South, which was dominated by the Bambara whereas the the Tuaregs and other Arab-speaking peoples fled the country to other neighbouring states in the Sahel and West Africa where there were significant Tuareg or Arab populations.

The post-war period in Mali was also characterised by food insecurity, something which affected the entire Sahel region after 2011 as a result of the drought that affected the region. This led to a drastic rise in the price of food items across the region, including in Mali.

Agricultural production experienced a massive decline in the entire region. A factor contributing to the situation was the failure of the governments in the Sahel region to foresee, anticipate or plan for the likely occurrence of such disaster. Lack of macroeconomic resilience to natural disaster was the underlying factor behind the food crisis in the Sahel even before the outbreak of the Mali war in 2012, which only further worsened the situation[292].

Another significant factor to consider in assessing the food insecurity issue in the region had to do with the never-ending succession of crises in the region. The impact of the crisis and instability in the region in 2005, 2008, 2010[293] and 2012 was disastrous and allowed the population no opportunity to build any livelihood[294]. The occurrence of crisis and conflicts over and over again weakened the population, as well as their capacity to cope with the situation. As such, the population continued to be impoverished as it lurched from one crisis to another. This was despite the fact the 2012 harvest was a good one owing to the high rainfall recorded between July and October, that resulted in floods in certain parts of West Africa and the Sahel region, affecting about 1.5 million people throughout the region. Despite the floods, however, gross cereal production in 2012/2013 increased by up to 37% as compared with 2011/2012, reaching an output of 22.5 tonnes[295].

Niger, Burkina Faso, and Chad recorded cereal production surpluses as did Senegal and Mauritania. Yet public and private stocks had shrunk owing mainly to the depletion in the previous seasons and for other reasons, including lack of funds, rebuilding the stocks proved to be a difficult task. As such, poor families who had no access to agriculture were forced to rely on the markets as the only source of supply for their daily needs. Thus as grain and other produce was more plentiful in most of the markets across the region after harvests in 2012/2013 period, prices of foodstuff decreased, particularly in Burkina Faso, Mali, and Niger. However indications were that the price of food might not fall significantly in 2013 due mainly to the decline in production witnessed in 2012 despite the good crop production recorded in the 2012/2013 season[296].

About 4.6 million people were reported to have been affected by food insecurity and malnutrition in 2012[297]. It was further reported that about 1.3 million people were affected in 2013 of which about 585,000 were located in the north of Mali. Apart from food insecurity, the Malian economy had shrunk by 15%. Most of businesses in the North had had to close down. The closure of the Algerian border, which was a major business link, contributed to this. The closure of such businesses led to a shortage in the supply of basic commodities such as milk, flour, sugar, and oil. The prices of those products skyrocketed as a result of the shortage in their supply.

The 2012 Tuareg war had also led to the emergence of a humanitarian crisis due to the collapse of social services in almost all the cities, with the exception of Bamako. It was perhaps only in Bamako that certain social services could be obtained, but even then, the influx of people into the city from other places overwhelmed them and rendered them inefficient and insufficient for the now greatly increased population. Many civil servants and health workers had been dislocated and those of Tuareg or Arab origin had fled to the North following the outbreak of the conflict and the intervention by France. The crisis disrupted the education of about 700,000 pupils across the country[298]. Health services collapsed completely and most health care centres were deserted, their facilities looted. Thus the collapse in social services came to contribute significantly to the migration and displacement of the Malian population and the restoration of basic social services continued to be a determinant of the possibility of return to Mali by the displaced population.

The issue of security and protection was another significant cause of the migration. During the conflict – including the French intervention – countless human rights violations were recorded. Acts of violence, against women and young girls, including rape, by armed groups were reported in many places, particularly in the north. Women were subjected to gender-based violence, forced into prostitution along with children and many were abducted or forcefully recruited into the rebel forces, among those supporting the Malian government. After the intervention, ethnic killings were also reported to have occurred in revenge against those seen to be of the same ethnic group as the enemy, whether rebel or government.

Generally speaking, migrations in post-conflict Mali were seen to have taken three major ways: large-scale internal displacement; cross-border flows into neighbouring states; the disruption of mobility patterns, largely affecting cross-border traders, pastoralists and nomads.

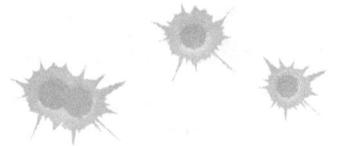

## CHAPTER SIXTEEN

# *Migrations*

*It is time that separates the beloved from those they love And when you think of them disturbing painful thoughts are all that come along.* Cler Achel [ I Spent the Day] Song.

– Tinarewen Musical Band
[Rebel Songs, The New Yorker]

I n January 2012, the start of the war in the North of Mali and the subsequent military coup caused a migration crisis of significant scope and size, both within and outside of Mali. By the time of the international military intervention in January 2013, 376,828 people had been displaced, including 228,920 (61%) internally displaced and 147,908 (39%) displaced into neighbouring countries. Given that the North of Mali is sparsely populated, this massive outflow represents a significant number of the overall population in the North (23%), estimated at 1.3 million people (or 8.6% of the total population of Mali) that had to flee the conflict zones to escape violence. Most of the IDPs who fled the North to the South lived with host families or in rented housing in Bamako (22%), Mopti

(18%), Segou (13%), Koulikoro (7%), Sikasso (6%) and Kayes (1%), which explains the absence of IDP camps.

Another characteristic of the displacement over this period has been its degree of fluidity: due to the necessity to check on family members, livestock and property in the original places of settlement, 19% of the displaced engaged in back and forth movements from their place of displacement to their area of origin. The Commission on Population Movement (Commission sur les Mouvements de Population, CMP) has reported that of the overall total of IDPs, 11% have been displaced within the Gao district, 13% within the Kidal district and 10% within the district of Timbuktu, including some people reportedly stranded at the closed border to Algeria[299]. During this period, IDPs were composed of individuals and groups with a variety of ethnic and political backgrounds. For example, civil servants (along with family members) originating from the South but working and residing in the North, were displaced to the South according to the CMP, where reportedly they continued to work following their integration into the local civil service. In general, the situation of IDPs has been marked by security and humanitarian constraints, including a lack of access to and limited availability of basic services and supplies, such as food, clean water and health care. About 26 special vulnerabilities among the displaced populations have also been identified, including more than 1,263 children separated from their parents across Mali according to UNICEF[300].

Thus, the majority were people who moved from the northern cities of Mali – the Gao and Kidal regions, as well as the district of Timbuktu - to the South. About 26% of them moved to Bamako, 185 people moved to Mopti, 16% to Segou, and 9% to Koulikoro. Another 45 were located in Sikasso and 2% in Kayes. Most of the internally displaced persons migrated to urban areas and dispersed. Had they gathered in one location it would have been easier for government or the many international donor agencies to provide them with humanitarian support or protection. About 65% of the displaced persons, according to a report of the International Migration Organization, rented houses, 27% lived with host families, and about 8% indicated 'others' living in community centres. Despite the ability of many people to move out of the northern cities, others were unable to move due to security concerns, lack of transportation, not being financially capable of migrating or vulnerable [old and disabled people] and unable to travel. The composition and vulnerability of the internally displaced persons is analysed below. [301]

According to the reports of the International Migration Organization, there were about 43,084 internally displaced households, which consisted of about 301,084 people. The census conducted in Mali in 2009 showed that the average size of a household consisted of five people. But in April, 2013, the number of registered households stood at about seven people per household, higher than the standard established by the 2009 census[302]. This was seen to indicate that most families now included extended family members or even non-family members living with them due mainly to the conflict, as well as to the intervention that followed. Figures indicate that about 51% of the internally displaced persons were women and 49% were men and that the majority of the displaced persons, 53%, appeared to be children under the ages of 18. Adults between the ages of 18 and 64 constituted 44% and about 2% consisted of people that were above 64 years of age. Only 21% of the total internally displaced persons were reported to have received humanitarian assistance, and even then it varied from region to region and the nature of the assistance received.

Regarding the vulnerable population, a total of 26,559 vulnerable persons were identified and they constituted about 13% of the total number of internally displaced persons in Mali. These people formed part of the 47.5% of the total households registered. 43% were separated and unaccompanied children with 11,295 separated children and 675 unaccompanied children[303]. Lactating and pregnant women made up 245 of the vulnerable displaced persons list while persons with chronic illnesses constituted 20%. The physically disabled people came to constitute a certain percentage, and unaccompanied old people were seen to have constituted only 1% of the total number of the vulnerable displaced persons.

About 38% of the households were reported to have no income at all at their places of displacement while 29% were said to be on regular income. About 50% of the displaced persons were identified as requiring food while 39% were seen to be in dire need of cash assistance. Most of the displaced persons in Bamako appeared to have been part of those that needed cash assistance, probably as a result of the metropolitan nature of the city, as the capital of Mali, whereas people in Segou and Mopti mainly required food assistance.

There were indications that return by the internally displaced persons to their original places of residence was possible at the end of 2013. About 93% of the displaced persons, according to a survey carried out by the IOM in February, 2013, indicated their willingness to return to their original residences. Out of this percentage, 62% said their decision to return would be determined by the security situation in Mali. By April 2013, 95% of the displaced persons still maintained that their return would be determined by the security situation. The lack of social services was identified as the immediate factor motivating the return of many of the displaced persons, especially as observed in Bamako and Mopti. Many decided in the absence of such social amenities to return to the North, which had been their place of origin before the outbreak of the conflict. Other returnees were encouraged to return as a result of the improvement in the security situation. Those that were seen not to have any willingness to return to the North were largely the victims of violence, including rape, amputations and torture. Some among the returnees to the north returned temporarily to see the situation as well as to repair their houses due to the approaching new season. Many houses were destroyed during the conflict. While some houses were partly damaged, others had to be completely re-built.

With regard to those who fled the country, the reports of the International Organization Migration indicated that as of the end of May, 2013, about 185,000 Malians had fled to neighbouring states. About 176,000 of this number had been registered as refugees with the United Nations High Commissioner for Refugees [UNHCR]. Most of the refugees were located in Niger, Mauritania, and Burkina Faso. A small number, about 26 - were located in Guinea and about 20 were in Togo. Algeria hosted in the region of 1,500 Malian refugees while 4,000 were reported to have fled to Cote d'Ivoire. The number of people migrating out of Mali continued to increase until the French military intervention. Even thereafter it continued but at a much lower rate.

The composition of the migrants indicated that the majority from among them were pastoralists, largely of the Tuareg and Maure groups. The groups preferred to migrate outside the country than move southwards within Mali owing mainly to the similarity in the pattern of livelihood and environmental conditions that pertained in those countries. Another advantage was their proximity and accessibility. Most of these refugees consisted of women and children since the men opted to stay behind in Mali to look after their family properties. The needs of these refugees were viewed with serious concern, according to reports of the UNHCR. About 80% of the children were reported to have lacked access to primary school education in the areas they migrated to. The schools around the various refugee camps could not cater for all the children, and other schools were located too far away for the children to attend. It was also observed that the influx of refugees had a significant impact on the local host communities. Especially given the food insecurity affecting many of the neighbouring states, the influx of refugees and sometimes their livestock worsened the problems their own communities were facing.

Mauritania was particularly hard hit. Reports of the UNHCR indicated that by May 2013, there were about 74,108 Malian refugees living within the country and an estimated 1,500 people crossed into Mauritanian every week from Mali. It was reported that the influx of refugees from Mali had particularly affected the southern part of the country. The presence of refugees with their livestock was seen to have overstretched both the economy and the physical environment of the host communities south of the country. The refugees were in dire need of shelter, water, sanitation, and health, as the risk of diseases remained high, especially since latrines were few and inadequate for the number of refugees present in their various locations[304].

Niger saw 50,515 refugees fleeing into the country while about 5,000 were located in the border cities of Niger and Mali. Tillaberi and Tahoau regions remained the areas most highly populated by Malian refugees. The refugees were said to be facing problems that ranged from food insecurity to malnutrition, shortage of water, sanitation, as well as health facilities, in the various places they were living. After the French intervention, about 10,000 were reported to have crossed over to Niger. Apart from this figure, about 3,991 Nigeriens that had been living in Mali also returned to Niger. Concerns in Niger were mainly associated with the unavailability of food. It was not readily available and supply from Mali was also not possible due to the security situation. At some point, however, the nutrition situation did improve in various refugee camps across Niger. Returns from Niger to Mali appeared highly unlikely, according reports by the International Organization Migration.

Burkina Faso was also affected by the Malian migration with reports indicating that about 40,975 Malian refugees were located in Burkina Faso by the end of April, 2013. The situation of the refugees, just as in Mauritania and Niger, remained the same in Burkina Faso. More financial and moral support was required to meet the growing needs of the refugees in various camps across the country. The population in the country also appeared to have been rendered vulnerable due to food insecurity as a result of the influx of refugees.

Guinea and Togo were two countries which recorded minimal influx of refugees. It was reported that only 26 refugees fled to Guinea while about 20 went to Togo. As such, there were no reports of a humanitarian crisis in these two countries arising from the influx of refugees as recorded in other states.

Algeria had, since the outbreak of the conflict in Mali, closed its borders with Mali. But despite this, many people still found their way into the country. UNHCR reports in April, 2013, indicated that about 1,500 Malian refugees were living in Algeria, mostly located in the cities of Timayawen and Tinzawaten, where they were said to have rented houses. No refugees were reported to have fled to Senegal and only very few to Côte d'Ivoire. The International Organization Migration, in collaboration with UNHCR, had made a contingency plan in anticipation of a massive influx of people to Cote d'Ivoire based on an assessment made by the two organisations in November, 2012, when about 4,000 Malians crossed the Algerian border. After crossing over, they stayed with family members and not as refugees as they did not seek asylum or refugee status throughout their stay. Most of them in fact might have returned to Mali after the security situation improved.

Reports indicate that there was no migration of refugees from Mali beyond the Sahel and West African regions. There is no record of Malians seeking asylum either in Europe or in the United States until the outbreak of the conflict in 2012. What is known is that Switzerland and France had removed Mali from the list of safe countries at the end of 2012, a situation that made it permissible for

Malians to apply for asylum in Europe. In the year 2012, about 2,531 Malians were said to have applied for asylum in Europe[305].

Many of the refugees outside Mali did not indicate willingness to return despite expressing their intention to return ultimately. Many believed that the security situation was still not favourable for their return. The main concern is related to protection as most of the refugees outside Mali are composed of the Tuareg and the Maure people, who were largely associated with the rebellion. After the military intervention by France, there were many reports of violations of human rights, as well as ethnic conflicts and revenge attacks, particularly against the Tuareg and other related people in the North who are sometimes wrongly associated with the rebels. This factor was responsible for most displacements, as well as for making it difficult for these people to return to Mali.

## CHAPTER SEVENTEEN

# Rights Abuses and The Rule of Law

*Universal human right is the most precious jewel of humanity. Most of it is buried in the mud, we simply have to uncover it.*

— Amit Ray.

It was almost five months after the French intervention in the Mali war before peace gradually came to be restored in the northern part of the country. As soon as peace and order were restored in the North, reports of issues related to human rights abuses or violations during the conflict, as well as during the stabilisation period in the post-conflict period, emerged. These reports appeared to indicate that the cited abuses and violations were carried out by both sides. The rebel's side were found guilty of these abuses just as the Malian army and its security forces were implicated and indicted in the reports. As a matter of fact, human rights violations were one of the main factors responsible for the migration of thousands of people from the north to within and outside Mali during and after the war. There were various allegations of human rights abuses that ranged from extrajudicial executions to enforced disappearances, torture, and other inhuman or degrading treatments, including rape[306]. Such violations or abuses constitute war crimes in humanitarian intervention law and as such are viewed with serious concern. As a result of the seriousness of these allegations, Amnesty International carried out a four-week mission into Mali to investigate and verify the said allegations. After the mission, the organisation released its findings, which discussed the nature of such abuses, the victims of the abuses, as well as the perpetrators of these inhuman acts.

According to the reports, there were more than twenty cases of enforced disappearances, as well as extrajudicial executions carried out by the Malian army in the north of Mali after the French intervention. These executions, according to reports, were carried out openly. They further indicated that about eleven people in the city of Timbuktu, which included Arab traders, were arrested by the Malian soldiers and extrajudicially executed. Some, according to the reports, may have been subjected to enforced disappearances[307]. The bodies of some of the many victims were found a few days after their arrests. Many of these bodies were discovered buried around the city's slaughterhouse a few days after their arrests by the Malian soldiers in Timbuktu[308].

In Kidal, it was reported that the Malian army launched an attack on a large scale that was said to have resulted in the death of many civilians that were suspected to be related to or supporters of the armed rebels. Testimonies collected in Gao Region by Amnesty International showed that the Malian soldiers targeted Tuaregs. Akiline ag Mossa, Aljounagh ag Bilal, Ghissa ag Algateck ag Mohammedu and Omar ag Algatheck were among those reported to have been arrested by the Malian soldiers in the house of a local family member only for their bodies to be found a few days later. A school teacher, Ibrahim Ahoudou, was also reported to have been shot from behind at a checkpoint after having revealed his identity and permitted to go.

Mohammed Hamedou ag Mohammed, Assaleh, and another Tuareg were also among those arrested by the soldiers five kilometres away to Gossi, were stripped naked, and forced to lie on the ground until another soldier intervened to secure their release. A few hours later, the same people were re-arrested at the Gossi market by about seven soldiers. Their bodies were later discovered in the bush about three kilometres from Gao and were buried by local inhabitants of the area. In the city of Niono, 350 kilometres north-east of Bamako, the Malian soldiers were reported to have abducted a man held by the military police. His body was only found three months later. Ousmane Yatassaye, a 40-year-old merchant, was arrested, also in January 2013, he was suspected of having some communications with Mauritania. He was taken by the Malian army and when Amnesty International enquired as to his whereabouts during its mission, it was informed that he had been handed over to the state prosecutor. However, three months later, his body was discovered in a mango orchard in Niono not far from the military camp.

Many testimonies collected by Amnesty International showed that the Malian army and security forces had been responsible for torture and other inhuman, degrading treatment after arresting individuals suspected of having links with the rebels[309]. About eighty detainees and children were interviewed by Amnesty International, and physical observation of injuries sustained confirmed the testimonies of the people interviewed[310]. Generally they claimed in their testimonies to have been tortured and maltreated by the soldiers and security forces after their arrests. In March, 2013, three Tuaregs were arrested in Gossi, according to Amnesty International reports, and were reported to have been beaten with cables and rifle butts and released without trial in April. Also a raid was reported to have been carried out by the Malian army in Kadji, in collaboration with the French forces. Following the raid, the Malian forces were reported to have looted certain houses under the pretence of searching for weapons and members of armed groups and in the process arrested about seventy people and detained them without trial. It was confirmed by Amnesty International that the army tortured and maltreated many people during the raid. There were reports of about fifty people who were beaten or tortured and were forced to confess being members of MUJWA[311].

Amnesty International further visited more than 80 male detainees, including children that were arrested in the North and accused of having links with the rebel groups. They were actually part of about 200 detainees in different locations across the country and in Bamako and consisted of different nationals, including Algerians, Nigeriens, Tunisians, and peoples of the Western Sahara. They appeared to have been held under the counterterrorism law that was adopted in July 2008 under the Malian penal code. Many of the detainees, including children, disclosed to Amnesty International that they had been subjected to torture and other inhuman treatment during their arrests and transfer to Bamako. Many of them showed scars and marks on their backs and chests to confirm their testimonies to the Amnesty International delegates that visited Mali.

Five of those arrested and detained from the north of Mali were reported to have died in detention. Before their deaths, most of them had complained to their fellow inmates of being beaten up before being transferred to Bamako. Most of these people, it is claimed, were denied access to medical treatment. These five people included Akassane Ag Hamina, who was arrested in Timbuktu on 4th April and died on 11th April in Bamako prison. Al Hassane Mahammedu, who hailed from Kadji, was arrested in Gao and moved to the Bamako prison on 4th April also and was reported dead on 11th April, 2013, in Bamako. Fellow inmates reported that soldiers trampled on him after he was arrested and he fell unconscious one week after his arrival to Bamako. Inha ag El Mahdi was arrested at Lere and he was reported to have arrived in Bamako prison on 4 April and died on 11th April, just as the three people previously mentioned. Another inmate of Moroccan origin, Dakane, who arrived Bamako prison on 4 April was reported dead on 12th April, 2013, while Houceiyn Traoré was also said to have arrived the Bamako prison on 4th April and died on 14th April.

The organisation made some effort to look into the condition of prisoners in the various prisons they were held. The results of the observation by the group indicated that the prisoners actually lived in very poor conditions. It was reported in the section where the five prisoners died, there were thirty-four and twenty-five people in only two cells, respectively, which were 5 x 5 metres in size. In the other sections, it was observed that there were about eight people in a single cell, which was 3.6 x 2 metres in size and not properly ventilated. The prisoners revealed to the group that they were locked up for 24 hours and not allowed to walk within the prison yard until after the death of the five prisoners[312]. There were also reports of prisoners being denied access to medical care and prisoners that sustained injuries during torture after their arrests. Some found parts of their bodies, their hands, for example, deformed due to lack of medical care.

It was also reported that children were among the detained persons. Under Malian law, it is forbidden to detain children in the same place with adults, as confirmed to Amnesty International by the Malian justice minister during their visit. The minister said he had ordered that the children be moved to a specific facilities centre.

The rebel groups were also accused of perpetrating acts that were considered as constituting human rights violations or abuses of different nature. According to information gathered by Amnesty International, civilians, including Tuaregs, were brutally killed by members of MUJWA due to the fact that they showed support for the French military intervention in the conflict. Many of those killed by the rebel groups disappeared after their abduction from their houses by the rebels, only for their dead bodies to be found inflicted with wounds and cigarette burns due to torture.

The rebel groups were further accused of forcing children to join their ranks and fight on their side. Information gathered revealed that children between the ages of 12 and 17 were given weapons, and some were charged with the control of checkpoints while others cooked or ran errands for the various rebel groups. Sometimes these children, according to reports, were sent to the frontline to fight. The children were reported to have been arrested by the Malian army after the capture of certain cities by the French forces, which forced the rebels to retreat. An estimated forty children between the ages of 12 and 17 were said to have volunteered for MUJWA in the hope of getting paid and underwent military training. The rebels openly enlisted children in villages while promising their families money but, in most cases, they were paid nothing.

Many acts of sexual violence were also reported to have been committed by the rebel groups during the uprising. According to Amnesty International reports, there were eighty-three cases of rape recorded against women and girls in Gao and Menaka after the occupation of the north by the MNLA. Again, between January and February 2013, eleven new cases of rape were documented in Gao; six were between the ages 6 and 13. In the Mopti Region, rape came to be considered very common. The Mopti hospital was reported to have treated about ten cases committed in Menaka in May alone, another two cases in Gao, and one in Timbuktu. Most of the cases reported were gang rapes by the MNLA, MUJWA, or AQIM members. The armed groups forbade their female victims to migrate south. They were only to move out to Algeria. But after the success of the French and the Malian forces, these victims had access to medical care and could move freely within the country to any region[313].

Generally, the Malian authorities responded to the allegations against them by admitting to Amnesty International that the violations of human rights and other inhuman acts really took place. The authorities also assured Amnesty International that investigations were still being carried out and those found guilty would certainly be brought to book[314]. However, the Malian defence minister maintained that the abuses reported to have been carried out by the Malian army were actually committed by elements that had deserted from the army but still wore their uniforms. The Malian government also confirmed to Amnesty International that a section of the Malian population was bent on taking revenge on people suspected to have links or supported the rebel groups. The Malian government further denied the killings at Gossi, attributing them to the Gandakoy militia. It also said that it was investigating five members of the organisation concerning the killings and that the army bore no responsibility. With regard to the issue of human rights violation by the Malian security forces, the Malian Minister of Justice confirmed to Amnesty International that an enquiry was ongoing on the alleged killings of sixteen Muslim preachers by Malian soldiers in Diabaly on 8th and 9th September, 2012. He further said that the body of Ousmane Yatassaye had been exhumed and a judge had been appointed to handle the case. It was, however, noted that nobody from either the Malian army or its security forces had been prosecuted or arrested since the outbreak of the conflict and the violations that followed.

Amnesty International was of the opinion that the Malian government should open a prompt, impartial, and effective investigation of those reported violations of human rights and abuses and identify those responsible and prosecute such persons. It further called on the Malian authorities to take adequate steps to prevent the occurrence of future violations and abuses, including torture and other inhuman treatment and suspend all members of the Malian army or security forces that were suspected or found to have been involved in the reported cases of abuse and violations of human rights across the country. The organisation also called on the Malian authorities to improve the conditions of its prisons, where suspects were being detained, as well as to ensure that detained persons were not tortured or subjected to other inhuman treatment during the detention. It also called for all detainees to be brought before a court of law at the time of arrest and be given a fair hearing and access to an attorney and that detainees have unlimited access to health care during the detention, as well as be allowed to be visited by family members. It further advised the Malian government to ensure proper care and protection to victims of rape and make an effort to establish with the collaboration of the UN, donors, and national and international non-governmental organisations programmes of humanitarian assistance to various rape victims and other forms of abuse. It also called for the government to make efforts to provide emergency health care programmes and rehabilitation to victims of abuses. And, finally, Amnesty International advised the Malian authorities to pay special attention to the issue of child soldiers and set up a programme that would facilitate their rehabilitation into their various communities and families[315].

## CHAPTER EIGHTEEN

# Rebuilding the North

*It is called destruction before reconstruction. People will have to see the danger of war, the hopelessness of war, before things can change.*

– Elizabeth Joyce.

The establishment by the United Nations of the Multidimensional Integrated Stabilization Mission in Mali [MINUSMA], was mainly aimed at achieving the objectives of ensuring a peaceful political transition and supporting efforts aimed at rebuilding Malian society in all areas, including security, stabilising key population centres, restoring state authority, deterring threats, as well as playing an active role in preventing the return of armed elements to all parts of the country[316]. In line with this objective, MINUSMA was able to conduct elections in July 2013, which were widely acclaimed to be free and fair and without rancour. The elections saw the transfer of authority from the Malian transition administration under Traoré to the newly elected democratic president, Ibrahim Boubacar Keita. Having succeeded in ensuring a peaceful transition, the newly elected government and the MINUSMA mission in Mali were now left with the responsibility of rebuilding the Malian society as a whole. Consequently, a roadmap was adopted by the Malian government that highlighted the humanitarian needs of displaced persons, as well as the need to ensure the facilitation of the return of displaced persons once the right conditions were put in place. The main focus of the recovery plan for Mali was seen to have centred on the needs of refugees and displaced persons, as well as returns and reintegration process. In order to achieve this noble objective, the Malian government needed the support of many international non-governmental organisations and donor agencies, which were seen to have one role or two to play in rebuilding the country.

The EU had carried out many humanitarian interventionist programmes in Mali through its Humanitarian Aid and Civil Protection Office[317] [ECHO] even before the outbreak of the 2012 war as part of its security and development strategy for the Sahel region. However, after the outbreak of the 2012 war and the intervention of France, which saw the end of the violence that engulfed the country at that time and the restoration of state authority and normalcy, the armed conflict appeared to have brought about serious humanitarian crises in it, especially the north of the country, which appeared to have been hit most by the conflict. As such, there was the need to rebuild the north of the country and provide relief and aid to many of the displaced and vulnerable population in it. The needs of Mali after the 2012 conflict were enormous, and there was also the need to raise sufficient funds to rebuild the country, as well as provide relief materials and aid to the vulnerable population. Consequently, the president of the European Commission José Manuel Durao Barroso, the president of France Francois Hollande, and the president of the republic of Mali Diocounda Traoré took an initiative and held a high-level donor conference for the development of Mali after the 2012 conflict[318].

The conference was supposed to provide an opportunity for Mali to present its sustainable recovery plan and request the support of the international community in financing such plan[319]. A detailed plan for the sustainable recovery of the country was drafted and presented at the conference in Brussels to the international community on 15 May 2013 after the intervention by France. The final version of the document identified twelve main areas of priority in the recovery plan that include ensuring peace, security, and public services everywhere; responding to humanitarian emergencies and the implications of the crisis; organising credible elections; increasing governance through decentralisation; ensuring a functional judicial system; supporting a public finance reform; rebuilding the economy by strengthening the private sector and agriculture; investing in infrastructure and providing employment; addressing the challenges of education; ensuring access to quality health services; supporting cultural projects; promoting the role of women; and, lastly, integrating environmentalism into policies and strategies. These were the milestones that Mali hoped to achieve in the recovery plan over time[320].

The conference, which came to be known as 'Together for a New Mali', was intended to provide an opportunity for Mali to present its sustainable recovery it plan and request the support of the international community in financing such plan[321]. It took place in Brussels and saw the participation of delegates from 108 countries and institutions, including about 13 heads of states and government, a large delegation of foreign ministers and senior representatives of regional and international institutions, and representatives of local authorities, civil society, the diaspora, and the private sector.

The Malian authorities informed the conference that the 2012 conflict had revealed to the Malian people and the rest of the world the weakness and fragility of the Malian state—its institutions, military, and governance—which led to corruption, lack of credibility and to the eventual loss of confidence in government by its citizens. After the conflict, the transitional authorities were faced with the task of re-establishing constitutional order and identified three immediate tasks: re-establishing the integrity of the national territory; reviewing public policies; and pursuing structural reforms with the aim of creating conditions for sustainable economic growth. The Malian authorities reiterated to the conference its aim to maintain the macroeconomic framework by trying to pursue a policy of moderating public expenditure by freezing appropriations where the returns in terms of revenue were not assured, a policy that was naturally lauded by both the World Bank and the IMF[322].

Presenting Mali's plan for sustainable recovery to the conference, the Malian authorities said drafting the document became necessary after the European Union and France had proposed to the Malian authorities that they would facilitate the organisation of the conference. The Malian authorities then drew up a document known as 'A Road Map for Political Transition, Strategic Growth and Poverty Reduction 2012–2017'. The strategic document was meant to create the foundation for a resilient economy and was based upon certain structural elements. First, among such elements were infrastructure investment programmes, such as roads and energy development, which were considered necessary for any meaningful economic development. The second element was improvement in the quality of administrative services in order to strengthen trust between the government and the citizens. The third element was the issue of food security in a country where about 70% of the population lives in rural areas. Improvements in agricultural methods and techniques and the establishment of functional markets as well as processing channels were considered necessary. The fourth and last element highlighted by the Malian authorities remained the provision of basic social services or amenities to the citizens, such as education, health care, and access to potable drinking water throughout the country.

Apart from those elements, which were considered the bases of any meaningful recovery plan in Mali, the Malian authorities presented to the conference twelve priority areas that needed immediate support in order to rebuild the Malian society[323]. The total amount of money required to finance the plan stood at 2.85 billion Malian francs. The twelve priority areas identified and mentioned in the introductory part of the chapter include the following:

- Ensure peace, security, and public service everywhere
- Respond to humanitarian emergencies
- Organise credible elections
- Increase governance through decentralisation and public service reform
- Ensure a well-functioning judicial system and the fight against corruption
- Strengthen the public finance system
- Rebuild the economy by strengthening the private sector and agriculture and investing in infrastructural development and youth employment
- Address the challenge of education
- Ensure access to quality health care services for all
- Support cultural projects for peaceful coexistence
- Promote the role of women
- Integrate environmentalism into policies and strategies

At the end of the conference, the donors, based on the twelve priority areas contained in Mali's recovery plan, agreed to donate the sum of €3.25 billion to Mali within a two-year time frame. However, the donors' support for the recovery plan and their budgetary commitments would depend on the Malian authority's determination to pursue vigorously a public finance reform that would ensure transparency. The EU made known its intention to continue to collaborate with the republic of Mali in the area of political dialogues and security. The collaboration, according to the EU, would be based on humanitarian response that was also based on the needs of the most vulnerable population in line with humanitarian principles. The conference called for political support for the peace talks and reconciliation in the country, as well as the modernisation of the state. In terms of co-operation, action was to be based on direct response to the most pressing needs of stabilisation and reconstruction in the post-conflict areas while maintaining a perspective of recovery and long-term development and taking into account regional dynamics affecting Mali with regard to security.

The EU had already expended almost a billion Euros on various projects in different areas in Mali between 2008 and 2014, the highest being in the macroeconomics and public sector reforms, which cost about €305 million. This was closely followed by the construction of a road network across Mali, which cost about €207 million. The EU had expended about €140 million on humanitarian activities in Mali just as it had spent millions in other areas that include elections, human rights, decentralisation, justice and security, environment, food security, health and social services and so on. As can be seen, the total cost of various projects carried out by the EU in many different areas within the period mentioned above amounted to about €993 million, very close to a billion. The EU also planned to spend another €615 million between the years 2014 and 2020[324].

The conflict appeared to have only affected the north, and as such, all activities were seen to have been concentrated in the region. The three main regions—Gao, Timbuktu, and Kidal—were prioritised by the United Nations and other partner agencies in an effort to assist and rebuild the Malian state.

## Gao Region

There were several challenges identified in the Gao Region in the post-war period, and by far, the most important among these challenges remained that of basic social amenities, which had to be rebuilt. Water, electricity, and education remained the major challenges but were gradually being rebuilt, though civil servants and other technical staff remained absent and were yet to return to the region. Livestock and food also remained a challenge in a region where about 150,000 of the population is pastoral. Displaced persons had started returning to the region and were making effort to restore their livelihoods; but they appeared to be under pressure due to lack of pasture for their livestock, which was seen as mainly due to drought.

MINUSMA deployed civilians and uniformed personnel to Gao City while the military personnel were based at Menaka and Asongo. MINUSMA also expanded its mission from mere support to that of security and other areas that included civil affairs, political affairs, human rights, the rule of law and electoral assistance. MINUSMA conducted outreach missions to other circles [subdivisions]. Again the United Nations police[325] established a co-location programme to mentor and support the Malian police. It was reported that about 600 UN police were scattered across the north of Mali and that out of this number about 11 individual police officers and 210 police units were put in place. The police units carried out joint patrols day and night in conjunction with the national police, gendarmerie, and the Garde Nationale[326].

Generally, the UN and its partners responded in a robust manner to the various challenges facing Mali in the post-conflict period and in rebuilding the north. The Office of the Co-ordination of Human Affairs [OCHA], as an organisation, was stationed in Gao and provided coordination support to all humanitarian partners on the ground, including military coordination. About 182 civilian and military personnel were trained by the UN in civil-military co-ordination in March 2013. The areas to secure for humanitarian actors, as well as the identification of all markets in these areas, were mapped out and shared with military actors in the region. The UN and its partners worked to promote human rights, fight against gender-based violence and promote peace and reconciliation. Some of the immediate problems were food insecurity and human rights issues as well as social amenities. The World Food Programme [WFP] responded to the issue of food insecurity appropriately, assisting close to 230,000 people, including internally displaced persons and returnees, through free food distribution for 87,260 beneficiaries. The organisation also made an effort to prevent acute malnutrition and treat victims of malnutrition in the region.

On March 2013, MINUSMA conducted three fact-finding and protection field missions to the Gao Region to document human rights violations and make recommendations to improve the situation. It also visited detention facilities about twenty times to assess the legal status of detainees and their conditions. In this regard MINUSMA's justice and corrections section was seen to be supporting the process of redeploying judicial and prison authorities to Gao Region. As a result, the tribunal and the prison in Gao Region was opened in February 2014. In partnership with the UNDP, the courthouse, which was partially restored by the French Serval forces in early 2014[327], underwent reconstruction just as efforts were being made to establish the remaining Justice of the Peace tribunals and prisons in the region and ensure access to justice. About ten monitoring and early warning committees were established by the UN and its partners to alert the authorities about sexual violence, forced marriages, and rape. Meanwhile, the MINUSMA child protection unit also continued to monitor violations against children and trained UN peacekeepers on child protection. It also conducted training sessions for the seventy-two Chinese and sixty-two Nigerien troops that were stationed in

Gao and further conducted a two-day workshop on monitoring and reporting mechanisms, which was organised by UNICEF[328].

The UN and its partners also focused attention on the social sector and gave attention to education and health care services in the Gao Region. Several communities, according to reports, had been unable to reopen schools due to insecurity. But as a result of an initiative led by the Malian government with the support of UNICEF and other partners, about 91,227 students returned to school in Gao compared to 100,307 in the pre-crisis period. About 2,023 teachers in the Gao Region reported to various schools out of 2,691 in the pre-crisis period and about 250 teachers underwent training in psychological support and about 350 in peace education with the support of UNICEF. In the area of health, the World Health Organization helped to strengthen disease surveillance and response in the Gao Region. And about 13,000 children were said to have been vaccinated against cholera in the region. In collaboration with other partners, technical support and medicines were provided to control the outbreak of measles in Asongo, which ended in March 2013.

The UN and its partners, such as the UNDP, also appeared to be strongly supporting the reconciliation process started by the Malian government. The UNDP launched a social cohesion and inter-community dialogue project in the north of Mali and deployed staff in Timbuktu, Gao, and Mopti. The UNDP further supported many local organisations that have been involved in dialogue and peace consolidation. These organisations received small grants to enable them to continue their mediation efforts and crisis management activities in Gao. The UN and its partners supported the broadcasting of messages of peace and reconciliation in many languages including French, Arabic, Amazigh, and Songhai on the local radio in Bourem. The UN Mines Action [UNMAS] also continued to mark and clear dangerous areas contaminated by the remnants of war. In March UNMAS, with the support of MINUSMA and Senegalese 'deminers', completed a battle-area clearance task within the future MINUSMA super-camp area in Gao, as well as the area that was to be allocated to the Niger battalion in Asongo. UNMAS was reported to have cleared a total of 467,617 square metres of land in Gao and identified and destroyed two unexploded ordnances. It was said that about 763 villages had been surveyed since February 2013 and this led to the destruction of about 1,100 UXOs and some 45,000 items of small arms ammunition by UNMAS. Meanwhile, starting in February, 2013, UNESCO undertook an assessment mission in Gao with the support of MINUSMA to rehabilitate certain historic cultural sites such as the tomb of Askia the Great, the Sahel Museum, as well as the Sanaye archaeological site. An inventory of intangible heritage was started through a project that came to be managed by the Ministry of Culture but funded by UNESCO, with logistical support provided by MINUSMA[329].

## Timbuktu Region

The United Nations agencies in the Timbuktu Region set up programmes and strengthened their presence and activities throughout the region. An inter-agency multi-sectoral assessment mission went to Agouni, Atilla, and Likraker on 27th March, 2014. Although the security situation was still not so good, security forces continued to be deployed throughout the region. Many civilians and uniformed personnel were deployed in the towns of the region, while MINUSMA military personnel remained stationed in the cities of Goundam and Gossi. MINUSMA's personnel on human rights and the rule of law, as well as the UN police and its civil affairs divisions, were all reported to have established their presence in Timbuktu, with outreach missions across the region. The numbers of UN police in Timbuktu included 11 individual police officers and 140 police units in the region. The Office for the Co-ordination of Humanitarian Affairs [OCHA] provided co-ordination support to humanitarian partners on the ground, including civil-military coordination. The UN and its partners continued to promote and support human rights and women, as well as to assist returnees while responding to protection needs in the Timbuktu Region. MINUSMA's human rights division was said to have conducted two fact-finding and protecting missions, including a joint protection mission with JMAC and UNHCR, to assess the overall human rights and security situation in the areas of Lere and Lerned. These also included the humanitarian needs of refugees and internally displaced persons. The division conducted nine visits to detention facilities in Timbuktu Region to assess the legal status of detainees and their detention conditions[330].

In the area of social services, the back-to-school initiative led by the Malian government, with the support of UNICEF and other partners, kicked off and targeted about 82,365 students and 2,199 teachers. It was reported that Timbuktu was ahead of the other regions in terms of progress recorded in the restoration of education in the region. About 84% of schools were said to be functioning in Timbuktu, or a total of about 483 schools out of 588[331]. Furthermore, about 350 teachers were said to have undergone training in psychological support while about 400 trained in peace education with the support of UNICEF. WFP assisted 44,561 schoolchildren in 328 schools with food through its feeding programme.

With regard to the health sector, the WHO trained health workers in Timbuktu on HIV treatment and care. It also supported health services and strengthened disease surveillance and response. Meanwhile, UNHCR supported the Timbuktu referral centre with five tonnes of drugs and four tonnes of medical devices as part of a programme to improve basic social services in areas of return, as well as to ensure equitable access to primary health care for the returned populations. UNICEF on its part ensured the vaccination of about 15,000 children across the Timbuktu Region. The International

Organization for Migration also distributed drugs in fifteen different communities to provide health care to vulnerable families[332].

In order to support the government's efforts towards recovery, economic reconstruction and social cohesion, several UN agencies, including UNDP, UNFPA, WFP, FAO, and the ILO, initiated a joint programme on youth and resilience, to create employment for the youths and other vulnerable groups, as well as to support micro enterprises. The WFP began to tackle the problem of food insecurity in the region, which showed that about 271,360 were food insecure in the region. The organisation was said to be at that time assisting about 39,820 people across the Timbuktu Region through distribution of food freely. And the FAO on its part targeted 2,500 households and distributed animal feeds and medicines and was reported to have distributed over 100,000 vaccines in the region. The programme also came to include reproductive health matters, including HIV/AIDS awareness-raising campaigns. About 600 youths were reported to have participated in the rehabilitation programme initiated by those agencies. The UNDP provided equipment and raw material for eighteen associations or 300 women for the processing of local products. The assistance was part of the implementation of the MDG-accelerated framework that would enable the rehabilitation of small businesses in the Timbuktu Region. The International Organization for Migration also provided 208 returned families with income-generating activities, including trade, herds or flocks reconstitution, livestock farming, market gardening, as well as agricultural activities in certain communities, including Soumpi, Soubourdou, and Lere. UNIDO, on its part, was seen to have initiated a programme in collaboration with the Ministry of Crafts and Tourism, a creative village project for the city of Timbuktu, whose objective was the promotion of tourism as well as to create jobs through small enterprises and trade-capacity building in the region. UNESCO also undertook activities aimed at rehabilitating and protecting cultural heritage centres in northern Mali. In this regard, a strategy for the reconstruction of mausoleums in Timbuktu was prepared and presented to the Timbuktu community in March, 2014. UNMAS continued to identify, mark, and clear dangerous areas that had been contaminated by explosives, remnants of the conflict in Timbuktu City. About ninety villages were surveyed in Timbuktu Region. UNMAS helped coordinate post-blast response, as well as investigate activities after improvised explosive devise incidents[333].

# Kidal Region

Kidal, unlike the rest of the regions, proved a little different to handle as a result of the nature of the security situation in the area. Insecurity was reported to have increased in March and April 2013 in the towns of Kidal, Aguelhok, and Tessalit. Access to roads in many areas in the region remained extremely dangerous as a result of improvised-explosive-device incidents. Many organisations such as ICRC and UNHAS were forced to fly to Kidal, with the ICRC planning to extend its coverage to Tessalit. It was reported that local authorities and security forces had difficulties returning and sometimes being deployed throughout the region.

Despite such challenges, the UN and its partners stepped up their activities in the region and organisations such as the ICRC, Médecins du Monde, Norwegian Church Aid and Solidarités Internationales continue to play a prominent role in many different fields in the area. Meanwhile, MINUSMA deployed civilian and uniformed personnel in Kidal and stationed soldiers at Aguelhok and Tessalit. All MINUSMA outfits, including its civil affairs, rule of law, electoral affairs, human rights, and public information, were present and very visible in Kidal. The number of UN police in Kidal was estimated at about 10 individual officers and 140 police units for the Kidal Region in its entirety[334].

The United Nations and its partners continued to support the redeployment of administration in Kidal and aimed to accelerate the provision of basic social services in the region. Among the major problems facing the region was food insecurity. About 25,410 people were said to be food insecure, 6,000 were in emergency condition, 18,000 were said to be in crisis, while about 45,000 were said to be under pressure in Kidal. WFP and its partner, Association pour l'Appui au Développement Global, responded to the food insecurity issue by assisting about 27,300 people with free food distribution. At the same time WFP was supporting about 8,900 children aged 6 months to 6 years through its malnutrition prevention programme and was also supporting about 1,366 pregnant and lactating women across the region.

To restore social services and other critical issues, technical service and the launch of tenders for the rehabilitation of public infrastructure, including offices of the prefecture, sub-prefecture, residences of the prefect, sub-prefect, and deputy prefect of Kidal Region, were all reported to have been carried out. MINUSMA continued to provide support in terms of both food and non-food items for a list of about 1,847 elements of signatory armed groups in three initial pilot pre-cantonment sites in Kidal since September 2013. Such activities were supported through the Trust Fund for Peace and Security in Mali. The UN Office for Project Services [UNOPS], which was an implementing partner, initiated the construction of the first three cantonment sites under a $3 million Peace-building Fund [PBF] project that was meant to ensure effective cantonment for elements of armed groups. This was seen as one of the confidence-building measures. Other parties continued to negotiate a global peace accord that would ensure the disarmament of the armed groups.

In terms of protection, the UN and its partners continued to promote human rights and women rights, as well as fight against gender-based violence across the Kidal Region. MINUSMA continued to monitor and report detention conditions in the detention premises run by MNLA and Haut Conseil Pour l'Unité de l'Azawad [HCUA] – a Tuareg organisation founded in 2013 - within their cantonment sites and also monitor the situation of detainees under the custody of the police. The human rights division of MINUSMA continued to document, investigate violations and abuse cases, and refer the victims to adequate services. About fifty police officers were trained by the UN human rights team on human rights standards. In Tessalit, the UN and its partners established a project for psychological and economic assistance for women and girls. The project was led by UN WOMEN. It was one of the activities carried out in the region that has benefited about 250 displaced women and girls; it also secured funding for 150 income-generating activities. UNICEF, on the other hand, continued to support activities that promoted mine risk education and psychological support for Gender-based Violence [GBV] survivors. And MINUSMA, as part of its child care protection, called on armed groups to vacate all occupied educational centres across the entire region. About 117 Chadian troops in Tessalit were further trained by MINUSMA's child rights division on child protection and child rights[335].

In the social sector, which includes education and health, seven schools in the Kidal Region were reported to be functioning out of a total of sixty-two schools that had functioned in the pre-crisis period. Prior to the conflict, there were 7,710 students in Kidal and about 398 teachers, but at the time of writing, there were only 772 students and 26 teachers present in Kidal Region. UNICEF and one of its partners, GARDL, had provided assistance to over 770 students and 22 teachers throughout the region while WFP and one of its partners, MUSTABAL, were making an assessment on the possibilities of restarting school feeding programmes in Kidal. In the area of health care, UNICEF and its partners, Médecins du Monde-Belgium, which was the only NGO providing health care in the region, continued to operate in the Kidal Region. WHO conducted a humanitarian mission to Kidal in March and provided over 100 consultations and 155 surgical interventions, including wounds caused by weapons such as land mines. About 2,000 children were reported to have been vaccinated with the support of WHO in the entire Kidal Region. The regional medicine depot was also reported to have been refurbished and the delivery of services improved throughout the region.

To support the reconciliation process, the UNDP launched a social cohesion and inter-community dialogue project. At the time of writing it had supported about three local organisations and involved them in the dialogue process and peace consolidations. The organisations received small grants that were expected to enable them to restart mediation and crisis management activities across the Kidal Region. Meanwhile, the UNMAS or Mines Action Organization had cleared thirty-six government buildings and their immediate surroundings and removed and destroyed over 440 remnants of the conflict. Also, about 487 personnel were reported to have received awareness training in Kidal regarding mines between January and March 2013. The WFP started activities that were aimed at the creation and rehabilitation of community assets, which include ponds, dams, water retention points, a sea wall, and market garden perimeters, which covered 2,730 beneficiaries across the region. MINUSMA embarked upon the rehabilitation of a centre for garbage collection in the urban centres in Kidal. It also rehabilitated the Gendarmerie and the police stations in Kidal, one for water and two were related to the rehabilitation of the gendarmerie and the police as well as a water project in the Kidal region. UNICEF, on its part, continued to provide support in the areas of water, sanitation, and hygiene initiatives in Kidal and had rehabilitated thirty-five water points in various communities. The project was targeting about 23,970 people in four districts of Kidal and was said to benefit women and children enrolled in nutritional programmes[336].

## CHAPTER NINETEEN

# *Disarmament*

*The world is over-armed and peace is underfunded.*

– Ban Ki-Moon [UN].

At the end of the French intervention, Operations Serval, and the recapture of the north of Mali from the rebel groups, many weapons were found or taken in the course of the encounter with the extremist groups. Some of the weapons were seized while others were abandoned by the groups in hurried attempts to flee the area due to the air strikes from the French forces. Many of the rebels' weapons had been captured from the Malian army. It was common knowledge that even in the previous wars the Tuaregs had always targeted and carted away arms and ammunitions from government military bases.

The 2012 Tuareg war differed in both intensity and scale from previous wars in 1963, 1990, as well as 2006 not only because of the involvement of Islamist rebels but also because of weapons the rebels possessed. Many different varieties and categories of weapons were reported to have been available to the groups. The origins of the weapons were diverse and difficult to identify. There was a general belief that most of the weapons probably originated from Libya after the overthrow of Gaddafi. This appeared quite logical - however, the weapons were manufactured in many different countries. The fact that many Tuaregs serving in the Libyan army returned to join the MNLA and start the rebellion was well known but was this sufficient to link all the weapons to Libya?

Weapons manufactured in Russia, Belgium or France came to be found in Mali. We need to document and inventorise these weapons in order to assess not only the nature of the conflict, but the capacity of the rebel groups militarily and the violence that erupted in Mali. It will further help us also to be able to assess the impact of the Libyan conflict on the violence in Mali, as well as to contribute to the research into the sources of the weapons for future reference.

The Conflict Armament Research in collaboration with the Small Arms Survey, making an assessment of the security situation in the region, categorised the weapons as: small arms; light weapons and ammunitions; larger conventional weapons and ammunition; and armoured military vehicles and were documented.

In the category of small arms, different models of the Kalashnikov-pattern 7.62 x 39 were found in Gao, Timbuktu, and the Ifogha mountain areas. Some were Russian but their exact provenance remained unclear. AR-M Bulgaria model 63 and 65, as well as the Romanian M-70 pattern and Serbian [possibly Iraq] type 56-1 and type 52 China made were also found and documented. The year of manufacture could not be identified from the film footage available[337]. FN FAL-pattern 7.62 x 51 mm rifles were also documented in the Gao Region between April and May 2012. The film footage does not make clear the country of manufacture[338]. G3 pattern 7. 62 x 51 mm rifles were found in the Gao Region. Again the film footage does not make clear the manufacturer[339]. Mat-49 9 x 19 mm submachine guns were also found in the Gao Region between April and May and may have been manufactured in France around the late 1940s to the 1970s. It was reported that many West African states were in the possession of that particular weapon, including Mali[340].

Other small arms found include the RPD-pattern 7.62 x 39 mm light machine gun, documented in the Gao Region - identification of factory or country of manufacture or year of manufacture was impossible to determine[341]. PK-pattern 7.62 x 54 mm general-purpose machine guns were also found in Gao between April and May 2012 and again at Aguelhok in January, 2013. Though the film footage does not make clear the country or year of manufacture, the film footage suggests widespread deployment of the weapon among the rebel groups. FN MAG-pattern 7.62 x 51 mm general-purpose machine guns were also discovered in Gao around April – again details impossible to determine.[342]. Barrels for 7.62 x 54 R MM RP-46 general-purpose machine guns were found in Diabaly on 24 January, 2013 after the recapture of the town by the French and the Malian forces. The identification was not so clear, but indications were that they may have been manufactured in the Soviet Union between the 1940s and 1960s. Dragunov SVD-pattern 7.62 x 54 R mm sniper rifles were documented in Timbuktu in April and again at Aguelhok in January 2012 – no details.[343]. PSL-pattern 7.62 x 54 R mm sniper rifles were located in Timbuktu and Aguelhok on April 2012 and January 2013, respectively. It was not confirmed if this was a Romanian FPK variant of PSL or an Iraqi al-Kasedih, which look similar[344]. SKS-pattern 7.62 x 39 mm rifles were found in Gao in April 2012. Again the film footage tends to suggest that a large number of these weapons may have been in circulation among the rebel forces[345].

Much small-arms ammunition was also found, and they include ammunition 7,62 x 39 mm, which were documented in Diabaly and Gao between January and February 2013 after the recapture of the area by the French and the Malian forces. In Diabaly, the ammunition was of two types. One type was manufactured by factory 31 in China while the other was manufactured also in China but by factory 61. However, it was not known when the weapons were transferred from China and who the recipient was. The ammunition in Gao, on the other hand, included M67, which was manufactured by Prvi Partizan, Serbia, in 1981 while the cartridges were manufactured in factory 711 in Russia or the Soviet Union in 1989. A third source may have been Arsenal in Bulgaria, dated 2011.

Beyond the dates and countries of manufacture, there was no evidence that indicated the sources of the weapon into Mali. Ammunition 7.62 x 54 rmm [relative molecular mass] was also documented in Gao on April 2012 and February 2013. The film footage did not provide for the identification of the manufacturer and date. However, better documented samples from a base abandoned by MUJWA included three types. One type was found to have been manufactured by Barnaul machine tools plant in the Soviet Union in 1988, the second was by factory 60 in Frunze, Kyrgyzstan, dated 1986 while the third was manufactured by Arsenal, Bulgaria, in 2011[346].

Light weapons documented included DSHKM-pattern 12.7 x 108 mm heavy machine guns found in Gao in April, 2012, and again in February, 2013. They were recovered by the French forces in the Adrar and Ifogha mountains on March 2013. The weapons were deployed on Toyota Land Cruiser 4 x 4 vehicles. Such weapons mounted on a variety of such vehicles appeared widespread among the rebel forces[347]. Type 8512, 7 x 108 mm heavy machine gun box were also documented in Diabaly on 24 January, 2013. Indications were that they might have been manufactured in China in 2007. No recipient country was indicated for transfer. KPV/KPVI-pattern 14.5 x 114 heavy machine guns were also documented in the Gao Region and again at Aguelhok during a rebel attack in January 2013. These weapons were mounted also on Toyota Land Cruiser 4 x 4 vehicles in single-barrel ZPV-I configurations in both Gao and Aguelhok. No manufacturer was indicated[348]. Also found included mortar 81/82 mm shown in Ansardine-released film footage of a military action during a rebel assault on Aguelhok in January, 2012. The footage did not provide for any identification of either manufacturer or year of manufacture[349]. PG-7 rockets were also documented in Diabaly on 24 January 2013. All the samples documented in the area indicated that they were manufactured in the Soviet Union from the 1960s. It was not clear when the rockets were transferred out of the USSR as well as the recipient of the transfer.

Other light weapons found included OG-82 and PG-82 rockets found in Diabaly around January 2013. They were found to have been manufactured in the Soviet Union and were used in the SPG-82 anti-tank rocket launcher, and it was suggested that they might have been manufactured before the 1970s. The OG-82 was said to feature a high-explosive fragmentation warhead for anti-personal use while the PG-82 featured a high-explosive anti-tank warhead. Mortar bombs 82 mm were also documented in the Adrar of the Ifogha mountains on 3 March, 2013 after the French and the Malian forces succeeded in taking over the area from the rebel forces. No manufacturer was identified from the film footage provided[350]. Again 120 mm mortar bombs were found in the same place. No manufacturer was identified.[351]. Unidentified nose fuses were also documented in Diabaly - no manufacturer identified. F1 pattern fragmentation grenades were documented in Diabaly and in the Ifogha mountain areas, identified as Soviet Union–designed F1, with UZRG-type fuses. It was reported that the production of grenades had been widespread among the other republics that made up the Soviet Union as well as in China. As such, it became difficult to determine the specific country of manufacture[352]. RPG-7 pattern launchers were documented in Gao in April, 2012, and again during a rebel assault in Aguelhok in January, 2013- manufacturer unknown[353]. SPG-9-pattern 73 mm recoiler guns were among other light weapons documented in March, 2013, and recovered by the

French and Malian forces in the Ifogha mountains in the north with no details available.[354]. M40 106 mm recoilless guns were also found and documented in Gao around April and May, 2012. The same weapon was said to have been photographed in two other areas, namely Diabaly and Konna – a weapon that was available in Libya but scarce among West African states. It was therefore suggested that the weapon may have been transferred from Libya in 2011.[355]

Light weapons ammunition documented included 12.7 x 108 mm ammunition, found in Diabaly on 24th February, 2012, and again in Gao in February, 2013. The cartridges indicated a Chinese manufacturer. In Gao ammunition box markings tended to indicate API ammunition manufactured by factory 41 in China around 2007[356]. Ammunition 14.5 x 114 mm was also documented in Konna on 26th January, 2013, and again in Diabaly on 24th January, 2013 – manufacturer unknown. However, certain features on the jackets that appears non-plated with a clear lacquer greyish appearance tended to suggest that they were manufactured in the Soviet Union or Russia. In Konna, marks on the ammunition box suggested that it was manufactured by factory 41 in China in 2007. Light weapon ammunitions NR-160 106 mm heat projectiles were documented in Diabaly and Konna in January, 2013. They were also reported to have been documented in Gao and the Ifogha mountain regions. Such ammunition was designed for use in M40 106 mm recoilless guns. There was an indication that the ammunition may have been manufactured in Belgium, as revealed by certain marks. It was reported that Belgium had weapons of this type to Libya since the 1970s. The weapon did not appear in the stockpile of weapons belonging to the Malian army and as such may not have been taken from the army by the rebels[357].

Larger conventional weapons featured various warheads found in the post-war period, including single-barrel 2A 14 23 x 152 mm cannons, documented in Gao and mounted on Toyota Land Cruiser

4 x 4 vehicles – no manufacturer identified.[358] Zu-23-2 pattern twin-barrel 23 x 152 rmm cannons were also documented in Gao in April and in May, 2012 as well as in film footage of a rebel military action in Aguelhok in January, 2013. According to the photographs of the ammunition for the weapon displayed, the weapon may have been deployed by the rebels in Diabaly area[359]. Type 63-pattern rocket launchers were among the large weapons found in Gao between April and May, 2012. They were mounted on civilian pickup vehicles and may have been manufactured in China, according to reports. Similar rockets of the same type were also said to be produced in Egypt, Iran, Sudan, and Turkey and appeared quite identical. UB-32 mm multiple rocket launchers, a weapon usually designed to be mounted on aerial platforms, like Mi-24 attack helicopter, was documented in Gao on 25th February. It fires 32-S-5 air-to-ground rockets and can also be mounted on a 4 x 4 vehicle. The same weapon was said to have been used by the Malian army and it was suspected as having been captured from the army by the rebels. The exact origin was not very clear[360]. Again D-30, a 122 mm towed howitzer was found in the Adrar and Ifogha mountain areas on 3 March 2013. The weapon was recognised to have been in use by the Libyan and Malian armies prior to the outbreak of the conflicts in both countries. As such, its origin remained unclear[361]. A BM-21 122 mm multiple-launch rocket system was also documented in film footage taken at the Gao international airport in April and again in May, 2012. Two BM-21 systems were documented, and one was said to be immobile while the second was said to be moving and loaded with thirty-four rockets of 9m 22 m type. The French forces were reported to have destroyed one BM-21 system and captured three more systems near Bourem. The total number of systems in the possession of the rebels was not known. It is possible that the rebels captured the systems from the Malian army[362].

The last category of weapons documented in the post-conflict period was ammunition for conventional weapons. These included

23 x 152 B mm ammunition, which was found in Diabaly on 24th January, 2013. It had a high-explosive incendiary load and was used in ZU-23-2 cannons – again no manufacture identified, though the box design suggested that either Bulgarian or Russian manufacture. Disintegrating links for 23 x 152 B mm ammunition belts were also documented in Diabaly on 24th January, 2013. The links indicated the redeployment of ZU-23-2 cannon by the rebel forces. Again Howitzer ammunition 122 mm was documented in the Adrar and Ifogha mountain areas in footage of weapons captured by the French and the Malian forces. The weapon was known to have been in the service of the Libyan and the Malian forces prior to the outbreak of conflicts in both countries[363]. Rockets 9 mm 122 mm were captured in Diabaly and the same type also came to be documented in Konna on 26th January, 2013, and in Gao on 25th February, 2013. The rocket was known to have a range of about 20 kilometres. It was generally used in the BM-21 multiple-launch rocket system and was of Soviet Union/Warsaw Pact origin, possibly manufactured between 1972 and 1988. It was not clear how it was obtained by the rebels.[364] A BRDM-2 armoured personnel carrier was documented in Gao around April and May, 2012, and may have been manufactured in the Soviet Union. It was thought that the rebel forces might have seized it from the Malian army during the 2012 operations. Mali had deployed sixty-four BRDM-2 vehicles prior to the 2012 rebellion, and Bulgaria was reported to have supplied Mali with about forty-four of them between 2007 and 2009[365]. Lastly, a BTR-60 armoured personnel carrier was among the equipment for conventional weapons captured by the rebel forces from the Malian army in March 2012. The Malian army was said to have deployed forty-four of the vehicles prior to the outbreak of the 2012 war. However, the colour of this particular vehicle differed from that of the Malian army, which was usually painted in a plain dark-green colour[366].

# Epilogue

*The World is Quiet Here.*

— Lemony Snicket

T he Sahel Region has remained in flames and turmoil since the outbreak of the Tuareg war in 2012. Despite the intervention of France, violence has continued to spread across borders. The activities of groups such as AQIM has continued to expand to the other countries. AQIM has continued to support other Jihadist groups operating in countries such as Burkina Faso, Niger, Chad, Northern Cameroun, and parts of Nigeria, including Boko Haram and recently ISWAP. The book has tried to shed light on the developments and violence in the Sahel region and Mali since the 1963 Tuareg war. The intervention of Paris has been explained from two perspectives: the French and the Malian perspectives. The French perspective was explained in terms of French economic interests not only in Mali but in the Sahel region as a whole. France feared that the instability in Mali was likely to affect other Sahel states where France was seen to have made significant economic investment. The Malian perspective, on the other hand, saw the intervention mainly from a security point of view and the weakness and inability of the Malian state to deal with the offensive of the rebel groups, hence, a request by the Malian president for Paris to intervene. It was basically from those perspectives that the intervention of France in the 2012 conflict in Mali was explained.

The book has not only investigated the 2012 Tuareg war in Mali and the intervention of France in the conflict, but it has also shown how Mali emerged as a nation in recent history, its ancient past, and the old Mali Empire, which reached its zenith under Mansa Musa. This was because it seemed impossible to discuss the 2012 Tuareg war in isolation from Mali's history and previous wars by the Tuareg group. The French incursion into Mali tried to show that French interest in the country was initially to have access to its possessions in the Senegal basin. The study also discussed the establishment of colonial rule in Mali, during which Mali came to be known as the French Sudan. The French Sudan, as it was known, came to include Mauritania, Burkina Faso, and Mali. Those entities, separated after the attainment of independence from the French in 1960. But until independence, they constituted what was regarded as the French Sudan. The policies of both the French regime and the post-independence administration of Modibo Keita and other successive regimes in Mali have been discussed. From this, it could be observed that the Tuareg revolt was rooted in colonial times. The history of the Tuaregs shows that foreign control or influence was alien and unacceptable to the group. In their history, the Tuaregs had never been under the influence of any other group or people; and that came to explain their initial resistance to the French, as Alla ag Albachir at different times succeeded in organising resistance against the French. As a result of such actions during the colonial times, the Tuaregs were exempted from many activities including forced labour and service in the colonial army. Although Alla Albachir's son, Elledi, started the 1963 war in the post-independence period in an attempt to avenge the killing of his father, which was in accordance with *egha* or revenge in the Tuareg culture, it should, however, be understood that the policies of the Keita regime were what first ignited hostilities between the group and the Malian authorities. The policies of the

Keita regime included many programmes that were similar to those of the colonial period, and as such, the revenge by Elledi of his father's death in the post-independence period only marked the outbreak of the revolt, but other factors motivated the group to take arms against the Malian government.

After the failure of the 1963 rebellion, the persecution of the Tuaregs by the Malian government led to their migration into other neighbouring states, although it was certain that the droughts of the 1970s and the 1980s also facilitated such migrations. The migrations and the emergence of a Tuareg diaspora were described as critical in explaining the second Tuareg war in 1990 that came to be known as Al Jebha. Long years of military training and preparation abroad appeared to have prepared the Tuareg, and they had the upper hand against the Malian army after one or two encounters, the Malian government was forced to open negotiations with the group.

Since Al Jebha, which lasted between 1990 and 1996, there were some other Tuareg uprisings; but among all of them, one came to be considered as a revolt that appeared to have laid the foundation for the outbreak of the 2012 Tuareg war. This revolt was known as the 2009 Tuareg revolt, and although a peace agreement was reached, certain parties among the Tuaregs remained unsatisfied and were bent on continuing with the rebellion. Among those people was Ibrahim Bahanga, who has been seen to be the mastermind of the 2012 Tuareg War. It was Bahanga, according to many sources, who started the plan for the 2012 war, which was greatly aided by the civil war in Libya and the fall of Gaddafi. After the fall of Gaddafi, the return of several thousands of Tuareg fighters from Libya to Mali resulted in the formation of the MNLA, and the war was declared.

So many factors also appeared to have favoured the starting of the rebellion and its success before the intervention of France. The situation in the Sahel region and the emergence of the smuggling networks, trade in drugs, and general organised crime that saw the emergence of groups such as AQIM, Ansardine, and MUJWA, who in alliance with MNLA launched the 2012 rebellion, were partly responsible for the outbreak of the war. The availability of weapons from Libya after the fall of Gaddafi had made it very easy for the rebels to overpower the Malian soldiers, and Mali had to seek the help from France to regain the control of its domains.

France responded to the request of the interim president of Mali by conducting air strikes that resulted in the retreat of the rebels to the Algerian border. The French action was supported by ECOWAS, AU, EU, and the United Nations as well as many other countries including the United States, Britain, Norway, Canada, and Germany. ECOWAS had been involved in negotiations with the rebels prior to the intervention of France and had called for the deployment of an African-led force, which was approved by the United Nations. However, the African-led force could not be mobilised in time, and the rebel advance was rapid. This explained why the Malian regime sought the help of Paris.

The intervention increased French presence and influence in Mali and projected French influence and interest not only in Mali but across the Sahel region as a whole. Several factors apart from that of security may have motivated Paris into quick action. These were explained above from the two perspectives that were identified. However, it is argued that all other factors were dependent on the security factor, considering that without the security factor no intervention would have taken place whatsoever. But, of course, many valid geo-strategic and geo-political reasons have been advanced to explain the French intervention. The presence of other countries economically and militarily in certain African countries that were seen as part of French sphere of influence played an important part in motivating Paris to take action. Another motivating factor was the struggle for control over mineral resources such as oil, uranium, and many others in some of the African states among the big powers such as USA, China, the BRIC states and France. The competition among these countries extended to trade in certain commodities that included textile and cotton. All these factors played a part in convincing France to intervene in Mali.

The intervention was viewed as successful despite the problems encountered. After the intervention, the United Nations approved the deployment of a UN multidimensional force, which played a prominent role in the rebuilding of the Malian society, especially the North, which was most affected by the conflict. Immediately after the restoration of peace, elections were conducted and authority was transferred from the interim administration to the new democratically elected government under President Boubacar in 2013. Many United Nations agencies and other international organisations concentrated their activities in the North, which was faced with a humanitarian crisis as a result of the war. Migrations and displacements both within and outside the country worsened humanitarian issues in the post-war period. As such, re-establishing and restoring basic social amenities and the provision of food as a result of insecurity remained a major challenge, especially in the north which suffered most in the crisis.

A document for the sustainable recovery of Mali was drafted; the plan was focused for the year 2013–2014. It contained both short-term and long-term plans for Mali and outlined major areas of concern. The first item on the list of the plan was the restoration of peace and security, as well as that of public services throughout the country. Response to humanitarian emergencies and elections were carried out in July, 2013, and came second on the list. The document further called for increased governance through decentralisation to achieve balanced development and reform of the public service. The fight against corruption was also highlighted as necessary in order to ensure the well-functioning of the judicial system. There was the need to rebuild the Malian economy through the strengthening of the private sector, agriculture, as well as investment in infrastructural development and youth employment. The educational sector, according to the document, needed to be addressed quickly; along with health care, which was considered insufficient and inaccessible to many people. The document further called for the support of cultural projects to promote peaceful coexistence among all groups. Promoting the role of women within the society was also identified as a key area that should be given attention. Environmental issues were the final item on the list. The document called for the formulation of policies and strategies which would improve on the environment, which it recognised as a priority, especially if the desert north was taken into consideration as a result of the food scarcity, which had constantly affected the country due to the poor climate that was linked to the environment.

A lot of progress was made by many of the organisations in collaboration with the Malian government. Organisations such as the UNMAS continued to clear the north of the remnants of dangerous weapons and mines, and a survey of the weapons seized and abandoned by the rebels is contained in the last chapter, demonstrating the variety and scope the weapons in rebel hands and their sources.

It was generally believed that if attention was focused on the identified areas, the rebuilding of the country would not take long, and it may in turn bring about peace all over the country. However, in order to avoid the outbreak of another Tuareg revolt, especially since the 2012 war did not end with any agreement, a factor which made the possibility of a reoccurrence high, it was necessary to look into the decentralisation of the country as a policy, as well as previous agreements entered into by the Malian government and the Tuaregs such as the National Pact and its provisions. Otherwise, the partition of the country into North and South was seen to be a possible solution to the lingering Tuareg conflict if all options failed.

It must be added too, that failure to resolve the Malian/ Tuareg issue will prolong the poor security situation in the Sahel region that has continued to worsen since the 2012 war in Mali. Countries like Nigeria have been poorly hit by the instability in Mali and Libya, which are related anyway, and so is Chad, Niger, and Burkina Faso among several other nations of the Sahel region that have so far remained in crisis. In Nigeria, the emergence of what is now termed as 'banditry' in the northwest and central of the country has added a new dimension to the operations of Boko Haram and the kidnappings that are already exist, and it remains linked directly or indirectly to the instability in Mali and Libya. As such the Sahel region as it is has come under fire from terrorist groups and other criminal elements. World leaders and governments have failed to investigate the environmental problems associated with minerals exploration and operations by multinational companies in the region that has put the population at risk because of radiation arising from uranium exploration, which is among reasons for the instability and uprising by the Tuareg. The poverty and neglect are a serious cause of concern in the region. A regional approach is likely to bring the situation under control. However, so far there has not been any successful coordinated approach by the Sahel states to bring this razing fire of violence under control.

*"A people divided will hardly reach its goal It may never be able to make an acacia tree with beautiful leaves A divided people will lose its way Each of its part will be an enemy unto itself"*. Toumast [The People] song.

– Tinarewen Musical Band
[Rebel Songs, The New Yorker].

# Notes

1   The Kanem-Bornu Empire was a middle African empire of the Chad Basin centred in modern Chad and Nigeria. It lasted from the ninth centuryADuntil 1900. At the height of its power, it comprised an area covering not only much of Chad but also parts of southern Libya, eastern Niger, North-Eastern Nigeria, northern Cameroun, Central African Republic and South Sudan with its capital at Bornu in present-day Nigeria.

2   The Fulani or Fulbe people were referred to by the French as Peul.

3   Rafael Grasa and Oscar Mateos, 'Conflict, Peace and Security in Africa: An Assessment and New Questions after 50 Years of African Independence', August 2010, p 9.

4   Ibid., p 11.

5   The terms are analytical categories that gained prominence in the mid 1990's. Policy makers and academics held the belief that potential or contemporary conflict is to be found within and not between states, among low capacity and low income states. The term failed states was coined by Helman and Ratner (1992), collapsed or collapsing state by Zartman (1995). Failing and failed states came to be widely disseminated by U.S. administrations and U.S. Policy analysts after 9/11 in 2001. The notion of fragile states came to be spread internationally among donors, technical agencies and various governments in the areas of development, humanitarian assistance and peace building.(Olivier Nay, Fragile States: Critical Perspective on Conceptual Hybrids, a paper prepared for 22nd IPSA World Congress of Political Science 8-12 July, 2010, pp 1-2).

6   Jackson Robert H, "Quasi-States, Dual Regimes, and Neoclassical Theory: International Jurisprudence and the Third World". I: International Organization nr. 4, p 523.

7   Claire Mcloughlin, 'Topic Guide on Fragile States', Governance and Social Development Resource Center, University of Birmingham, UK, p 9–12.

8   Jackson Robert H, "Negative Sovereignty in Sub-Saharan Africa. I: Review of International Studies nr. 4,10. 1986, p 250.

9   W. Zartman, 'Introduction: Posing the Problem of State Collapse in Collapsed States: The Disintegration and Restoration of Legitimate Authority, Boulder, London, UK, 1995.

10  Francis Rodd, "Origins of the Tuareg", The Geographical Journal, Vol 67, No 1, November, 2013. p 27.

11  'El Merabat' [Arabic *al-Murābiṭūn*] means "those dwelling in frontier garrisons".

12  'Mali: Defending Democracy: A Global Survey of Foreign Policy Trends 1992–2002', Democracy Coalition Project, pp 1–2.

13  Rafael Grasa and Oscar Mateos, 'Conflict, Peace and Security in Africa: An Assessment and New Questions after 50 Years of African Independence', 2010. pp 7–8.

14  Ibid.

15  Freedom C. Onuoha and Alex Thurston, 'Franco-African Military Intervention in the Mali Crisis and Evolving Security Concerns', Al Jazeera Center for Studies, 19 February 2013, pp 2–5.

16  Bakare Sambe, 'The Crisis in Mali: Origins, Developments and Impact on the Sub Region', KAS International Reports, December 2012, pp 119.

17  Dona J. Stewart, 'What Is Next for Mali? The Roots of Conflict and Challenges to Stability', United States War College Press and Strategic Studies Institute November2013, p 6.

18  A reg is described as a plain of sand and black, red, or white gravel.

19  Humans are said to dwell in the sand stone cliffs, which rise to about 1,000 metres.

20  'Mali in Perspective: An Orientation Guide', Defense Language Institute Foreign Language Center, Technology Integration Division, 2011, p 4.

21  Ibid., pp 5–6.

22  Population Division of the Department of Economic and Social Affairs of the United Nations Secretariat, 'World Population Prospects', 2010 revision.

23  http://microdata.worldbank.org/index.php/catalog/dh.

24  Ibid., p 36.

25  The complexion of this group of people differs slightly with that of the southern population. While the population in the south is typical of the Negroid race, the light skinned in the north look more like the Arab people.

26  Pew Forum and Public Life, 'The World Muslims: Unity and Diversity', 9 August 2012.

27  'International Religions Freedom Report 2008: Mali'.

28  It should be understood that the Bambara do not constitute 80% of the population of Mali but that about 80% of the people of Mali speak the Bambara language, including non-Bambara people.

29  It is a family of languages in the Afro-Asiatic languages and considered a single language in the past, especially in French tradition. It is spoken by about 14 million people scattered in the Maghreb states.

30  One of Africa's finest epics tells the story of Sundiata's victory over Soumaora, who ruled over a number of kingdoms before the founding of the Mali Empire. This epic legend came be passed down from generation to generation by the griots [bards] of Mali. The oral epic was finally written down by D.T Niane as *Sundiat: An Epic of Old Mali*.

31  Ibid., pp 8-12.

32  Sundiata epic

33  Dona Stewart, 'What Is Next for Mali? The Roots of Conflict and Challenges to Stability', United States Army War College Press and Strategic Studies Institute, November 2013, p 9.

34  Leo Africanus has sumptuous accounts of ancient Mali, Timbuktu and Gao in his *History and Description of Africa*.

35  Ibid., p 10.

36  For detail of Ibn Batuta's travels see; Ibn Batuta, 'Travels in Asia and Africa, 1325–1354', Translated and selected by H. A. R. Gibb with introduction notes, George Routledge & Sons Limited, London, 1929.

37  It was a medium of exchange that was used in the Arab world in those days that Ibn Batuta tried to equate in describing the value of the exchanges that he witnessed in different commodities in Mali.

38  For details of Ibn Khaldun's works, see Ibn Khaldun, *Histoire des Berbères et des dynasties musulmanes de l'Afrique septentrionale; traduit de l'Arabe par le baron W. M. de Slane [1852-1856]*, Algiers.

39  Mansa Kankan Musa was the tenth *mansa* or ruler and is considered the most famous ruler or emperor of the wealthy Mali Empire, which flourished between twelfth and sixteenth century. Musa reigned between 1280 and 1337.

40  Ibid., p 11.

41  'The Wealth of Africa: The Kingdom of Mali Students Worksheet'. British Museum, .www.britishmuseum.org, p 4.

42  Ibid., p 5.

43  Jackson Family, 'Mossi People', www.memfamily.com/clark-history.

44  The Soghai was another ancient empire that rose to power and defeated Mali and took control of many of its cities.

45  African History Online, 'Songhai Empire', www.sahistory.org.za/topic/songhai-african empire-15th-16th century.

46

47  Dona Stewart, 'What Is Next for Mali? The Roots of Conflict and Challenges to Stability', United States Army War College Press and Strategic Studies Institute, November 2013, pp 16–21.

48  Ibid., pp 16–21.

49  Ibid., p 19.

50  Ibid., p 20.

51  Dorothea Schulz, 'Praise without Enchantment: Griots, Broadcast Media, and the Politics of Tradition in Mali', *Africa Today*, October–December 1997, p 446.

52  Ibid., pp 447–450.

53  Lord Frederick Lugard [1858-1945], High Commissioner and Governor-General of Nigeria between 1900 and 1919.

54  Wallace G. Mills, 'French Approaches in Colonial Policy', St Mary's University www.saylor.org, pp 1–4.

55  Dorothea Schulz, 'Praise without Enchantment: Griots, Broadcast Media, and the Politics of Tradition In Mali', *Africa Today*, October–December 1997, p 445.

56  Wallace G. Mills, 'French Approaches in Colonial Policy', St Mary's University. www.saylor.org, p 6.

57  Dona Stewart, 'What Is Next for Mali? The Roots of Conflict and Challenges to Stability', United States Army War College Press and Strategic Studies Institute, November 2013, p 23.

58  Vichy France – the puppet government led by Marshal Pétain set up in two thirds of the country as a result of the German conquest of France in 1940.

59  This principle meant that the Africans were ready to risk their lives and go to the war and fight for the French in exchange for the freedom of their respective states from French control.

60  The indigenet is a set of laws, creating in practice an inferior legal status for natives of French colonies from 1887 until 1944–1947. It was applied across the French colonial empire between 1887 and 1889.

61  The French Sudan refers to the French colonial territory in the Federation of French West Africa that emerged around 1880 until 1960 when it became the independent state of Mali. It comprised of eight French colonial territories of Mauritania, Mali, Senegal, Guinea, Ivory Coast, Upper Volta, Dahomey, and Niger.

62  Baz Lecocq, 'The Disputed Desert; Decolonization, Competing Nationalisms and Tuareg Rebellions in Northern Mali', Afrika-Studiecentrum series, p 28.

63  Ibid., p 29.

64  Dorothea Schulz, 'Praise without Enchantment: Griots, Broadcast Media, and the Politics of Tradition in Mali', *Africa Today*, October–December 1997, p 451.

65 When the Keita government invited the Algerian FLN fighters it hadn't the slightest idea that a kind of relation will develop between it and the Tuareg group in the north which is where the training camp of the FLN is also located. And it was not so easy for the government to ask the FLN to vacate Mali since there isn't any evidence of any collaboration or plan between it and the Tuaregs against the Malian state at the point.

66 It must be understood that the Tuaregs had not shown any interest in being part of the Malian state since its creation. Although the Keita regime did try to pursue a policy of integrating them, the group preferred the colonial period due to the fact that they did not participate in all negative colonial policies like forced labour and enlistment in the army. And the group further despised the Malian state partly as a result of the new policies introduced by the Keita regime of volunteer labour, which resembled the forced labour during French rule. Unfortunately, the Keita regime, unlike the French, did not exempt the Tuaregs from these new policies, which became a major source of dissatisfaction with the Malian state and the Keita regime by the Tuaregs.

67 Dorothy Schulz, 'Praise without Enchantment: Griots, Broadcast Media, and the Politics of Tradition in Mali', *Africa Today*, vol 44, no 4, December 1997, p 455.

68 Dona J. Stewart, 'What Is Next for Mali? The Roots of Conflict and Challenges to Stability', United States Army War College Press and Strategic Studies Institute, November 2013, p 25.

69 It was following the rebellion that Touré, who was head of Traoré's personal guards, arrested the president and later announced himself as the new president in Mali. So it was not a military coup as such, but the rebellion provided a good opportunity from Touré to seize power.

70 www.africansuccess.org, 'Biography of Alpha Oumar Konare'.

71 www.berkleycentre.georgetown.edu, 'Resources on Faith, Ethics and Public Life: Ahmadu Touré'.

72 www.aljazeera.com, 'Mali Mutiny 'Topples' President Toure', March 2012.

73 Francis Rodd, 'Origins of the Tuareg', *Geographical Journal*, vol 67, no 1, November 2013, p 27.

74 Rodd explains in his article that the spread as well as the physical characteristic of the group distinguishes them from other groups, and for this he concluded that the group constitutes more than a tribe and may only be referred or considered as a race.

75 Ibid., p 29.

76 *Mendacious* is a word that is used to mean either dishonest, especially when it is habitual, untruthful, deceitful. It originated from Latin word *mendacium*, which means *lie*.

77  The *dolichocephalic* category describes the Tuaregs as having a straight forehead with prominent eyebrow bones. They are of tall stature, face tapering from temples, with unobtrusive cheekbones, thin long nose, and straight chin. They also have an unobtrusive muscular developmentbut dry and sinewy limbs, broad shoulders, and slender waists, the trunk forming a reversed cone.

78  Ibid., p 34.

79  Ibid., p 38.

80  Tewsit explains the general organisation in the Tuareg federation that is made up of several clans. This organisation on the basis of clan is what is known as tewsit.

81  Tamasheq refers to the Tuareg people or their language. The Tuaregs themselves, throughout the various records of their history, refer to themselves as the Kel Tamasheq, which literary means 'those that speak Tamasheq'.

82  J. S. Lecocq, 'The Desert is Our Country: Tuareg Rebellions and Competing Nationalisms in Contemporary Mali', Ph.D. Thesis, Faculty of Social and Behavioral Sciences, University of Amsterdam, 2002.

83  Ibid.

84  Baz Lecocq, 'Disputed Desert: Decolonization, Competing Nationalisms and Tuareg Rebellions in Northern Mali', Afrika-Studiecentrum Series, vol 19, p 77.

85  J. S. Lecocq, 'The Desert is Our Country: Tuareg Rebellions and Competing Nationalisms in Contemporary Mali', Ph.D. Thesis, Faculty of Social and Behavioral Sciences, University of Amsterdam, 2002, p 45.

86  Baz Lecocq, 'Disputed Desert: Decolonization, Competing Nationalisms and Tuareg Rebellions in Northern Mali', Afrika-Studiecentrum Series, vol 19, p 78.

87  See G. Klute, 'Herren und sklaven, Zur frage der kolonialen sklavenpolitik in Franzosisch-West Afrika', H. Willer, et al. [eds.], 'Macht der identitat=identitat der Macht. Polische prozesse und kulturller wandel in Afrika'[Munster, 1995], pp 53–241.

88  It is important to understand that despite the fact that slavery had been banned by the French colonial regime since 1905, the Tuaregs still maintained slaves, and it was known by the authorities. And so the emerging post-colonial political parties whose programmes were against slavery could not garner the support of the Tuaregs.

89  As mentioned previously, the reluctance of the colonial regime to stop the Tuareg group from continuing to maintain slaves as well as their exemption from other policies of the French like forced labour and enlistment in the army made it clear that they were favored by the French among other groups in the French Sudan.

90 'Les partis politiques en AOF et les consultations electorates de 1945 a 1955', No 8: Sudan. ANSOM-1 Affpol/2263/6.

91 'Elections generales de 10 Novemeber 1946' Cercle de Kidal. ANM-FR 7D-67.

92 Known also as the amenokal, he is the leader of the Tuareg group. The amenokal is a position that has been occupied by different people from among the Tuaregs.

93 see M. A. Ag Attaher Insar, 'La scolarisation moderne comme strategie de resistance', H. Claudat-Hawad [ed.], 'Tuaregs exil et resistance', REMMM 57[1990], pp 91–97.

94 Ibid.

95 Ibid.

96 W. Jones, 'Planning and economic policy: Socialist Mali and her neighbours', Three Continental Press, Washington, 1974, p 115.

97 W. Jones, ' The rise and demise of socialist institutions in rural Mali', Geneva-Afrique 11, pp 19–44.

98 It was, of course, known to the regime that the Tuaregs, among other groups, may not welcome the new policies, which resembled the forced labour policy of the French that the group strongly resisted under colonial rule.

99 SNED ['Societe Nationale d' Etudes pour le Development'], 1980, p 44.

100 C. Bogosian, 'The Little Farming Soldiers: The Evolution of a Labour Army in Post Colonial Mali', Mande Studies 5, 2003, pp 83–100.

101 Labor migrations first started during colonial rule, and many tried to escape colonial forced labour by migrating either within or outside the country.

102 C. Bogosian, 'The Little Farming Soldiers: The Evolution of a Labour Army in Post Colonial Mali', Mande Studies 5, 2003, pp 83–100.

103 It is not clear if they still lived there or not. It is known that many Tuaregs did not return to Mali especially after the outbreak of the first rebellion and its end; thereafter, a Tuareg diaspora was known to have developed in many West African countries.

104 The Bambara people are part of the Mande people and constitute the majority among the Mande people. About 80% of the Malian population speaks the Bambara language regardless of ethnicity as a result of the dominance of the group over other groups, particularly among the Mande people.

105 See P. Campmas, ' L' Union Soudanaise R.D.D: L' histoire d' un grand parti politique africain'. Communications Intercontinental, Abidjan, 1978.

106 Baz Lecooq, 'Disputed Desert: Decolonization, Competing Nationalisms and Tuareg Rebellions in Northern Mali', Afrika-Studiecentrum Series, vol19, p 62.

107 Baz Lecooq, 'Disputed Desert: Decolonization, Competing Nationalisms and Tuareg Rebellions in Northern Mali', Afrika-Studiecentrum Series, vol 19, p 116.

108 At this point, the group did not make clear their intention or at least not openly, but the actions of the group clearly showed that they were not interested in the new arrangement. But at the same time, they did not declare if they wanted to be independent or not. These were just grievances being expressed by the group and may form reasons for future disagreements with the Malian state.

109 Baz Lecooq, 'Disputed Desert: Decolonization, Competing Nationalisms and Tuareg Rebellions in Northern Mali', Afrika-Studiecentrum Series, vol 19, p 117.

110 The Keita-led US-RDA had tried to win the support of the Tuaregs; however, after the elections and subsequent introduction of new policies, the Tuaregs and the Keita government fell apart.

111 Ibid., p 70.

112 'Une nouvelle etape dans l' affirmation de la personalite de notre jeune nation', l' Essor, 03/07/1962.

113 Baz Lecooq, 'Disputed Desert: Decolonization, Competing Nationalisms and Tuareg Rebellions in Northern Mali', Afrika-Studiecentrum Series, vol 19, p 71.

114 Ibid., p 70.

115 Ibid.

116 J. S. Lecocq, 'The Desert is Our Country: Tuareg Rebellions and Competing Nationalisms in Contemporary Mali [1946–1996]', Faculty of Social and Behavioral Sciences, University of Amsterdam, p 101.

117 This was money being paid for membership by the public to the Keita-led US-RDA, which was the political party in power at that time.

118 J. S. Lecocq, 'The Desert is Our Country: Tuareg Rebellions and Competing Nationalisms in Contemporary Mali [1946–1996]', Faculty of Social and Behavioral Sciences, University of Amsterdam, p 78.

119 It is clear that the rebellion did not take place overnight, and moreover, it is important to look at the history of the Tuaregs themselves as a people that have been described as a war-like nation, whose principal occupation was raiding, and then look at other development such as how the group found itself under colonial rule and other conditions that accompanied such colonial occupation and the post-independence developments as well.

120 These are all clans within the Tuareg federation. As discussed, the Tuareg society is organised along tewsit [clans] lines; and these are many in the Tamasheq [Tuareg] world, bearing different names as seen with the Ifogha and the Adagh above.

208

[121] M. Valet, 'Les Tuoregs du Hoggar entre decolonization et independences 1954–1974'.

[122] J.S. Lecocq 'The Desert is Our Country: Tuareg Rebellions and Competing Nationalisms in Contemporary Mali [1946–1996]', Faculty of Social and Behavioral Sciences, University of Amsterdam, p 104.

[123] J. Guillemin, 'Les campagnes militaires francaise de la decolonization en Afrique Sud-Saharine' Mois en Afrique XVII, 1982, p 136.

[124] Based on Chef d' Arrondissement de Tessalit a Commandant du cercle de Kidal. 27/08/62, Confidential no../AT/CF.ACK.

[125] Gouverneur de Gao a Commandant du cercle de Kidal, 20/05/1960.ACK.

[126] Ibid.

[127] J. S. Lecocq, 'The Desert is Our Country: Tuareg Rebellions and Competing Nationalisms in Contemporary Mali [1946–1996]', Faculty of Social and Behavioral Sciences, University of Amsterdam, p 118.

[128] Ibid., p 129.

[129] Probably these slaves were among those taken away from the Tuaregs at independence since slavery had been banned since the colonial period, but the Tuaregs continued to have slaves and the French colonial masters did not do anything to stop them. But the coming Malian regime insisted on the policy of banning slavery and as a result took away many slaves and freed them from the Tuareg group.

[130] Baz Lecocq, 'Disputed Desert: Decolonization, Competing Nationalisms and Tuareg Rebellion in Northern Mali, Afrika-Studiecentrum Series, vol 19, p 157.

[131] Ibid.

[132] Ibid., pp 157–158.

[133] Dicko, ' Process verbal de compte rendu de mission', n.d [+/-30/10/1963]. ACK.

[134] Questions poses pae le Capitaine Diarra, Commandant la C.S.M er le Cercle de Kidal, 'au rebelle Amouksou ag Azandeher', Kidal, 04/10/1963.ACK.

[135] Baz Lecocq, 'Disputed Desert: Decolonization, Competing Nationalisms and Tuareg Rebellion in Northern Mali, Afrika-Studiecentrum Series, vol 19, p 160.

[136] Questions posées par le Captain Diarra, Commandant la C.S.M. et le Cercle de Kidal, 'au rebelle Amouksou ag Azandeher', Kidal,04/10/1963.ACK. There was no formal contact actually between the either the French or the Algerians and the Tuaregs. However, there are indications that some informal relations definitely existed between the group and the Frenchand the Algerians as well. First, if we will recall, some of the injured Tuareg fighters were mostly treated by French doctors or citizens at the French nuclear facility in Algeria. Secondly, it is well known that the Algerian border was widely open for the

Tuaregs, and they mobilised all attacks from Algeria. It is unimaginable that the Algerian authorities may have not been aware of the group's movementand did not make any attempt to stop or arrest any member of the group.

137 Questions posees par le Captain Diarra, Commandant la C.S.M. et le Cercle de Kidal, 'au rebelle Amouksou ag Azandeher', Kidal,04/10/1963.ACK.

138 Elledi ag Alla is considered to have started the rebellion because he was the first to attack and kill a gourmier. He is considered to have inspired the revolt proper against the Malian state.

139

140 J. S. Lecocq, 'The Desert is Our Country: Tuareg Rebellions and Competing Nationalisms in Contemporary Mali [1946–1996]', Faculty of Social and Behavioral Sciences, University of Amsterdam, pp 140–141.

141 Ibid., p 140.

142 Interrogatoire du prisonnier rebelle Eladi ag Alla par le Captaine Diby Silas Diarra, Commandant d'armes et du Cercle de Kidal, 13/03/1964.ACK.

143 Ibid.

144 This was based on Mali, 'Tableau des forces armee et forces publiques du Mali au 1er mai', 1964.CHETOM-15 H 77-2c.

145 Declaration de Kaza ag Larlar, Kidal, 08/02/1964.ACK.

146 Questions posees par le Captaine Diarra, Commandant la C.S.M et le Cercle de Kidal, au rebelle Amouksou ag Azandeher, Kidal, 04/10/1963.

147 P. Boiley, 'Les Touaregs Kel Adagh Dependence st revoltes du Soudan francais au Mali contemporain' Paris, 1999, p 318.

148 This is based on Interrogatoire du prisonnier rebelle Eladi ag Alla par le Captain Diby Silas Diarra, Commandant d'armes et du Cercle de Kidal, 13/04/1964.ACK.

149 Ibid.

150 Declarations des deux rebelles rendus avec leurs armes le 10 juillet 1964 au chef de tribu Bissaada-I/ Declarations du nomme Salia ag Bakarine, fraction Imerade Intalla. ACK.

151 'Kidal a celebre la fete nationale avex un eclat particulier', L'Essor Hebdomadaire, 28/08/1964.

152 H. Claudat-Hawad, 'Coups et contre-coups: l'HONNEUR EN JEU CHEZ Tuaregs, les Touaregs, portrait en fragments', Aix-en-Provence, 1993, pp 13–27.

153 J. S. Lecocq, 'The Desert is Our Country: Tuareg Rebellions and Competing Nationalisms in Contemporary Mali [1946–1996]', Faculty of Social and Behavioral Sciences, University of Amsterdam, p 153.

154 Courier de l'UNESCO, April 1975, no 11.

155 J. Derrick, 'The Great West African Drought, 1972-74', African Affairs LXXVI-305, 1977, pp 537, 586, 561.

156 The Tuaregs had been fed up with the Keita regime, and when the Afellega failed, all hope for independence were dashed. As such, the fall of the Keita regime, in the imagination of the group meant, an end to the Malian nation or in any case signalled a possibility for independence again.

157 In the material consulted, there was only a reference to the Gaddafi speech, and it was not clear where he made the speech and on which occasion or for what reason he declared Libya as the country of origin of the Tuaregs. This is despite the fact that at the beginning of the chapter, Rodd had indeed confirmed that the Tuaregs did originate from Libya as claimed by Gaddafi.

158 J. S. Lecocq, 'The Desert is Our Country: Tuareg Rebellions and Competing Nationalisms in Contemporary Mali[1946–1996]', Faculty of Social and Behavioral Sciences, University of Amsterdam, p 178.

159 Griots are traditional praise singers. They very famous in Mali and are known to have played prominent role in government in the pre-colonial period.

160 The Tuareg communities that developed outside Mali came to be called the Ishumar in the Tuareg language, which is similar to diaspora. They were found in Niger, Algeria, Nigeria, Burkina Faso, and Mauritania, as well as some countries in North Africa.

161 The Ishumar is used in describing the Tuaregs, the new culture that began to emerge among many of the economically and politically marginalised Tuareg youths, rebellious or revolutionary in nature, and reasserting cultural pride.

162 J. S. Lecocq, 'The Desert is Our Country: Tuareg Rebellions and Competing Nationalisms in Contemporary Mali[1946–1996]', Faculty of Social and Behavioral Sciences, University of Amsterdam, 2002, p 190.

163 It is a Tuareg word and a synonym of the word *revolution* or *revolutionary*. It can also mean struggle at the same time.

164 N. Belalimat, 'Le rapport a l'histoire dans les chants de lutte de la resistance Tuaregue contemporaine,' Les cahiers de l'IREMAM 7/8, 1996, poem 1.

165 Ibid., poem 2.

166 Azawad is the name of a valley that is located at the heartland of the Tuareg area in northern part of Mali. The adoption of such name appeared full of meaning and the desire of a Tuareg country or nation.

167 It was an organisation for the liberation of the Western Sahara that sought to balance Algeria's relation with other North African states like Morocco.

168 It is worthy to note that Gaddafi did not consider the Tuaregs as Arabs; however, one cannot dismiss the fact that the Tuaregs have often been mistaken as a Berber group, an Arabic group, as a result their resemblance, but they speak different languages. It is possible that Gaddafi viewed this relation from racial terms and perhaps religion since the Tuaregs were Muslims, just like the most Arabs.

169 It is also known as the Popular Front for the Liberation of the Greater Arab Central Sahara [FPLSAC].

170 Note that a Nigerien comes from Niger and a Nigerian comes from Nigeria.

171 In 1971 a group of young Sahrawi students in the universities of Morocco began organising what came to be known as The Embryonic Movement for the Liberation of Saguia el-Hamra and Rio de Oro. After attempting in vain to gain backing from several Arab governments, including both Algeria and Morocco but only drawing faint notices of support from Libya and Mauritania, the movement eventually relocated to Spanish-controlled Western Sahara to start an armed rebellion. The Polisario Front was formally constituted on 10 May 1973 with the express intention of militarily forcing an end to Spanish colonisation. Its first secretary general was El-Ouali Mustapha Sayed. On 20 May, he led the Khanga raid, Polisario's first armed action in which a Spanish post manned by a team of Tropas Nomadas [Sahrawi-staffed auxiliary forces] was overrun and rifles seized. Polisario then gradually gained control over large swathes of desert countryside, and its power grew from early 1975 when the Tropas Nomadas began deserting to the Polisario, bringing weapons and training with them. At this point, Polisario's manpower included perhaps 800 men and women, but they were suspected of being backed by a much larger network of supporters. A UN visiting mission headed by Simeon Ake that was conducted in June 1975 concluded that Sahrawi support for independence [as opposed to Spanish rule or integration with a neighbouring country] amounted to an overwhelming consensus and that the Polisario Front was the most powerful political force in Morocco - https://en.wikipedia.org/wiki/Western_Sahara_War.

172 J. S. Lecocq, 'The Desert is Our Country: Tuareg Rebellions and Competing Nationalisms in Contemporary Mali[1946–1996]', Faculty of Social and Behavioral Sciences, University of Amsterdam, 2002, p 219.

173 See B. Haghebaet, 'De wereld volgens Khadafi', Breda, 1986; and R. Oyatek, 'La politique africaine de la libya 1969–1985]', Paris, 1986.

174 J. S. Lecocq, 'The Desert is Our Country: Tuareg Rebellions and Competing Nationalisms in Contemporary Mali [1946–1996]', Faculty of Social and Behavioral Sciences, University of Amsterdam, 2002, p 227.

175 Ibid., p 234.

176 Nous, Touaregs du Mali [Paris, 1990].

177 Ibid.

178 G. Klute, 'Die Rebellionen der Tuareg in Mali und Niger', Habilitationsschrift University, 2001, pp 480–486. It was described as man to man, in a form of a guerilla style, a physical combat, like in battlefield, face to face as in ancient warfare.

179 The pact offered many special privileges to the Tuaregs and appeared to have appeased the group at that particular time; it was supposed to be implemented over time. The pact had promised some kind of autonomy to the group. Although it is known that in the past autonomy had been promised under the Tamanrasset agreement, but the agreement was never fully implemented by the Malian government, and so it was not immediately clear if the National Pact will also be fully implemented. And many among the Tuaregs remained sceptical about the full implementation of the pact, especially as it relates to autonomy, despite the fact that they officially accepted the pact and the ceasefire agreement.

180 P. Boilley, 'Les Kel Adagh. Un siecle de dependances, de la prise de Tombouctou [1893]0au pacte National 1992', These de doctorat d'histoire, Universite Paris VII, 1994.

181 The Gandakoy emerged to challenge the Tuaregs but was explained also to have come about after the Malian government signed the National Pact with the Tuaregs. The Gandakoy initially enjoyed government support, but later on, they saw the national pact as favouring the Tuaregs and intensified their struggle against the Tuareg and requested to be incorporated into the provisions of the pact, so they could also benefit from the socioeconomic integration plan offered to the Tuaregs by the Malian government.

182 See G. Klute, 'Die Rebellionen der Tuareg in Mali und Niger', Habilitationsschrift, Siegen University, 2001.

183 'Extract du no 00 de La Voix du Nord: organ de combat des peuples sedentaires', [n.p. n.d]. The Ganda Koy at some point became a problem to the Malian state despite the fact that their fight was directed at the Tuaregs who are seen as the perceived enemies of the Malian state. However, at some point, the Malian state was interested in peace and the general stabilisation of the country, and the Ganda Koy at this time appeared to have made such peace impossible. These did not go down well with the Malian authorities even though there wasn't any confrontation between the state and the Ganda Koy.

184 The Malian government had contemplated engaging the military to bring about an end to the Tuareg-Ganda Koy problem but realised it would not be feasible and therefore chose to engage the group in a dialogue and ultimately involved the group in the peace negotiations that were offered to the Tuaregs under the National Pact.

185 J. S. Lecocq, 'The Desert is Our Country: Tuareg Rebellions and Competing Nationalisms in Contemporary Mali[1946–1996]', Faculty of Social and Behavioral Sciences, University of Amsterdam, 2002, p 295.

186 Signe Marie Cold-Ravnkilde, 'War and Peace in Mali: Background and Perspectives', Danish Institute for International Studies, report 33, p 30.

187 This was an agreement that was signed between the Malian government and the Tuaregs after the outbreak of Al-Jebha rebellion on 6 January 1991. The agreement considered a ceasefire, transfer of prisoners and civil servant between the north and south of Mali, as well as autonomy for the north. It took place at Tamanrasset in Algeria and came to be known as the Tamanrasset agreement.

188 'Tuareg-Mali 2006-2009', www.globalsecurity.orh/military/world/war/tuareg-Mali-2006.

189 Ibid., p 32.

190 A subsidy is explained as a financial assistance granted by a government or private organisation for the purpose of promoting an enterprise that is considered beneficial to the public welfare. Subsidies are often granted to keep prices low, to maintain incomes, or to preserve employments. Algeria lifted its subsidies in response to the usual dictates of an IMF Structural Adjustment Programme according to reforms free up the market and limit government control.

191 Wolfram Lacher, 'Organized Crime and Conflict in the Sahel Sahara Region', *Carnegie Papers*, Middle East Carnergie Endowment for International Peace, September 2012, p 4.

192 Ibid., p 5.

193 Ibid.

194 Ibid., p 6.

195 Ibid., p 7.

196 Signe Marie Cold-Ravnkilde, 'War and Peace in Mali: Background and Perspectives', Danish Institute for International Studies, report 33, 2013, p 36.

197 Ibid., p 36.

198 Wolfram Lacher, 'Organized Crime and Conflict in the Sahel-Sahara Region', *Carnergie Papers*, Middle East, Carnergie Endowment for International Peace, September 2012, p 8.

199 European nations were usually ready to negotiate and pay ransoms to secure the release of any captured or kidnapped citizen, and as a result of this, they became the victims of the kidnapping enterprise, although sometimes the kidnapping of foreign nationals, particularly Europeans, was explained as a form of a protest against perceived exploitation of natural resources and general economic misfortune and instability facing many African states.

200 Ibid., p 9.

201 Afrique-Drogue, 'Mauritanie: un trafiquant de drogue francais en cavale', 16 September 2011, http/afriquedogue.blogs.rfi.fr/article/2011/09/16/mauritanie-un trafiquant-de-drogue-francias-en-cavale.

202 The decision to reverse the prison terms was seen as a way to make things a little easy for drug pushers, and this is because relatives of the former president have at one time or the other been involved in drug-related issues. This further confirms the involvement or support that crime in the Sahel region enjoyed from the leaders of the various states.

203 Scheele, 'Tribus, Etats et Fraude', pp 87–88.

204 Diplomatic Cable, US Embassy, Bamako, 18 March 2009, www.wikileaks,org/cable/2009/03/09BAMAKO163.html.

205 Wolfram Lacher, 'Organized Crime and Conflict in the Sahel-Sahara Region', *The Carnergie Papers*, Middle East, Carnergie Endowment for International Peace, September 2012, p 12.

206 The Malian government at some point was supporting certain Arab groups in the north against the Tuaregs, trying to use these groups to check the Tuaregs. This support appeared to have aided the perpetuation of unofficial organised crimes and instead of putting a check on the Tuareg led to the escalation of the Tuareg grievances with the Malian state.

207 Ibid., p 13.

208 Interview with Pierre Berret, UN consultant to the MINUSMA force in Mali, 11 April 2014.

209 David J. Francis, 'The Regional Impact of the Armed Conflict and French Intervention in Mali', Norwegian Peace building Resource Centre Report, April 2013, p 4.

210 Freedom C. Onuoha and Alex Thurston, 'Franco-African Military Intervention in Mali Crisis and Evolving Security Concerns', Al Jazeera Center for Studies', 19 February2013, p 2.

211 Alexander Thurston and Andrew Lebovich, ' A Handbook on Mali's 2012–2013 Crisis', Institute for the Study of Islamic Thought in Africa [ISITA] Working Papers series, no 13-001, Roberto Buffett Center for International and Comparative Studies, Northwestern University, 2 September 2013, p 28.

212 BakarySambe, 'Crisis in Mali: Origins, Developments and Impact on the Sub-Region', Kas International Reports, p 117.

213 Freedom C. Onuoha and Alex Thurston, 'Franco-African Military Intervention in Mali Crisis and Evolving Security Concerns', Al Jazeera Center for Studies, 19 February 2013, p 4.

214 Lori-Anne Theroux Benoni, 'Situation Report', Institute of Security Studies, 25 February 2013, p 1.

215 The African Union was the successor of the Organization of African Unity, which was founded by the former Ghanaian president Kwame and Nkrumah and his counterpart from Ethiopia, Hailes Selassie. The same idea was also revived in the 1990s under the leadership of Muamar Gaddafi at the Sirte declaration in 1999, followed by the Lome summit in 2000 where the African

Union Act was adopted. The African Union is a geopolitical entity covering the entire African continent with the exception of Morocco.

216 On May 1975, fifteen West African heads of state met in Lagos, Nigeria, to sign the ECOWAS Treaty. The idea of forming a regional body is credited to Liberia's former president William Tubman around 1965. The ECOWAS was founded to promote and achieve economic integration among West African states.

217 KwesiAning, Frank Okyere, and Mustapha Abdallah, 'Addressing Emerging Security Threats in Post Gaddafi Sahel and the ECOWAS Response to the Malian Crisis', Kofi Annan International Peacekeeping Training Centre policy brief, 1 May 2012, p 4.

218 Ibid., p 5.

219 Ibid.

220 Bakary Sambe, 'Crisis in Mali: Origins, Developments and Impact on the Sub-Region', Kas International Reports, p 127.

221 African Union, ' Report of the Chairperson of the Commission on the Operationalization of the Rapid Deployment Capability of the African Standby Force and the Establishment of an African Capacity for Immediate Response to Crises', sixth ordinary meeting of the Specialised Committee on Defence: Safety and Security, preparatory meeting of chiefs of staff, Addis Ababa, Ethiopia, 29–30 April 2013, p 4.

222 Freedom C. Onuoha and Alex Thurston, 'Franco-African Military Intervention in the Mali Crises and Evolving Security Concerns', Al Jazeera Center for Studies, 19 February 2013, pp 4–5.

223 African Union, ' Report of the Chairperson of the Commission on the Operationalization of the Rapid Deployment Capability of the African Standby Force and the Establishment of an African Capacity for Immediate Response to Crises', sixth ordinary meeting of the Specialised Committee on Defence: Safety and Security, preparatory meeting of chiefs of staff, Addis Ababa, Ethiopia, 29–30 April 2013, p 4.

224 Ibid., p 5.

225 Freedom C. Onuoha and Alex Thurston, 'Franco-African Military Intervention in the Mali Crises and Evolving Security Concerns', Al Jazeera Center for Studies, 19 February 2013, pp 4–5.

226 Paul Melly and Vincent Darracq, 'A New Way to Engage? French Policy in Africa from Sarkozy to Hollande', Chatham House, May 2013, p 8.

227 Ibid., p 10.

228 The French president may have relied on this circle of advisers probably as a result of the sensitivity of the military action required and also partly due to the emergency nature of the request from the Malian president, which did not give room for long consultations with either parliament or anybody

for that matter. Also, it is difficult to say which body was more influential in taking any decision. Both the ministry and the advisers appeared to have worked in consultation with another and took all decision together based on the situation on the ground and what needed to be done.

229  Ibid., pp 10–11.

230  Voice of America, 'French Military Operations in Africa Unpopular at Home', 14 January 2014, www.voanews.com/content/french-military-operations-in-africa-unpopular-at-home.

231  Parliamentary Oversight of Armed Forces, 'Mali and Operation Serval', http// parliamentaryoversight.wordpress.com/2013/01/28/Mali-and-operation-serval/.

232  African Union, ' Report of the Chairperson of the Commission on the Operationalization of the Rapid Deployment Capability of the African Standby Force and the Establishment of an African Capacity for Immediate Response to Crises', sixth ordinary meeting of the Specialised Committee on Defence: Safety and Security, preparatory meeting of chiefs of staff, Addis Ababa, Ethiopia, 29–30 April 2013, p 6.
     The countries belonged to different regional bodies; and these bodies had different rules regarding movement, trade, and military exercises. This created coordination problems among the states. For example, while Mali and Burkina Faso were ECOWAS members, Algeria and Mauritania were not ECOWAS states, and do not have agreements with ECOWAS or member states regarding issues such as military exercises, trade or free border movements of goods and services.

233  Papa SanbaKare, 'Mali: The Forgotten War', Al Jazeera, 6 September 2014, www.aljazeera.com/indepth/opinion/2014/09/Mali-Forgotten-War.

234  Chad deployed about 2,000 troops, one infantry regiment with 1,200 soldiers, and two support battalions with 800 soldiers to Mali. The Chadian army is considered as one of the best in Africa and was considered to lead together with the French army for this reason. The Chadian army is seen to be experienced in fighting in the desert climate and had in the past suppressed many numerous internal rebellions in environments similar to that of Mali. Between 1983 and 1987, Chad fought and won a border war with Libya.

235  The MNLA initially started the rebellion in alliance with the Islamist groups of al-Qaeda, Ansardine, and MUJWAbut disagreed with the other groups after the capture of the north and specifically after the groups insisted on establishing Islamic rule in the north. The MNLA is not considered as a terrorist groupbut is rather seen as an organisation of the Tuaregs, seeking better conditions for the group under the Malian nation, and is seen as a regional pressure group.

236 International Crisis Group, 'Mali: Security, Dialogue and Meaningful Reform', Africa Report, no 201, 11 April 2013, Brussels, Belgium, pp 6–12.

237 The United States would appear only to lend support to the French action but generally supported the intervention by Franceand provided intelligence and patrol aircraft, which were lacking in the operation against the rebels.

238 Maj. Gen Olivier Tramond and Lt. Col. Philippe Seigneur, 'Early Lessons From France's Operation Serval In Mali', Army, June 2013, pp 42–43.

239 Claire Mills, Arabella Lang, and Jon Lunn, ' The Crisis in Mali: Current Military Action and Upholding Humanitarian Law', International Affairs Section, House of Commons Library, SN06531, 11 March 2013, p 4.
Ibid., p 11.

240 Claire Mills, Arabella Lang, and Jon Lunn, ' The Crisis in Mali: Current Military Action and Upholding Humanitarian Law', International Affairs Section, House of Commons Library, SN06531, 11 March 2013, p 4.

241 Ibid., pp 5–6.

242 This a battlefield and ground surveillance aircraft used by the Royal Air Force of England.

243 Ibid., p 6.

244 Stewart Webb, 'Mali: The growing conflict', esprit de corps, vol 20, March 2013, p 20.

245 Thomas Donilon, 'The Need for a Stronger U.S. Policy towards the Crisis in Mali', memo to President Obama, White House, 15 February2013, p 6.

246 AFISMA is a military mission organised by the Economic Community of West African States [ECOWAS] sent to support the government of ECOWAS member nation Mali. The mission was authorised with UN Security Council Resolution 2085, which was passed on 20 December 2012, and authorised the deployment of an African-led international support mission in Mali for an initial period of one year.

247 The mission appeared to have run out of supplies that were initially projected to last for up to 90 days. But the terrain proved difficult, and logistical problems led to shortage of supplies including food and fuel that were considered necessary for the sustainment of the operation.

248 United Nations Security Council, 'Report of the Secretary-General on the Mali Situation', S/2013/189, United Nations, 26 March 2013, p 9.

249 Ibid., p 9.

250 United Nations Security Council, resolution 2085[2012], adopted on 6898th meeting, 20December 2012, S/RES/2085[2012], p 4.

251 ECOWAS Commission, 'Report of the 30th Meeting of the ECOWAS Mediation and Security Council', forty-third ordinary session of ECOWAS Authority of Heads of State and Government, Abuja, 17–18 July 2013, p 8.

252 United Nations Security Council, 'Report of the Secretary-General on the Mali Situation', S/2013/189, United Nations, 26 March 2013, p 10.

253 ECOWAS Commission, 'Report of the 30th Meeting of the ECOWAS Mediation and Security Council', forty-third ordinary session of ECOWAS Authority of Heads of State and Government, Abuja, 17–18 July 2013, p 8.

254 See detail of MINUSMA mandate in appendix A after the general conclusion.

255 IsalineBergamaschi, 'MINUSMA: Initial Steps, Achievements and Challenges', Norwegian Peace building Resource Centre Policy Brief, September2013, p 1.

256 Ibid., p 2.

257 IsalineBergamaschi, 'MINUSMA: Initial Steps, Achievements and Challenges', Norwegian Peacebuilding Resource Centre policy brief, September 2013, p 2.

258 'Mali: A Neo-Colonial Operation Disguised as Anti-Terrorist Intervention. French war in its historical context', Europe Solidaire Sans Frontières, 17 July 2013, p 6.

259 Ibid., p 6.

260 DorotheeFouchaux, 'French Hard Power: Living on the Strategic Edge', American Enterprise Institute for Public Policy, no 1, February 2014, Washington, p 2.

261 Ibid., p 7.

262 Ibid.

263 A careful look at the Pan-Sahel Initiative will clearly reveal the United States' strategic military plans in the Sahel region where almost all the countries were colonised by France. Although the initiative was to be implemented in collaboration with other stakeholders, it, however, shows the interest of the United States in the area and in these former French colonial states. And it is true that the United States had been involved militarily in other parts of Africa, and though the French may not have openly been against the US penetration, nevertheless, it is natural that they may want to remain in control of these areas.

264 Mary Jo Choate, 'Tran-Sahara Counter-terrorism Initiative: Balance of Power', US Army War College report, 30 March 2007, p 5, http://pdf docs/PCAAB627.PDF.

265 Dona J. Stewart, 'What Is Next for Mali? The Roots of Conflict and Challenges to Stability', United States Army War College Strategic Institute Press, November 2013, p 46.

266 FouadFarhaoui, 'The Crisis in Mali: The Great Power Struggle for Africa', International Strategic Organization, Center for Middle Eastern and African Studies, report no 13-03, April 2013, p 34.

267 Henri Plagnol et Francoise, 'La Situation Securitairedans les pays de la zone Affaires Etrangeres', 6 Mars 2012, p74.

268 Brics

269 Paul Melly and Vincent Darracq, 'A New Way to Engage? French Policy In Africa from Sarkozy to Hollande', Chatham House, May 2013, p 17.

270 Vivian C. Jones and Brock R. Williams, 'U.S. Trade and Investment Relations with sub-Saharan Africa and the African Growth and Opportunity Act', [CRS], Congressional Research Service, areport for Congress, 14 November 2012, p 18.

271 Charles-Louis Labrecque, Hugo Bourassa et Gerard Hervouet, ' La modernisationmilitairdernisation de la Chine- Uneanalyse des capacitesactuelles et des efforts de montee en puissance', Hautes etudes international, Universal Laval, Canada, June 2011, p 27.

272 Fouad Farhaoui, 'The Crisis in Mali: The Great Power Struggle for Africa', International Strategic Organization, Center for Middle Eastern and African Studies, report no 13-03, April 2013, p 49.

273 A military rule or incorporated into its policies or constitution.

274 Ibid., pp 52–53.

275 Thomas Cooper Patriota, 'Le Bresil, Un Partenaire de L'Afrique qui S' affirme-Les relations Bresil/Afriquesous les gouvernements Lula [2003–2010]', L'Institutfrancais des relations Internationales, Paris, France, p 21.

276 Antonin Tisseron, 'Enchevetrementsgeopolitiques author de la luttecontre le terrorismedans le Sahara', Hérodote, no 142, 3 e Trimestre 2011, p 101.

277 Ref.

278 Fouad Farhaoui, 'The Crisis in Mali: The Great Power Struggle for Africa', International Strategic Organization, Center for Middle Eastern and African Studies, report no 13-03, April 2013, p 37.

279 Ibid., p 38.

280 Benjamin Auge, ' Les nouveaux enjeux petroliers de la zone sahariene', Hérodote, no 142, 3e trimestre, 2011, p 201.

281 CSS Analysis in Security Policy, 'France's New Strategy: The 2013 White Paper', Center for Security Studies [CSS], no 139, September 2013, pp 1–4.

282 'EU and Mali', http://eeas.europa.eu/delegations/mali/eu_mali/index_fr.htm.

283 Council of the European Union, 'EUCAP Sahel Mali: EU Support Mission for Internal Security in Mali Established', 15 April 2014, p 2.

284 Ibid., p 4.

285 David J. Francis, 'The Regional Impact of Armed Conflict and French Intervention in Mali', Norwegian Peacebuilding Resource Centre report, April 2013, p 10.

286 T. Fessy, 'Ghaddafi's influence in Mali in Mali's coup', BBC Africa, 14 January 2013.

287 Ibid., p 11.

288 AllAfrica.com. 2013. 'Mali: fourth French soldier killed in Mali, Sarkozy criticizes intervention', 6 March 2013, www.allafrica.com.

289 'France probes suspects linked to African jihadists', 9 February 2013, www.bbc.co.uk/news/world europe-2139907.

290 See J. Keenan, 'The Dark Sahara: America's War on Terror in Africa', Pluto Press, London, 2009.

291 Seay Laura, 'Mali is not Afghanistan', 30 January 2013, www.foreignpolicy.com/articles/2013/01/30/Mali_is_not_Afghanistan_fr.

292 Food and Agricultural Organization, 'Sahel Update: The Sahel Crisis', 22 April 2012, p 1.

293 The entire region had witnessed drought prior to the outbreak of the 2012 rebellion. And in Mali, in particular, there were instabilities in the form of uprisings by the Tuareg group at one time or the other, which greatly affected agricultural activities in the country and were seen to have greatly contributed to the food insecurity facing the country, particularly after the outbreak of the 2012 rebellion.

294 Food and Agricultural Organization, 'Sahel Update: The Sahel Crisis', 22 April 2012, p 1.

295 Ibid., p 2.

296 Ibid., pp 1–3.

297 Diana Cartier, 'Mali Crisis: A Migration Perspective', International Migrations Organization, June 2013, p 11.

298 Ibid., p 12.

299 IDMC, Mali: No Where to Run: Fleeing Malians Struggle to Find Safety and Assistance, January, 2013. www.internaldisplace-ment.org.

300 OCHA, Mali: Complex Emergency Situation Report, No 25, February, 2013.

301 Also see Disaster Needs Analysis -2011/2012, 'Northern Mali: Conflict and Food Insecurity', Emergency Capacity Building Project, pp 3–5.

302 Many vulnerable persons were affected by the conflict and as such were among persons displaced by the conflict and the intervention after a study by the IMO was carried out after the intervention.

303 OXFAM Briefing Paper 167, 'Mali's Conflict Refugees: Responding to a Growing Crisis', 22 January 2013, p 10.

304 Diana Cartier, 'Mali Crisis: A Migration Perspective', International Migrations Organization, June 2013, p 16.

305 Ibid., pp 16–17.

306 Human Rights Council, 'Reports of the United Nations High Commissioner for Human Rights on the Human Rights Situation in Mali', Human Rights Council twenty-third session, 6 June 2013, p 3.

307 Ibid., p 9.

308 Amnesty International, 'Mali: Preliminary Findings of a Four Week Mission, Serious Human Rights Abuses Continue', Amnesty International Publications, 2013, p 9.

309 Human Rights Council, 'Reports of the United Nations High Commissioner for Human Rights on the Human Rights Situation in Mali', Human Rights Council twenty-third session, 6 June 2013, p 9.

310 Ibid., p 11.

311 MUJWA is among the rebel terrorist groups operating in the north Mali and may have been responsible for many kidnappings and other related issues in the north, including trafficking in the Sahel region.

312 Amnesty International, 'Mali: Preliminary Findings of a Four Week Mission, Serious Human Rights Abuses Continue', Amnesty International Publications, 2013, p 18.

313 Ibid., p 24.

314 To see measures taken by the Malian government regarding Human Rights abuses, see Human Rights Council, 'Reports of the United Nations High Commissioner for Human Rights on the Human rights Situation in Mali', Human Rights Council twenty-third session, 6 June 2013, p 15.

315 Amnesty International, 'Mali: Preliminary Findings of a Four Week Mission, Serious Human Rights Abuses Continue', Amnesty International Publications, 2013, p 25.

316 Diana Carter, 'Mali Crisis: A Migration Perspective, International Organization for Migration, June 2013, p 19.

317 EU and Mali, 'Humanitarian Aid', ttp://eeas.europa.eu/delegations/mali/eu_mali/humanitarian/index_fr.htm.

318 International Donors Conference, Together for a New Mali, Brussels, 15 May 2013, joint chairs conclusions, p 2.

319 Ibid., p 2.

320 Republic of Mali, 'Plan for Sustainable Recovery of Mali 2013–2014', final version, International Conference, Brussels, 15 May 2013, p 7.

321 Ibid., p 2.

322 Republic of Mali, 'Together for a New Mali International Conference', Plan for the Sustainable Recovery of Mali 2013–2014, Brussels, 15 May 2013, p 6.

323 Ibid., p 7.

324 EU-Mali, Humanitarian Aid: http://eeas.europa.eu/delegations/mali/projects/index_fr.htm. Accessed 4/01/14

325 The United Nations usually deploy policemen from member nations to crisis areas when needed. Many police officers from different countries serve as UN police in conflict states for the purpose of maintaining security and stability in those areas.

326 United Nations Mali, 'United Nations and Partner Activities in Northern Mali: Gao', 15 April 2014, p 1.

327 Before the Serval operations by the French, the courts had been non-functional and physically destroyed during the conflict. The intervention saw the restoration of the premises while reconstruction work continued to be carried out by the Malian authorities and other partners.

328 Ibid., p 2.

329 Ibid., p 3.

330 United Nations Mali, 'United Nations and Partner Activities in Northern Mali: Timbuktu', 15 April 2014, p 2.

331 Ibid., p 2.

332 Ibid.

333 Ibid., p 1.

334 United Nations Mali, 'United Nations and Partner Activities in Northern Mali: Kidal', 15 June 2014, p 1.

335 Ibid., p 2.

336 Ibid., p 3.

337 Ben Rabie/Echoruc, 'Northern Mali Taliban Stronghold in Africa? TV, Part II 'Gao', 18 June 2012, www.youtube.com/watch?v=yAx5AtLUgW8. It is visible in minutes 11:19–11:37, 12:59–13:06, 13:16–13:17, 20:42–20:44, 36:49–36:50, and 38:25-38-26.

338 Ibid. It can be viewed from minutes 12:28 to 12:30.

339 Ibid., minutes 12:28–12:30.

340 Ibid., visible in minutes 02:10–02:20.

341 Ibid., minutes 02:39–02:43.

342 Ibid., visible in minutes 04:14–04:18, 04:38–04:46, 11:44–11:50, 12:15–12:20, 12:28–12:30, and 12:35–12:43 and can also be viewed on AFP [Agency France-Presse], 'Islamist Fighters Call for Shariah Law in Mali', 14 March 2012, www.youtube.com/watch?v=OM1AyelRLP0, minutes 00:08–00:11.

343 NBC News, 'Mali Islamist Rebels Seize Town Despite French Fighting', 14 January 2013, www.nbcnews.com/video/nightly-news/50461319#50461319. Is visible in minutes 02:11–02:15.

344 AFP [Agence France-Presse], 'Islamist Fighters Call for Shariah Law in Mali', 14 March 2012, www.youtube.com/watch?v=OM1AyelRLP0, minutes 00:26–0029.

345 Ben Rabie/Echoruc, 'Northern Mali Taliban Stronghold in Africa?, TV, Part II 'Gao', 18 June 2012, www.youtube.com/watch?v=yAx5AtLUgW8, minutes 37:29–37:44.

346 Ibid., in minutes 11:37–11:41.

347 Ibid., minutes 10;10–10;14,10:32–10:38, 10:53–11:00, 12:33–12:35, and 12:49–12:52 and [2] AFP [Agence France-Presse], 'Islamist Fighters Call

for Sharia Law in Mali', 14 March 2012, www.youtube.com/watch?v= OM1AyelRLP0, minutes 01:24–01:32;[3] BFMTV, 'QUAND l' armee recupere les armes abandonnees par les islamistes, 25 February 2013, www.bfm.com/video/bfmtv/international/mali-larmee-recupere-armes-abandonnees-islamistes-25-02-113446, minutes 00:14–00:15; [4] Francetv, 'L'impressionant arsenal des jihadistes au Mali', 4 March 2013, www.francetvinfo.fr/video-l-impressionant-arsenal-aqmi-au-malli_274103.html, visible in minutes 00:28–00:33 and [5] BFMTV, 'QUAND l' armee recupere les armes abandonnees par les islamistes', 25 February 2013, www.bfm.com/video/bfmtv/international/mali-larmee-recupere-armes-abandonnees-islamistes-25-02-113446, minutes 00:23–00:30.

348  Cahier du RETEX, 'Les rebellions Touaregues au Sahel', Paris: Ministere de la Defense, Centre de Doctrine d'Emploi des forces', January 2013, p 1, www.cdef.terre.defense.gouv.fr/publications/cahiers_drex/cahier_recherche/Rebellions_Touareues.pdf and Ben Rabie/Echoruc, 'Northern Mali Taliban Stronghold in Africa?', TV, Part II 'Gao', 18 June 2012, www.youtube.com/watch?v=yAx5AtLUgW8, minutes 00:02–00:05.

349  NBC News, 'Mali Islamist Rebels Seize Town Despite French Fighting', 14 January 2013, www.nbcnews.com/video/nightly-news/50461319#50461319, visible in minutes 02:09–02:11.

350  Francetv, 'L'impressionant arsenal des jihadistes au Mali', 4 March 2013, www.francetvinfo.fr/video-l-impressionant-arsenal-aqmi-au-malli_274103.html, visible in minutes 00:04–00:14.

351  Ibid., visible in minutes 00:04–00:19.

352  Ibid., minutes 00:04–00:19.

353  Ben Rabie/Echoruc, 'Northern Mali Taliban Stronghold in Africa?', TV, Part II 'Gao', 18 June 2012, www.youtube.com/watch?v=yAx5AtLUgW8, is visible in minutes 00:09–00:13, 12:21–12:26 and 13:08–13:11 and [2] NBC News, 'Mali Islamist Rebels seize Town Despite French Fighting', 14 January 2013, www.nbcnews.com/video/nightly-news/50461319#50461319, minutes 02:09–02:11.

354  Aemee francaise, 'Operations de fouille dans le massif de l'Adrar', Armee francaise-operstions militaire OPEX [page offiecielle], Facebook, www.facebook.com/photo.php?v=51064348981384, visible in minutes 00:15–00:24.

355  Ben Rabie/Echoruc, 'Northern Mali Taliban Stronghold in Africa?', TV, Part II 'Gao', 18 June 2012, www.youtube.com/watch?v=yAx5AtLUgW8, minutes 11:00–11:25.

356  Armee francaise, 'Operations de fouille dans le massif de l'Adrar', Armee francaise-operstions militaire OPEX [page offiecielle], Facebook, www.facebook.com/photo.php?v=51064348981384, visible in minutes 00:44–00:46.

357 C. J. Chivers, 'Looted Libyan Arms in Mali May Have Shifted Conflict's Path', *New York Times*, 6 February, 2013, www.nytimes.com/2013/02/08/world/africa/looted-libyan-arms-in-mali-may-have-shifted-conflicts-path.html? r=2&<; [2] Ben Rabie/Echoruc, 'Northern Mali Taliban Stronghold in Africa?', TV, Part II 'Gao', 18 June 2012, www.youtube.com/watch?v=yAx5AtLUgW8, minutes 11:14–11:22; and [3] Francetv, 'L'impressionant arsenal des jihadistes au Mali', 4 March 2013, www.francetvinfo.fr/video-l-impressionant-arsenal-aqmi-au-malli_274103.html, visible in minutes 00;18–00:20.

358 Ibid., can be viewed in minutes 12:07–12:10.

359 Ibid., minutes 12:51–12:53; and NBC News, 'Mali Islamist Rebels Seize Town Despite French Fighting', 14 January 2013, www.nbcnews.com/video/nightly-news/50461319#50461319, minutes 02:02–02:07.

360 BFMTV, 'QUAND l' armee recupere les armes abandonnees par les islamistes', 25 February 2013, www.bfm.com/video/bfmtv/international/mali-larmee-recupere-armes-abandonnees-islamistes-25-02-113446. And can be viewed in minutes 00:00–00:21.

361 Francetv, 'L'impressionant arsenal des jihadistes au Mali', 4 March 2013, www.francetvinfo.fr/video-l-impressionant-arsenal-aqmi-au-malli_274103.html. It is visible in minutes 00:25–00:27.

362 The Guardian [Online edition], 'Footage of French Airstrikes on Mali, Video', 24 January 2013, www.guardian.co.uk/world/video/2013/jan/24/footage-mali-airstrikes-video.
The video shows a laser-guided GBU munitions being dropped on a BM-21 launch vehicle and a pickup truck coming under fire from a tiger helicopter.

363 France tv, 'L'impressionant arsenal des jihadistes au Mali', 4 March 2013, www.francetvinfo.fr/video-l-impressionant-arsenal-aqmi-au-malli_274103.html. It is visible in minutes 00:17–00:20.

364 Ben Rabie/Echoruc, 'Northern Mali Taliban Stronghold in Africa?', TV, Part II 'Gao', 18 June 2012, www.youtube.com/watch?v=yAx5AtLUgW8. Visible in minutes 37:59–38:08, and also on BFMTV, 'QUAND l' armee recupere les armes abandonnees par les islamistes', 25 February 2013, www.bfm.com/video/bfmtv/international/mali-larmee-recupere-armes-abandonnees-islamistes-25-02-113446. It is visible in minutes 00:10–00:12.

365 AFP [Agence France-Presse], 'Islamist Fighters call for Shariah Law in Mali', 14 March 2012, www.youtube.com/watch?v=OM1AyelRLP0. The film footage can be seen in minutes 00:17–00:24
Ben Rabie/Echoruc, 'Northern Mali Taliban Stronghold in Africa?', TV, Part II 'Gao', 18 June 2012, www.youtube.com/watch?v=yAx5AtLUgW8. Here the arms are seen in minutes 11:54–11:55, 12:33–12:35, and 12:54–12:57, respectively.

366 Ibid., minutes 10:23–00:31.

# *Index*

www.ingramcontent.com/pod-product-compliance
Lightning Source LLC
Chambersburg PA
CBHW021714120626
46545CB00004B/1562